SBN 671-21674-0
LIBRARY OF CONGRESS CATALOG CARD NUMBER: 73-13388
DESIGNED BY EVE METZ
MANUFACTURED IN THE UNITED STATES OF AMERICA

1   2   3   4   5   6   7   8   9   10

THE AUTHOR AND PUBLISHER WISH TO EXTEND
THEIR GRATITUDE FOR PERMISSION TO REPRINT FROM
Anne Frank: The Diary of a Young Girl,
copyright 1952 by Otto H. Frank.
Used by permission of Doubleday & Company, Inc.

The
Obsession

MEYER LEVIN

SIMON AND SCHUSTER · NEW YORK

*We do not know if we live in apathy or terror,
in conspiracy or moral incompetence.**
—NORMAN MAILER

*New York Sunday Times Book Review, March 11, 1973

1

IN THE MIDDLE OF LIFE I fell into a trouble that was to grip, occupy, haunt, and all but devour me, these twenty years. I've used the word "fall." It implies something accidental, a stumbling, but we also use the word in speaking of "falling in love," in which there is a sense of elevation, and where a fatedness is implied, a feeling of being inevitably bound in through all the mysterious components of character to this expression of the life process, whether in the end beautifully gratifying, or predominantly painful.

In my "fall," too, there lurks the powerful sense of the inevitable. Through the years of this grim affair it has always seemed that the process had to come, that it was the inevitable expression of all I ever was, all I ever did, as a writer and as a Jew; that it was in itself virtually artistic in its construction, its hidden elements, its gradual summoning up and revelation of character both in myself and others, and in its exposition of social forces.

The long trouble contained confrontations, even a public trial, and at various points I told myself it was over with, it had to be ended, that I was ejecting the entire cancerous growth from my psyche. But to every human being there remains, I believe, one final, ineradicable motive. This is the need to unravel the three-threaded intertwinings of fate, manipulation, and one's own will. "What happened to me?" is our unrelinquishable puzzle. "Exactly how did it, how could it have, come about?" we demand. Was all this from within myself? one asks, or from outside? Was there some hidden, secret force working on me so that no matter what I did through the normal ways of society I could not prevail?—Ah! paranoia!—But if I trace back and find that there really was such a force?—Witches! Demons! The conspiratorial view of history!

Four times I sought to trace it all out within myself, through analysis. Before beginning to write this account, a year ago, I was in session with my fourth analyst. I was telling of the courtroom trial that had taken place, already some fifteen years back, and of an incident at the close of the trial, which involved my sister Bess in Chicago. All these fifteen years I had freely told this incident. Now as I came to the key words, I couldn't utter them. I was suddenly choked with anguish. I turned my head away, trying to regain self-control.

The case in court had arisen from my difficulties over *The Diary of a Young Girl* by Anne Frank. Continuing from my war correspondent experiences my intense absorption with the Holocaust, I had helped Otto Frank to secure publication for the Diary in English, and had dramatized it. Mr. Frank had come to New York, to see to the authenticity of the staging, but at that point the prominent playwright Lillian Hellman and her producer, Kermit Bloomgarden, had persuaded him, he told me, that as a novelist I was no dramatist, that my work was unstageworthy, that it had to be discarded and another version written.

From the start I had strongly suspected that some doctrinaire formulation rather than pure dramatic judgment had

8

caused Miss Hellman's attack on my play, and after the substitute work written under her tutelage was produced, I became convinced that I had been barred because I and my work were in her political view "too Jewish." The Broadway play omitted what I and others, including several serious critics, considered essential material in the Diary. But also, while my work had been flagrantly smeared as "unstageworthy," the Broadway play proved identical in staging, with important scenes startlingly parallel to mine. The whole affair increasingly appeared to me as a classic instance of declaring an author incompetent, in order to cover up what was really an act of censorship. And in this, not only I, but Anne Frank was involved, as well as the public. Yet because of rampant McCarthyism, I could not then make public what I saw as the real issue: doctrinaire censorship of the Stalinist variety. Even at the trial I did not bring this issue out, for fear of supplying material to McCarthy's inquisitors.

Continual requests, mostly from noncommercial groups, for permission to perform my version were refused by the Diary owners. Appeals from literary personalities, community leaders, and even a massive petition from the rabbinate had failed, and I had finally gone to court. I won a jury verdict awarding me a high sum for damages, but as my opponents, with virtually unlimited funds at their disposal, kept up the costly litigation, I accepted a lesser settlement, so long as it assured me "moral victory." Only to find that the play remained suppressed.

Thus, I was not freed from the problem. Here I sat, seven books, fifteen years afterward, face averted from Dr. Erika.

"Let it come," the analyst said unobtrusively, meaning the weeping. As a knowing repeater in analysis, I was aware that this was to be counted as a breakthrough; only once before, quite long ago, with the first analyst—also a woman—had I wept. But that analysis had begun years before "the trouble," and the weeping then had come because of a clear, stark horror, the suicide of Mabel, my divorced wife. Then the source was primary. The analyst led you softly to the abyss, and you looked down in, and wept. An achievement, a natural reaction—you were human, you must feel released.

This time also I had been telling of a death—my brother-in-law, his name Meyer, like mine. (Ah, identification! One's own death! Weeping!) On the last day of the trial in New York, as I sat in the courtroom hearing my lawyer make his summation, a message came from my sister Bess in Chicago saying that Meyer had died. His third heart attack.

I couldn't possibly leave the courtroom, whispered my counsel at the table. Think of the effect on the jury if I walked out on our own summation! I must be here for the judge's instruction—that was mandatory. Nor could we ask for a recess at this point; our case was difficult. If the judge explained the reason, it would sound like a play for sympathy. After the jury went out the next morning, I could leave for Chicago.

And so it was, I had been telling the analyst, that I arrived too late for the funeral. The family was back in the house. The phone rang; my nephew Martin said the call was for me from New York. As we stood there by the kitchen wall-telephone and I heard and repeated the jury's verdict in my favor, my sister cried out, "I'm sure it was because my Meyer—"

I told the story that far, and couldn't say the rest. I repeated "Bess said, 'I'm sure my Meyer—' " and choked up again. I could not bring out what my sister had said about her husband, buried that day.

I had been describing Bess and Meyer so glibly. "Tell me something about your early life, your family." The fourth time around. The analyst had come to her question at the beginning of the session, as though she had prepared this aspect for today: *Family.*

I considered that the family material was not essential to

10

our particular exploration; right from the first session, I had explained, and Dr. Erika had agreed to it, that our objective was an immediate and limited one. At my age—though she shrugged this aside—I felt I could scarcely expect any radical character change. To embark again on any sort of depth-analysis, to try once more to relate temper tantrums in early childhood to unquenchable fury at literary suppression? Still another time to resift recollections, like some archeologist yet again putting the discard-pile through the sieve?

Perhaps only the basic facts of my life history would have to be recapitulated? To simplify this, I had given Dr. Erika my autobiography to read; that was at least one use for the half-forgotten *In Search*. I had really come to her, I explained, for a specific purpose. In a few months my latest novel, *The Settlers*, would appear. I wanted to be under some sort of control during those months, to make certain that I would not do anything rash in this critical prepublication period that could prove damaging to the reception of the book.

This novel was my biggest effort. At my age I had to consider that it might prove to be my last work. Just as I had completed the final proofreading, the ancient devilment had sprung out at me anew, intensified—the old obsessional trouble, the Anne Frank case. Day and night, I was invaded with a buzzing of plans, new protest projects, appeals to the P.E.N. Club and further legal actions.

There was a "reality situation," too; once more a community group wanted to present my play, and as so many times in these twenty years, it was forbidden.

I would go back to court, I would at last make a big scandal of the whole thing, I would succeed this time in bringing out the political side of the suppression; once and for all, I would show how the same gang had been cutting away at me during all these twenty years, denigrating my work, how one book after another had been sneered down by whispering campaigns, by passing the word on Levin.

11

—Paranoia! Fantasy!

—No, I had instance after instance, proof—

—Then if not fantasy, it was clearly my old masochism. The self-destructive mechanism. Here, with my new book coming out, with every chance in my favor for a great success, I wanted to provoke and arouse my enemies, granted they were real—

"Yes, I do believe you about the political side," said Dr. Erika. "I know quite a lot about this situation, and I believe you."

She was from Israel, so my particular subject was not strange to her. This was one of the reasons for my having selected this analyst. Another reason—she was a specialist in the analysis of writers, a happy combination for me, and she had given me to understand that she was quite well up on the intrigues of the literary world. On both counts there needed to be only a minimum of preliminary explanation. Dr. Erika had, for my situation, the exact qualifications.

We could get right to the question: the pressure in me to reopen the Anne Frank affair—was it rational or irrational? While working on *The Settlers,* I had, over several years, held down the obsession; now it was shouting in me: "You promised, as soon as you had the book out of the way!" Accusing: "Your play is still suppressed! You have a duty! Fight!"

Was this a cunning form of masochism, to arouse my enemies and endanger the big book itself?

On the contrary, I argued, that crowd didn't need to be aroused. They'd go after my book anyway, as they had done on so many others, and even more poisonously this time, since *The Settlers* was about Zionists. Instead of keeping silent, wouldn't it be a clever move for me to bring the whole case to public attention precisely at this time, to expose the literary politics, which people would now at last understand? In that way I could raise an alert against attacks on *The Settlers.*

12

No. By reopening the Anne Frank affair, I would simply be calling attention anew to my obsession, and so make it easy for the other side to sneer me down with my new book as well—Levin is a complainer, a loser, a freak.

Agreed, it was an obsession. Admitted. There it sat under my skull with my mind gripped in its tentacles. Sometimes dormant. Sometimes awakening and squeezing. Again I would react, send out protests and petitions. That was all very well for suppressed Russian writers, from prisons, from labor camps, that was all highly noble for a Solzhenitsyn, but for a free American writer to complain for twenty years about a so-called act of suppression was obviously obsessional.

I knew what was said. The poor fellow couldn't write any more—all he could think or talk about was his Anne Frank case; he had become a hopeless paranoiac. Any attempt to conquer my trouble by proving the case only fed this accusation: There Levin goes again. Obsessed.

Thus put, there is logic in shipping a protesting writer off to an insane asylum! The same for a Jew-mania. For example, there was the case in Leningrad where a protesting Jew, a brilliant young mathematician, set himself on fire in protest against emigration restrictions. Under any system wouldn't such a person—a person who set himself on fire—be sent off for psychiatric observation? A routine matter. Under all systems certain practices can seem the same. Similar causes, similar results. Here with us, the protesting writer, instead of receiving state psychiatric care, or incarceration, voluntarily betakes himself, through another kind of social mechanism, to his analyst. The fellow doesn't seem able to accept the normal, necessary practice of a certain degree of censorship of ideas. He screams "Suppression!" Infantile tantrums!

Gripped by obsession, the mind nevertheless pulses, creates. In these years I had written the novel by which I was most widely known, *Compulsion,* and the novel by which I had hoped to dispel my whole trouble, *The Fanatic,* and a dozen

13

more books, plays, films. And yet, in spite of all this product, and now with the completion of the most extensive task of all, *The Settlers,* I knew that if I took up the case, word would go out that Levin, hopelessly consumed, unable to write, was once more screaming his fixation.

Again and again the trouble had taken me to the analysts, reexamining the pathways of my mind, perhaps like some road map that has to be undoubled vertically and untripled horizontally before one can sort out the segment that shows one's way.

In this choked-up moment I sat with Dr. Erika, toward whom, if I felt two positive factors, I also felt two uncertainties. The lingering uncertainty of a man delivering his worldly complexities into the hands of a woman, and the question of this doctor's being, in years—it could also be in wisdom—so much younger than myself.

With this last misgiving, why was I here? Why hadn't I gone back to my first analyst, Dr. A, who was also from Israel, and who was now in New York? Dr. A was my own age, and an image of wisdom as she sat with her embroidery, her head slightly bowed, her hair severely parted. With Dr. A there would have been nothing to dredge up and repeat, for I had been her patient at several intervals over the years, the last time three winters ago. All that winter, struggling to begin on *The Settlers,* I had remained blocked. Dr. A, perhaps trying to shock me out of the impasse, had, one evening in the analytical cubicle, raised her eyes from her embroidering, fixed her gaze on me, and declared flatly that if I went on harboring my obsession, I was succumbing to my paranoia and would inevitably deteriorate until I was lost.

Then she had agreed that I should try with someone else, perhaps a man.

I had already done this some years before. Three times each week, in that hallucinating period encompassing the Anne Frank trial, I had gone to an elegant East Side apartment, en-

14

tered the cubicle, and sat beside the desk, facing on the wall that same tenderly brooding picture of Sigmund Freud, the icon of analytical cubicles. There I had talked to Dr. Sulzberger—obese, overflowing his chair, gossipy, with his casual manner of a colleague interested in the theater, the arts, with his curiosity about girls, and with his touch of the imperious. A man who bore the name of an exceedingly powerful German Jewish family, he was the maverick of the clan. Dr. Sulzberger had since died. But even were he still living, would I, in my present crisis, have gone back to him? Sophisticated though he had been about my problems in the literary and theatrical world, I had never felt more than a superficiality in our talks. But there is one admonition I cherish from him: "Fight! Yes, fight them! But with joy! Enjoy the fight!" Perhaps he had believed the whole time he could turn me into an Irishman.

And so from the second analyst, Dr. Sulzberger, I had returned to the first, Dr. A, and then had gone on to the third, again a man. All this time I was writing my books.—Amazing, how these writers carry on, running from one analyst to another, the way, after a pessimistic medical diagnosis, one runs to another specialist in search of a different finding!

For my third analyst I had found an elderly psychiatrist, a benign man, a father-figure to be sure, even though I myself had reached sixty. He was a Polish Jew, brought up in a Zionist family, hence not unfamiliar with the political background of my trouble. Again I had gone over my tale, and also combed over all those fearful childhood experiences in a Chicago gangland neighborhood; I had told of my mother, my father, my sisters Bess and Bertha, my first wife Mabel and the divorce, and her remarriage and redivorce and eventual suicide. I had told of my marriage to Tereska, of the terror and depression that came over her if the name of Anne Frank was so much as uttered. And then I spoke of my need to go on with my protests and of my efforts to free my work from suppression. "It's only when I actually do something, take some action, that I feel a release from the obsession and am able to go on with whatever I'm writing." Dr. Bychovsky had quite simply put me on a pill.

When I was at last making progress on *The Settlers,* Dr. Bychovsky suddenly dismissed me. The paranoia? The fateful deterioration? "No, maestro," he had said—somewhat to my discomfiture, this therapist had from the start, with a kind of old-world courtesy, called me "maestro"—"No, maestro, you do not have a paranoia. All artists are somewhat paranoid, but that is quite another thing than a paranoia. The enemies you tell of are undoubtedly real. The question is, are they worth all the trouble you give yourself over them?"

When the trouble re-asserted itself, I didn't go back to him. His pill helped me to finish the book and that was everything, but toward the end of the writing, I had barely been able to stave off the obsession. When I would lie on my back to let story-scenes come into my mind, there would come instead new plans, new actions to take, people to see, and all this would crowd out the images of my characters. I found myself carting out to my work-place, a barnloft near Nyack, the old cartons filled with files and folders of the Anne Frank affair, which I had kept out of sight in our basement so as not to arouse Tereska.

Just as I was finishing *The Settlers* I read of a conference of writers to be held at Town Hall, embracing the Authors League, the P.E.N. Club, and several more unities. Though I recognized from the usual names on the letterhead that my case would receive little help from this group, I was at it again, writing and mimeographing. I saw myself arriving early at Town Hall, putting my appeal on every seat. I had a self-addressed postcard for writers to sign, a petition for lifting the suppression from my play, "in recognition, so appropriate to the Diary, that not only human beings but their works have

16

a right to life." It had already been signed over the years by such illustrious names as Albert Camus, Norman Mailer, I. B. Singer, and all the rest. So as not to upset Tereska, I rented a post-office box in Nyack, and put this address on the cards. What if I shouldn't be allowed to distribute my appeal? I saw myself rushing up to the platform, creating a scene—

But the other side of me—the healthy? the cowardly?—demanded, "Won't this hurt *The Settlers*?" Answer: "Didn't Solzhenitsyn appeal to his fellow writers? Come on! How scared can you get!" Retort: "Okay, Levin the custodian of the rights of man, freedom of expression and all that shit! But here is your big chance on a big book. Do you have the right to risk a new gang-up without consulting your publisher? After all, on *Compulsion* you took Jack Goodman's advice to go away, and it worked out for the best." Oh, sure, Michael Korda, my present editor, had long known about the case. But the whole Anne Frank affair had taken place years ago. It was sheer fantasy to believe that some sort of politico-literary gang-up against me continued. I had no such enemies, Korda insisted, but still, I must do nothing to arouse them. Not until after the big book was published. And reviewed. And well on its way.

How, I cried with noble and genuine indignation, could the situation exist in America where the literary fate of my novel might depend on my silence about the suppression of a play? No literary Mafia existed, but I must not provoke its revenge!

No, no, that was not what he meant at all. It was just that I should not divert attention from the book itself. Why risk arousing an old animosity?

And so again in such miasmic circumstances, I had to seek help. I wanted to be careful not to risk injuring this book which had taken so long and come with such difficulty.

I didn't go back to Dr. Bychovsky, for, knowing that he would prescribe cautionary silence, the protesting side demanded a fair chance for revolt. Despite his flattering

17

"maestro" act, this side insisted, Dr. Bychovsky had never really recognized that my obsession was inbedded in the one absolute of art—freedom of expression. Raise the writer's flag! If the heroic Russian authors could risk their lives, why shouldn't I have the courage to risk the bestsellerdom of a book?

In my dilemma I was reminded of the Ben-Gurion slogan at the start of the Second World War, when the British imposed their White Paper terminating Jewish immigration to Palestine. To fight against the British White Paper as though there were no war, and to fight alongside the British in the war as though there were no White Paper. A fine slogan, but refugees died in the face of the immigration ban. For twenty years I had been trying to do my writing as though there were no Anne Frank case, and I had been trying to fight the suppression as though I had no other writings.

When the two conflicted, which came first? I had promised I would do nothing about the case until *The Settlers* was out, and here I had my protest ready for the writers' conference. Was I really going over the border with my obsession? Was Dr. A's grim prediction coming true? Was I deteriorating into helpless paranoia?

I must not accede to panic. Having lived with Old Obsession for twenty years, I knew it well—I knew when its demands were within reason, and when it was pressing me out of bounds. Had I not proved myself in court, before a jury? Were the jurors infected with my trouble to decide in my favor? What of the critics when the play was illegally presented in Israel? Had they too been infected, or had they written honest reviews?

It had to be recognized that there are two common misunderstandings about obsessions. The first is that they are inevitably all-devouring. Had I not gone on with my work, written my books? Everyone is, when he thinks of it, acquainted with persons who are touchy on one certain point but "otherwise normal." And one day it may turn out that even the touchiness was reasonable and justified. For the second common misunderstanding, the one that brings the greatest irritation to the obsessed, is a curious primary assumption that being obsessed is being in the wrong.

Examples to the contrary are part of every folklore. "He was proven to have been right, the whole time!" Belatedly, we praise the obsessed for integrity and perseverance. Piously, we cite them as examples. We tell our children the tales of these justice-seekers who, for principle alone, fought their cases through to the final triumph! Even if only a penny was involved! Even if it took a lifetime! From pulpits, from academic platforms, we continually call on the justice-obsessed to pursue their issues, to be the one voice against the whole world, to go to jail if necessary—while in living experience we do the opposite: the moment we sniff an obsession, we shun the culprit, the infected one; we whisper that the poor fellow is demon-ridden, an injustice collector, and we even refuse to listen to, or to examine, his cause, for the simple reason that he is "obviously obsessed with it."

Worse, the obsessed individual, himself a part of society, argues to himself against his own convictions: even if in some cases a one-man fight proves justified, does this mean that all such fighters are justified? Most of them, sadly, really are cranks. Isn't it possible that I too belong among the cranks, as my distinguished enemies proclaim with pity? "Unfortunately Levin has become obsessed," they tell persons who try to intervene, as though that settles the matter. You cut off a man's hand and then sigh, "Unfortunately he has become a cripple."

So I had come to my fourth analyst. All I wanted, I said, was to be sure I didn't go off the beam in this crucial interval before the book was out.

I had heard of Dr. Erika from a friend whom she had helped through our professional malady, the writer's block.

Her methods were unorthodox. She mingled socially with her patients, went to the same parties. Indeed, I had met her a few times. A psychological, not a medical, analyst, with her office still on the West Side. Quick, intuitive—"I use laser beams," she liked to say.

So she beamed them into my issue of the moment. As to the leaflets at the writers' conference, since I already had them prepared—okay, I could go that far.

Standing just inside the door at Town Hall, I handed one to each arrival for the session on censorship and suppression. Several of the crowd knew me, some even knew of the case and had a sympathetic word, some smirked. On the platform, Arthur Miller exhorted all writers faced with censorship or suppression, "Fight! Shout! Picket! Protest! Make a nuisance of yourself! Bring your case to the P.E.N. Club!"

I belonged to P.E.N. Members of the P.E.N. Club pledged themselves "to oppose every form of suppression of freedom of expression" in their country and community.

I had written to Arthur Miller as International President of the P.E.N. clubs. He had not replied. What was I to think? Was I really out of my mind?

In the post office box at Nyack I found my cards, signed by one out of six. "An excellent statistical return, anyone would have to agree!" said Dr. Erika. Still, just now I must do no more.

A letter had come from a student at Brandeis who wanted to stage the play at the university. Here was a perfect opportunity! Make a test case of it! Have him ask the Diary owners for the rights. Again would come a refusal. This time I would bring out the whole Stalinist motivation in the banning of this work. What did she think? Do it?

No! No! "Tactics!" Fight, but with clever tactics. I must wait a few months, as I had promised my publisher. Until the big book was out and well on its way. Again she cited the example of the war on the White Paper and the war against the Nazis. Tactics!

My new analyst too, then, was advising silence. Had she only been humoring me by letting me pass out my petitions? Did she too believe I was paranoiac, and was she only "handling me" more cleverly, giving me a longer leash?

Then the students themselves decided they did not want to make a test case—they simply wanted to put on the play. They would rehearse without publicity and stage the performance without asking for the rights. Once more I bottled up my anger. Galleys of *The Settlers* were going out to the book clubs and to important review media.

Thus we had come to the day of "Tell me something about your childhood." Times four. Not counting two or three exploratory contacts with other psychiatrists at one time or another. I turned on "childhood and early reationships": my father, the little tailor, my mother with her hysteria, my two sisters, and how Bess got herself a nice young Jewish doctor, and how her Meyer and I became close friends. And finally his heart attacks, the trial—and there I was, choked up.

Presently I was able to turn my head back to the analyst and repeat to her the words my sister Bess had said to me, there by the kitchen phone, just after the trial verdict came, just after her Meyer's funeral.

But to understand what Bess said, the whole trouble must be known.

The publication of *The Settlers* came, with curious results. From the publishing point of view the book had to be called a success, with sales of over 50,000 copies, though more had been estimated. From readers, both Jewish and Gentile, I received the most enthusiastic letters in a lifetime of writing. Then of what could Levin complain?

Of accumulating literary denigration.

The book had broken through to the public in cities

21

where it received attention, but only weakly in the area of the New York literary establishments. There, the silent treatment and the put-down prevailed. Deservedly?

Everyone had expected a well-placed review in the New York Sunday *Times* as what *The Settlers* deserved. Doubtless the reviewer would be a Michener, a David Schoenbrun, or some other writer who was knowledgeable about the background—Walter Lacquer, Amos Elon, Gerold Frank, Yael Dayan. The choice of reviewer is the whole decision, and the Sunday *Times Book Review* counts as much as all the other media put together. *The Settlers* was relegated to the back pages with a perfunctory review by Granville Hicks, guru of the "proletarian" school in the thirties! Tepid, dull in itself, the review breathed indifference, though even Hicks admitted, with a sigh of reservation, that *The Settlers* was my "most ambitious" work and "in all likelihood" my best.

In the daily *Times*? Nothing.

Time magazine? Nothing.

Newsweek? Nothing.

Even the *Saturday Review*?

Silence.

So it was with every national magazine—*Harper's, Atlantic Monthly, The New Yorker,* all. My previous books had been widely reviewed, not each in all of them, but none in none of them. It is the cumulative effect of reviews in such media that determine the status of an author.

Throughout the country there were magnificent newspaper reviews. In Chicago, Los Angeles, Philadelphia, Boston, the word "epic" kept being repeated, *War and Peace* kept being remembered, the characterizations, the writing, the insight— all were praised. But reviews in the daily press need reenforcement. The silent treatment in every single magazine—could this have come about by accident, as sheer coincidence, without some assiduous word-passing? Was I already so far denigrated that silence was automatic?

Then came the same pattern on the air in the all-important New York area. Once outside of it, on the prescribed promotion tour to Cleveland, Chicago, Denver, Los Angeles, San Francisco, I was welcome on every local talk show. In New York, popular commentators who had interviewed me with virtually every previous book, passed *The Settlers* by. Again and again the publisher's contact man would call the broadcasters, only to receive vague standoffs. "I simply can't make it out," he told me. "You rate. The book rates. I get nowhere." Excuses echoed the McCarthy period. "I've just done an Israel book." "I'll get back to you."

Months later I was to meet one of these commentators, Barry Farber, on a platform where we were taking part in a protest against the treatment of Russian Jews who wanted to emigrate.

Since an author's absence from "guesting" on the air can hardly be expected to be noticed by the public, I had been surprised, at more than one lecture appearance in the New York area, to have women in the audience (particularly some who said they habitually followed Barry Farber's program) ask me why I hadn't been on the air to discuss *The Settlers*. So now, while we waited our turn, I asked Farber why I hadn't been able to get on his program since the book came out? He'd never heard of any such request, he said. "I'm not pushing to get on your program. I'm mystified because it is not only you, but a half dozen New York commentators on whose programs I've appeared with every previous book." "Let's talk about that," he said. "I'll call you." He wrote down my number. When we left the platform, he repeated, "I'll call you." I even thought he might.

Unquestionably I was getting the silent treatment. Yet some of these commentators were known to be friendly to Israel. What could be affecting them? Was there something being said about me, more poisonous than anything before?

Oddly, that season there came a series of impressive articles in *The New York Times* about the very kind of trouble from which I was suffering—literary denigration, combined with the silent treatment, politically motivated.

First came the remarkable sections of Solzhenitsyn's Nobel Prize Award essay. Again and again Solzhenitsyn stressed the validity of particularism, of nationalism within internationalism, of man's special group heritage as the source of cultural growth, the particular as the source of the universal. Through literature, he said:

we have been given a miraculous faculty: to be able to communicate despite differences in language, customs, and social structures the life-experience of one whole nation to another whole nation . . . Thus literature, along with language, preserves the national soul.

In recent times there has been much talk of the leveling of nations, of the disappearance of peoples in the caldron of contemporary civilization. I do not agree with this . . . the disappearance of nationalities would impoverish us no less than if all people were to become identical, to possess one single, identical personality, one identical face. Nationalities are the wealth of humanity; they are its crystallized personalities; even the smallest among them has its own special coloration, hides within itself a particular facet of God's design.

But was he not speaking directly to me, of my efforts to write of the Jews, speaking of my own long struggle, my own obsession?

But woe to that nationality whose literature is cut short by forcible interference. This is no mere simple violation of "freedom of the press." This is a closing, a locking up of the national heart . . .

And then he spoke of the political methods of regimentation in the arts, of systematic denigration and repression of writers, that became "not only their personal misfortune but a sorrow for all nationalities, and a danger for all nations."

24

I was in no such extreme case as the Russian writers he cited—I was published and had even reached a large audience. But there remained the suppressed play, and then the whole question of literary denigration.

The Sunday *Times Magazine* took up this theme with a vivid article by the poet Joseph Brodsky, exiled from the Soviet Union and now in residence at the University of Michigan. Explicitly he told how the literary downgraders worked. The silent treatment. Down to the method of the shrug.

Then in the same magazine came the posthumous publication of a preface written by George Orwell for *Animal Farm,* showing how the interference of doctrinaire literary influences had almost kept that classic from being published at all, and how systematic literary denigration could be effective even against authors of established quality.

I was experiencing the same treatment from the same ideological sources. In Orwell's case the difficulty arose because the book was being published during the Second World War, when the USSR was an ally, and thus a satire of Stalinism was considered out of place. In my case the trouble started during the McCarthy era, when again, if for different reasons, an exposure of Stalinism was inopportune. But the trouble persisted. While the *Times* published these important articles about the literary-political process in the Soviet Union and in England, not a word, it seemed, could be uttered about my troubles here, for fear of reawakening McCarthyism! Thus, in a reverse manner, McCarthyism was still having its effect on me. In my case, it was abetting Stalinism!

I had to break out, yet nowhere could I tell my story. In my frustration, I recalled a novel of Silone's about Italy under fascism in which a pent-up radical, even though he knows his act is futile, yet feels he must make some outcry, some gesture, if only to show himself that he exists. One night he hastily chalks a slogan on a wall.

I placed an ad in *The New York Times.*

25

I had promised myself during those years of writing *The Settlers* that if "the treatment" extended even to this book I would make an outcry. I had even written such ads and stowed them away. It would be thrown-away money, and a large sum too, for I took a half page. My publisher was against the idea. Everyone said I'd be making a fool of myself.

The headline asked:

CAN A LITERARY MAFIA INFLUENCE YOUR CHOICE OF BOOKS?

I told my story not for itself alone but in terms of mind manipulation, of hidden censorship, of propaganda by omission as well as by repetition. It can even come down to book reviews, I said. Thus "a politicized literary mafia with an anti-Israel position" considered me "too Jewish" a writer.

There came quite a number of letters, cheering me on, asking for reprints of the ad. Some, quite understandably, asked how it was that other Jewish authors had no such complaints. The explanation was simple. I was the one who fought. During twenty years I had drawn down upon myself a vengeful animosity.

Other letters asked what I meant by saying I was dubbed "too Jewish."

I published a second advertisement: "It is simply being Jewish that is 'too Jewish' for some persons," I said, "including some Jews."

No, the ads didn't change anything. To have an effect, I was told, I would need perhaps a hundred thousand dollars for a real campaign.

But at least I was fighting in the open, obsession or not.

And what about obsession? As I have already pointed out:

An obsession is not automatically an aberration. People confuse the two.

26

A justice obsession is frequently well-founded. The entire struggle of Jewry is a justice obsession.

All Christianity began with a justice obsession—a justice obsession on the part of a group of people who saw a horror of injustice in the Crucifixion. The theology developed later.

Perhaps, then, it will help to an understanding of this condition for me to tell my story.

Not that the consequences in this single case could be in any way decisive. Isolated by itself, the instance could not by a hair change the course of history—though one young woman did, out of nowhere, recently write to me that *The Diary of a Young Girl* had indeed changed the course of her life. On reading the Diary she had first become aware of herself as a Jew, and this had led her to Israel. Years afterward, on a visit to the Anne Frank house in Amsterdam, she had been startled and troubled by what had been made of its meaning through the way the memorial house was presented and used. Where was the Jewish essence? She had heard that I might be able to explain what had happened.

There was my whole issue, in that young woman's letter. My aim in tracing this hairline of history is not only to show the course of one man's obsession, but also to dissect a case of the political manipulation of a work of literature, practiced with audacity and complete success on the unsuspecting world audience. For often it is not the obvious slogan, but the propaganda of omission that manipulates our minds. We are more and more subjected to such uses, and our only, if tenuous and perhaps ultimately inadequate, defense must be through alertness and awareness.

In Search left off in 1948. Though written as an autobiography, much of the book told of my encounter with the Holocaust, for during the war years, I had become totally im-

27

mersed in the fate of the Jews of Europe; as a war correspondent I had asked for the one special assignment—to
uncover what had happened to the Jews—and I had sought
out every survivor I could unearth, from the first who emerged
from the subcellars of Paris, to the living cinders of the death-
camp crematoria. Immediately after the war I had written a
symbolic story of the Jewish fate, *My Father's House,* and had
gone to Palestine to film it. After that, I had set off for Poland,
to film the underground movement of surviving Jews across
Europe; I had managed to show them, led by Haganah men,
slipping through border forests, making their way over the
Alpine snows, and then crossing the Mediterranean, packed in
the hold of an "illegal" ship. The making of this historic
document was a culmination for me; perhaps, above anything
I have written, it remains the most important thing I have ever
done. The film completed, I sat down to think myself through,
by writing *In Search.* One thought that I set down in the
autobiography was to become germinal for the whole Anne
Frank problem. No one, I wrote, not even those of us who had
immersed ourselves in the aftermath of the Holocaust, really
could make the world aware of its meaning: "From amongst
themselves, a teller must arise."

It would take decades, I said, for the psychic chasm of the
Holocaust to begin to be encompassed by mankind. If this
massive suffering was not to be relegated to the area of the
grotesque, there was an absolute need for it to be communi-
cated in all its depth.

Since then, many tellers have arisen from amongst the
survivors, and a vast literature has been created, but the Diary
of Anne Frank was the first, in all its youthful candor, to bring
home the Holocaust to the world public, to mankind, and it
remains to this day the most widely known and influential of
all such works. It was not an insignificant matter, then, that
Anne Frank's reincarnation for stage, film, and television, an
incarnation affecting a far more numerous audience than the

book itself, should be true. The transference had to be true in its deepest rather than its surface sense; it had to be true especially in its Jewish essence, for this was the particularism that gave Anne Frank her universality.

This has been the issue; this remains the heart of my obsession. At the outset there was a man's compelling need to defend the quality of his work, and a love for that work, but soon it became clear that what is more importantly involved here is essentially a political issue, an ideological issue, and a real example of the fiercest struggle of our time, the struggle for freedom of identity. In this particular example, the entire Jewish problem is seen in microcosm, and with it the universal human problem of the preservation of the self.

To the wide, accepting public, moved to tears by the popular Broadway play and film, my concern may seem absurd. To those who are aware of the techniques of distortion, my protests seem valid, but by now a matter of the past. A lost cause. It would have been better, they agree, if, in the only way for Anne Frank to be reincarnated, to speak and live again briefly each time she was created on the stage, she could have been allowed to be truly herself. "I would gladly and willingly do whatever possible to put back Anne Frank in her true light," Elie Wiesel wrote, in my support. There would have been a certain cleansing value, too, people admit, in having her passionate outcry as a Jew, her declaration of faith, heard by tens of millions all over the world. And the censorship of those words was indeed a shame, for they epitomized all our baffled striving for meaning in the Holocaust, the entire tormenting question of God and the Six Million. These, then, are the stage-censored words in *The Diary of a Young Girl* that crystallize the whole issue:

Who has made us Jews different from all other people? Who has allowed us to suffer so terribly up till now? It is God who has made us as we are, but it will be God, too, who will raise us up again. If

29

we bear all this suffering and if there are still Jews left, when it is over, then Jews, instead of being doomed, will be held up as an example. Who knows, it might even be our religion from which the world and all peoples learn good, and for that reason and that reason only do we have to suffer now. We can never become just Netherlanders, or just English, or just . . . representatives of any other country for that matter, we will always remain Jews, but we want to, too.

These words, so purely written by an adolescent girl, are actually forbidden utterance on the stage, even now, and it is over this I am obsessed.

In their place Anne Frank is made to say, "We're not the only people that have had to suffer. There have always been people that have had to . . . Sometimes one race . . . sometimes another."

Yes. Everyone concurs, though this is not what she wrote, nor is it what was in the heart of every Jew facing annihilation in the Holocaust. And when I came upon this substitution, I could think only of Babi Yar, where no word has been permitted to declare this a mass grave of Jews.

Why had her Jewish avowal been censored on the stage? It is an essential statement, epitomizing the entire mystery of God and the Six Million, a pure and perfect expression of the search for meaning in the Holocaust, for all humanity, Jewish or not. Nowhere in the substitute drama is this touched upon. This brazen example of the inversion of a dead author's words epitomizes the programmatic, politicalized dilution of the Jewish tragedy. Millions of spectators the world over were unaware they were subjected to idea-censorship.

Effectively, perhaps, all this is past—and why cling to my trouble? Because by some peculiar force of resurrection, a paradigm of the Jewish experience itself, the issue does not die: it is not I who will not leave the issue alone, it is the issue that will not leave me alone. Each time I have tried to put it from my mind there has come a letter, or an attack on me, or an application by some group that wants to put on my version of the Diary, up to this very day. The issue epitomizes nothing less than the entire question of particularism, and for me, of Jewish continuation. In projection, the question arises not only around a drama forbidden to be heard, but around every book I write, around my life activity. The question reflects the whole problem of Jewish continuation, as confronted by assimilation, sometimes freely chosen, sometimes forcibly imposed, sometimes subtly but schematically hastened.

Coming into my hands soon after I had written, in *In Search,* that "a teller would arise," the Diary was like a direct, personal answer. It was Tereska who put the book into my hands, shortly after it had been published in French, and doubtless she has long felt this to have been a perversity of fate, for the trouble centering on the Diary has been the greatest cause of strain between us. At one time, just before the trial with Otto Frank, it all but destroyed our marriage, and again and again times have come when she has agonizedly cried out, "It's me or Anne Frank! Choose!" as though this were some rival love I could abandon at will (Masochist, clinging to your pain-giver!). But can one by an act of will banish what invades one's mind?

All that was vulnerable in both of us was to be awakened, as it must be in any profound struggle, and though the issue had an outside life of its own, it brought forward the most remote and unexpected flaws in our beings, as a physical struggle brings forward muscular flaws due to some forgotten childhood illness, or some imperfection from birth.

I must again make the exposition of the prolonged literary fight, and the obsession.

Appropriately enough, the history begins just where the earlier part of this autobiography leaves off. Since I started *In Search* with the words "This is a book about being a Jew"—

31

more correctly, it turned out to be about being a writer and a Jew—I may say that that theme continues here, for the experience has unfolded with inevitability. "Something like this was bound to happen to him," any reader of *In Search* would say, but the beauty, yes, the macabre beauty, of the unfolding has been the unfailing inventiveness of events, adhering always to the central theme. This, even while in the grip of such events, a writer must admire, just as one can react in awe at the ghastly inventiveness displayed in the history of human tortures.

For there became involved in this single history of the suppression of a play the shimmering, interlocked puzzle of the Jew in the world, and, related to this, the increasingly active issue of political conformism in art. The whole process of image deformation and of the subtle manipulation of ideas in the public mind, the saturation power of mass media, was exemplified. And also, the manipulation of culture through a determined—and biased—elite.

2

THAT SUMMER we were living in a cottage near Antibes, while I worked on a film adaptation of my early novel, *Yehuda,* for Yehudi Menuhin. I hoped to restore my fortunes with this, for I had nearly exhausted my reserves in publishing *In Search* on my own in Paris. I had come to this point after difficulties in finding a publisher for the book in New York; I had attributed these rejections to certain frank passages about the publishing world, until there came a last, a peculiar, refusal that was later seen to fit into the pattern of my "mania."

A week before I was to return to Paris, I had handed the book to Nat Wartels, of Crown, who had told me many times he was an admirer of *The Old Bunch.* In a few days he called. Acceptance. I rushed to his office and had one of those pleasurable sessions in which you are told how good your book is. Both Nat and his brilliant young editor, Hiram Haydn, were full of praise; Haydn declared the autobiography a breakthrough in the use of self-analysis, as well as a startling document on the Jewish experience. A contract, said Wartels, would be drawn over the weekend.

Then, as I stood in the going-down elevator, glowing and

gratified and relieved of long tension, I was tapped on the shoulder, and turning, I looked up into an affable Irish face I at first didn't recall. The Irishman reminded me. Prewar days. Chicago. *Esquire.*

Of course! We had tried to start a union, and every one of our ten members had been fired. It was the heydey of unionization, in the Roosevelt era, and this Irishman, then working out of New York for another publisher, had got a few of us to try to start a unit at *Esquire-Coronet.*

Now he was at Crown—and what was I doing here? "I just placed a book with you," I happily announced. "My autobiography!"

"Well! Great! I'll have to read it right away!"

On Monday Nat Wartels called. "You'll put me down for a shit, but I've got to renege—"

As soon as I got back to Paris, I had *In Search* printed on my own. A crazy, impractical thing, I knew. Conceited, too—trying to put myself among the Paris-published geniuses, the Joyces and Henry Millers. Still, printing was cheap in France, and I had to get the book off my mind.

I sent copies to such illustrious personalities as Thomas Mann and Albert Einstein, and behold, received remarkable jacket quotations. Nevertheless, having no means whatever of distribution, I was stuck with virtually the entire edition. Hearing somewhere that Yehudi Menuhin was eager to appear in a film in Israel, I dug out my early novel, *Yehuda,* about a fiddler in a kibbutz. He liked it, and he even had a producer, the one who had made *Carnegie Hall,* Boris Morross. I was to meet them at the Salzburg festival.

Packing the family and our Siamese cat into the Quatre-Chevaux, I drove to Antibes to adapt the story. On the way the cat leaped from the car and vanished: a bad omen.

It was then, in Antibes, that Tereska gave me the Diary, just published in French from the original Dutch. The book had received warm reviews and attained a *succès d'estime,*

34

without, however, attracting a wide readership. As the Diary dealt with what so absorbed me, she had bought it—and from the first page the seizure was complete. Here was the voice I had been waiting for, the voice from amongst themselves, the voice from the mass grave. As I read on, I became certain—this was the needed document. For here, instead of a remote story-book Jewry, was an urban family with which every American reader could feel empathy. "There I go, with my sister, with my mother and father."

I wrote to Otto Frank at once, in care of the French publisher. It was a simple, practical note, for throughout my contact with survivors the feeling had grown in me that expressions of commiseration were embarrassing to both sides, perhaps in some way presumptuous, since no expression could be adequate. I quite simply asked whether publication in English was arranged, whether Frank might want help with publisher contacts, and even offered, if need be, to do the translation, though it would have to be from the French.

Very quickly there came a reply from Otto Frank, to Tereska and myself. For she, too, had impulsively written him of how deeply she had been touched.

He would welcome contacts in the publishing world, he wrote, for already several American and British book houses of highest standing had rejected the Diary. Unfortunately, they all said, the subject was too heartrending; the public would resist, the book would not sell.

This was what I had anticipated, so I began a campaign to find a publisher. I sent the Diary to a half dozen editors whom I knew. The reactions were uniform: they were personally touched, but professionally they were convinced that the public shied away from such material. I wrote a plea for publication of the Diary that appeared in the annual literary issue of *Congress Weekly,* the organ of the American Jewish Congress. This, it later turned out, had an effect.

Meanwhile a copious and warm correspondence had developed with Otto Frank. I saw the Diary as a play and film, I wrote, for in that way its impact would be enormous. The transfer to stage and screen must be done with utmost simplicity and authenticity; perhaps the film could be made in the hiding-house itself. At first Otto Frank replied that he "could not see" the Diary in dramatic form, but that, as he knew my film *My Father's House,* he would trust me to go ahead. Presently, he began to "see" and even to make suggestions for assuring absolute fidelity.

There is a constant pull in me, as I write this after so many years of conflict, to turn my account only into a self-justification. In *The Fanatic* I observed that self-justification becomes the overriding motive in man. Yet in itself it has no virtue. One hears it not only from the injured, but from every criminal; one reads it in the final mad legacy of Hitler.

What should be noted here is simply Otto Frank's concurrence that fidelity was the first requirement.

While still seeking a publisher for the Diary, I began to approach producers as well. On the way to New York, where an American edition of *In Search* was at last appearing, I carried an extra suitcase filled with copies of the Diary, which I took around Broadway. The one who came nearest to "seeing" was Herman Shumlin, but he sat back and decided, "It's impossible. You simply can't expect an audience to come to the theater to watch on the stage people they know to have ended up in the crematorium. It would be too painful. They won't come."

I felt differently. The very origin of our theater was in religious plays of martyrdom. What of the *Passion Play*? And in the modern theater, what of *Saint Joan*? Yet at least one factor this man of the theater saw as I did: the play, if done, must be a reincarnation. In the persistence of the living spirit each spectator would feel a catharsis. When the spirit reappeared before him, indestructible, the crematorium was negated. Precisely because of this sense of reincarnation, the

36

distortions that came later on literally haunted me. One critic, writing in *Commonweal,* was to imagine Anne Frank witnessing the Broadway play and rushing home to write furiously in her diary, "No, no, it wasn't like that at all!"

But why, I have ceaselessly been reproached, why should you, personally, be so disturbed over this? After all, the Diary itself was not your creation! An opposing lawyer was given to quipping, "Levin has the hallucination that he actually wrote the Diary."

My sense of violation, unabated all this time, even in the case of a drama derived from a book written by someone else, is nevertheless an aspect of creativity. The play had, in today's phrase, become "my thing." It was I who had first conceived of the Diary as drama, clinging to the idea and insisting, when everyone else denied the possibility.

Wasn't my disappointment commercial?—Come on, Levin, aren't you really sore because you had your hands on a "property" that was worth millions, and let it be taken away from you?

Hadn't I been promoting? Was I in any way different from that legion of adaptors, agents, and producers who "fall in love" with a "property" and peddle it around, hoping eventually for success and great profit? Hadn't I been virtually broke at the time and desperate for a project?

From the very first I tried to face the money issue. In the end, I am more angry that people who curtailed its content made great amounts of money from the Diary than I am that to me it has only been costly. Angry too, because all this time the public has been led to feel that the Diary was being handled altruistically. Yes, all this has contributed to my obsession.

There were even rumors that I had a money-share in the book. Over and over I had suggested to Otto Frank that he employ a professional agent for the book and the play, but he had insisted that he preferred to have me represent him. I could only accept what came to me as adaptor, I told him, and even in that capacity, should the Diary become enormously profitable, I would set a reasonable limit beyond which the money should be donated to a public cause—perhaps the aid of survivors. So much for self-justification on the money question.

As things turned out, the Diary has been a constant drain on me, not only in actual outlays for legal help, for printing, for dissemination, but in such indirect costs as fees for analysis, worktime, and in the unmeasurable area of career erosion. Of emotional costs one cannot speak. But at least on the financial side, so far as it concerns me, the issue has retained a certain purity.

The British publisher of *In Search* was taking the Diary. And at last, Frank wrote, he had an offer from an American publisher! He was coming to Paris; we would finally meet! At that time we were living in an impressive apartment on Quai Henri IV, facing the Ile St. Louis, acquired just at the end of the war by a lucky stroke at a modest price. (We thought the owner, who seemed so eager to divest himself of the place, had perhaps been a collaborator.) From the flea market, then still a treasure-trove, we had furnished all six rooms for a total of a hundred and fifty dollars. With its period pieces, and its classic view of the spread-fingered flying buttresses of Notre Dame, the apartment made a decided, if uncalculated, impression of status. In considerable tension, we waited for our first sight of Anne Frank's father, and, as Tereska opened the door to him, he appeared to be someone utterly familiar, tallish, thin, a man who had mastered his tragedy but in whose presence you could not help but sense it. He carried a doll for Dominique— a little girl, playing on the rug before her parents and their guest.

After lunch, I would drive him around Paris on his errands. But what can I truly say about Anne Frank's father, whose personality was unfortunately to occupy so huge a place in the distortion of all these years of our lives? First of all, he is a survivor and as such, in certain areas of behavior, sacrosanct. I have known many other survivors, and with several I have come to be very close. With one, I wrote a book—*Eva*—about her experiences in the Holocaust. Nothing in her life was withheld from me. Another, Dr. Leon Wells, who was of the age of Anne Frank when he was pressed into service in a body-burning *Kommando*, I count as a constant friend. The same may be said of Yechezkiel Dinur, an Auschwitz survivor, author of *The House of Dolls* and other searing works of the Holocaust experience, who signs his books under the number ineradicably etched into his skin. Through these friends I have tried to understand Otto Frank, and by their support in a sense received sanction to write with a minimum of reserve.

True, every survivor stands as though ringed by eternal fire in the unapproachable area of those who have endured an experience that puts them beyond our judgment.

To attempt to understand is permitted and necessary. There has been at least one instance of character penetration—Bruno Bettelheim, himself an emergent from the concentration camps, and therefore more readily permitted to do so than an outsider, wrote an analysis, drawn from the content of the Diary, of the personality of the father, finding, in the whole plan of hiding, a regressive quality, something of a child's impulse to hide or even to return to the womb. This impulse was shared by a host of persons who hid, and there were those who succeeded, even if this was regression, in thus saving themselves. And so Otto Frank had done at the end in Auschwitz, by managing to keep out of sight in the sick-barracks when the evacuation march was ordered.

As he related this, the German word was more apt, applying also to the hiding in Amsterdam—*versteckt*. Stuck away. The hiding impulse later proved to be a character point; it

39

extended to a considerable secretiveness, and had I understood this earlier, much grief would have been avoided.

There was also to come to my attention, when I was far into the trouble, a remarkable study called *Human Behavior in the Concentration Camp,* by Dr. Elie Cohen, a psychiatrist deported to Auschwitz. He was, like Otto Frank, from Amsterdam, though they had never met. In my perplexities, his book proved illuminating.

But for me as for the world, Otto Frank was the warm, patient, self-denying personality portrayed by his gifted young daughter, and so vivid was the image she created, so universally has it become accepted through her book and through stage and screen actors who assumed the physical appearance of Mr. Frank, that throughout the whole trouble this portrait remained the reality of him, and the difficulties that arose had to be regarded as caused entirely by others, including my own erring self.

One does not, one must not, add further wounds to those a survivor has suffered. Yet once, after an unbearably tormenting night, I found myself, in a wild effort to shock Otto Frank into reality, bitterly writing, "You have been my Hitler." How dared I, who had never been touched, allow myself such a cry! What could have driven me that far? I am no longer sure whether I sent the letter—after the release of writing, one tears up, one puts aside, one writes over, omitting. Even in that extreme, I told myself that what I wrote was written not in hatred but in shock.

Ah, then, one analyst after another could readily suggest, was I not all this time reacting in anger because I had made of Otto Frank a father image, and was not my rage the archetypical hostility of the disappointed son who, at any defeat in the world, feels that his father somehow set him off wrong? Neatly as it seems to fit, such analysis was never able to help me in my trouble.

On that day in Paris it was quite simply the father in the Diary who arrived at our apartment, modest, upright, with the reddish touch high on his cheeks characteristic for me of German Jews. He spoke a fluent enough English, and it emerged that as a young man Otto Frank had come to America from Frankfurt-am-Main, and spent some time with a young relative in New York, clerking at Macy's. Only when I was to find myself facing the pressure of the whole upper-class Jewish establishment did I realize that the "young relative" had been Nathan Straus, Jr., of the owning-family of Macy's.

During lunch, Tereska and I were wary of touching on his Holocaust experiences, until Anne's father himself declared that he did not mind speaking of these things, and told us of the fates of all those seized in the hiding place. His own survival, he explained, was a piece of sheer good fortune; one day, too feeble to go out with the labor *Kommando,* he had been sent to the sick-barracks. From there, I knew, few ever returned. But by good fortune, Mr. Frank related, the attending prisoner-doctor happened also to be from Amsterdam, and because of this bond, had protected him and prolonged his stay even after he was able to get on his feet again, so he could gain strength. In the meantime, poor Van Daan had been among the last sent to be gassed; shortly afterward, the death chamber was closed down. Then, from the women's side, word had come that both Mrs. Frank and Mrs. Van Daan had fallen ill and died. As we knew, Anne and Margot had remained alive in Auschwitz and been sent on the evacuation march to Bergen-Belsen. When the march was ordered, and the bombardment was already heard of the Russian troops approaching Auschwitz, young Peter Van Daan, Anne's sweetheart, had come to Otto Frank in the sick-barracks. Peter had luckily received a post in the prized *Kommando* known as Canada, where incoming parcels were sorted, most of them addressed to persons already dead. And from these parcels he had brought food to Otto. They had discussed whether to join the evacuation march in the hope of escape on the way. No, Otto had counseled Peter, it was certain to be a death march. Peter had best stay behind; Otto could arrange for him also to be *versteckt* in the sickroom. The boy had chosen to go on the march, and never been heard of again. Nor was the death-circumstance known of Dussel, the dentist.

Released and repatriated by the Russians, Otto Frank had returned to that very house, the hiding place, where all had transpired; no, he did not find it painful to live there—in a way it was the right place to live, and besides he was not alone—the young Dutch couple, Miep and Henk, who had been the most constant outside contact and provisioners, were sharing the house with him.

From me, he was eager to know about the methods of making a book successful, and what the chances were of the Diary's reaching a wide audience. This was his remaining mission in life: that Anne's words be heard.

His pledge echoed in me; wasn't this the very kind of work that I too had been trying to do, since encountering the Holocaust?

We stopped at one point, that afternoon, before a sumptuous residence in the most aristocratic quarter of Paris, while Otto visited a relative. It was a Rothschild house or something equally elite, I told Tereska on coming home, and I recalled that Anne, in the Diary had related how her father came from a wealthy family, and how they had lived in splendor in Frankfurt-am-Main before the Nazis came. It was true, Tereska agreed, that although Otto was entirely unpretentious, something of the aristocratic manner remained, despite even the experience of Auschwitz—and, nasty as this seems—I must put down that even on that day there arose in me a faint doubt as to his view of me, a doubt that I at once sup-

pressed with shame, as being due to my early Chicago preju-
dices against German Jews, who persisted in their superiority-
attitude toward us *Ost-Juden* from Poland or Russia. The
distinguished apartment on Quai Henri IV, we decided, would
have been enough to dissolve any such attitude, even if it
could have remained in Mr. Frank after the Holocaust. O,
world! To this day I accuse myself of this counter-prejudice
against German Jews, yet I cannot rid myself of the feeling
that I am seen by them as a Yid.

We had parted in warmth, and only at the door did Otto
Frank bring up a question that might have been an augury of
the future. Could I advise him as to which was a better publisher, Little, Brown or Doubleday? He had just received an
offer from Doubleday, in addition to the one from Little,
Brown.

Both were excellent, first class, I told him, the first having
perhaps a more distinguished imprint, but Doubleday being
the largest and most powerful of book houses. Then he asked,
since Little, Brown's offer had come some time ago, was he
still in a position to accept the other? There had been only
letters, but no contract. He wanted the best for Anne.

Finally he chose Doubleday.

At this time suddenly I had to return to New York. The
Frank affair was to draw everything, private and public, into
such a tight web that my relations at home, my relations with
my work and my relations with the world became totally inter-
mingled. Perhaps this becomes the truth for everyone. So I
must tell of the suicide of Mabel.

By the beginning of the war we had become estranged, and
decided on divorce. During the war Mabel remarried, and a
few years later, again divorced. Our son was with her. In a
gallant effort, she had gone to teach at the University of Hono-
lulu, but again had been drawn down. There were suicide
attempts. Her last struggle was in New York. A series of

43

analysts had failed with her. Two suicidal car collisions took place, one with our son in the vehicle.

There is a fallacy in the saying that those who make many attempts at suicide never really do it.

Tereska brought the children over from Paris, and we set up house in New York. It was a difficult period. I didn't have enough money to see me through a novel and had to spend much of my time and energy in that endless kind of appointment-keeping and sample-writing that besets writers who have to do a bit of everything to earn their living: magazine articles, radio scripts, television. With an occasional short story in *Colliers* or in *Commentary,* which had just been started by Eliot Cohen, my first editor in *Menorah Journal* days, I somehow managed.

The Menuhin film meanwhile suffered a fate at least grotesque enough for a grim laugh: one day Tereska brought in the paper, asking, "But isn't this your producer? Boris Morross?" The moonface stared at me from the *Times;* I had last seen it in a café in Salzburg when, our film project ready for signature and the passing of a check, Morross had pocketed the papers and vanished. Now his odd behavior was clarified: here was Boris Morross in the headlines—a double-agent! He had used his film-producing feints as a cover for hustling around Europe to entrap a small cluster of American Communists who, in France, passed information to him in his role of Soviet agent! Yehudi Menuhin and I had been, in our moment, part of his window-dressing.

As to the Diary, I had meanwhile brought the book to Eliot Cohen, urging him to serialize it in *Commentary* before book publication, and this I was able to write to Otto Frank would be done.

In place of our gracious apartment on Quai Henri IV, I had been able to find only a rather dismal sublet in one of those oldish buildings, squat-looking despite their fifteen stories, that stretch without an airspace between them, along West End Avenue. There was still a doorman, wearing a uniform-jacket with frayed cuffs; his principal task seemed to be to keep the entrance free of black tots from the welfare hotel around the corner. As our apartment was on the first floor, Tereska would help them climb in through the Ninety-ninth Street window to play with Gabriel.

Also, the apartment was shared. In the last stages of the desperate hunt, I had answered an ad offering an apartment, all but a consultation room, which was to be retained by our landlord, an analyst named Reuben Fine. Dr. Fine had come to analysis after attaining renown as a chess master, and between sessions with his patients we could hear him typing away at his latest chess book.

As is common for writers in New York, the maid's cubicle behind the kitchen became my workroom. This, and two bedrooms, opened on a dismal areaway shared by the welfare hotel; scarcely a night passed without screams, brawls, ambulance and police sirens; once a woman jumped from a high window. We stayed there for over a year, and in this atmosphere the trouble developed.

Combined with the gritty physical atmosphere in which we found ourselves was the psychological malaise of the time; McCarthyism was at its apogee. For me, it was to be intertwined with the Frank affair, and in an inverse way, determinative. An entire generation has passed, and while McCarthyism is still a familiar term, it is necessary, as with the Depression, to describe the basic aspects for those who did not live through it.

There is a similarity between the two eras. In the sense one had of trying to survive in a world in which some supportive element has fallen away, living through the period of Mc-

Carthyism was like living through the Great Depression. It was a world where one might at any moment in one's life-balancing act be tilted into the void.

In the Depression, however, you clearly knew the physical supporting element that was pulled out from under you—a job. In the McCarthy era it wasn't the loss of a job alone that projected you into the abyss, for you lost also the psychological supporting sense of knowing what was true. We were confronted with the manipulation of truth on a massive, pervasive scale. An insinuation became a truth. To have associated socially with a communist friend, or—in the new language—with someone suspected of "subversion," became disloyalty to America. Even more deeply disturbing than loss of employment was the loss of life-orientation.

There was created the pervasive atmosphere of a conspiratorial world, in which you could never be sure you were being told the truth in matters that affected your friendships, your employment, or your beliefs.

Joseph McCarthy—to orient younger readers—was a Senator from Wisconsin who had become the chairman of a long-standing Washington committee whose function it was to accumulate information on whatever the committeemen suspected might be "un-American activities." They gathered investigative material and testimony that presumably would enable them to propose laws to stop such activities. Suspected un-American activities might range anywhere from membership in the Ku Klux Klan to membership in a labor union, but the hunt was spectacularly concentrated on Communists, particularly in the communications arts—films, television and radio. The usual device was to subpoena a suspected "subversive" to appear before the committee, and there demand if he was or ever had been a member of the Communist Party.

The impression persists that McCarthy sent people to prison for being Communists. It was and still is legal to belong to the Communist Party in the United States, and to hold and propagate Marxist views, nor did the committee have direct authority to send people to jail.

But if a witness admitted membership in the party, he could be asked the names of others in his unit. If he refused to "name names," he could be cited for contempt and tried in the federal courts on this charge and, if convicted, sent to prison. Thus, indirectly, the committee could and did get people jailed.

In the same period, though not in connection with the McCarthy Committee, a group of Communist Party officials were tried and imprisoned on the charge of advocating the overthrow of the government by force. Though an ordinary rank-and-file member of the Party might not readily be accused of advocating the overthrow of the government by force, the conviction of the top leadership had left this a tenuous question, so that a real terror existed in these red hunts. Never certain of what might be its status in a rise of reaction in America, the Communist Party had always been partly underground.

Those called before the McCarthy Committee faced the moral dilemma before all partisans. While they were not, in America, in the acute physical danger that faces political partisans in other lands, they could, quite simply, have their lives broken. The Committee's most prominent early victims were Hollywood writers and directors, some of whom had already been listed by a California state investigating committee of the same sort. Like so many demagogues, McCarthy was not original—he had simply picked up a headline-getting idea. A group of screenwriters who, as the Hollywood Ten, were to become cultural heroes defiantly refused to answer the committee's political questions, and were sentenced to a year's imprisonment. Many directors and scenarists were fleeing to Europe or to Mexico to avoid appearing before the dreaded inquisition, while blacklists of suspected "subversives," even if they had not been summoned by McCarthy, were being used in film, television and radio production offices, and then in colleges and public schools, destroying the careers and livelihoods of hundreds of persons, most of them nonstructured liberals.

My own first apprehensiveness, on returning to New York, came with a chance encounter at an airport. I was hailed by an old friend from my high school days, indeed a central character in *The Old Bunch*. Ben and I had virtually run the school between us, he as student-mayor, I as editor. He had become a lawyer, and in the Depression an active radical; he represented a number of unions, including one in the theatrical field in Chicago, and was rather openly a Communist. Indeed, during our union-organizing difficulties at *Esquire,* I had turned to Ben for advice, only to be treated to a complex analysis of the crisis in the sponsoring union in New York, just then torn between Communist and Trotskyite factions.

Ben was now a labor lawyer in New York. There was another side to his activities that had always touched me; Ben was a frustrated creative personality—he wanted to write, he wanted to act, he had been a member of our early little theater group, The Philistines. In recent years Ben had discovered himself as a painter; he kept a studio on Fourteenth Street where he produced wildly colored sex-symbol compositions of goats, caves, and weirdly animalistic flora.

'Look!" Ben cried out at our chance meeting. He produced a book from under his arm. "I'm famous at last!" The book was entitled *Red Channels*.

This directory, offered as a listing of Communists and fellow travelers who were active in radio, film, theater, and television, was soon to become widely known as the bible of McCarthyism. There, among the big and little "reds," was Ben's name as lawyer for a theatrical union.

I didn't take the directory too seriously at the moment—a crank publication brought out by some rabid red-baiter. We even checked to see whether I was in it. I wasn't. However, another of our Philistines, who had escaped his father's dream that, with his mellifluous voice, he become a rabbi, and instead had made a successful career as a character actor in theater and radio, not only was listed but was to become one of the first to challenge *Red Channels* in the courts.

This directory, Ben explained, had been compiled by an America-Firster, a wealthy woman who must have gathered together the letterheads of leftish labor unions, organizations to aid Spanish Loyalists, organizations against war and fascism, all having scores of sponsors and committee members. Every communications executive was, presently, to keep a copy of *Red Channels* in a desk drawer, along with other lists by specialists who sprang into the field. *Red Channels*, with its viciously haphazard inclusion, became one of the "authentic" tools of the McCarthyists.

Though I was not listed, I soon heard from a good friend, Bill Zimmerman, a New York film executive who had helped with our production of *My Father's House,* that he had been visited by an FBI man who wanted to know whether I was a Communist. "I said I was sure you weren't."

Meanwhile I heard a story about myself from Bernie Geis, who had lasted longer than I with Dave Smart at *Esquire.* One day, after I had been forced to resign, my name had come up in conversation, and Dave had cried out that I was an out-and-out red—that I had tried to set up a Communist union in the place. He knew for certain I was a party member. "I held Meyer's red card right here in my hand!"

In the flat on West End Avenue we turned on the television one evening, and there was the renowned Senator McCarthy addressing a patriotic society. "I hold here in my hand—" he began.

So I had been a premature victim of the McCarthy method.

When I came home the next day the television, a heavy table set, lay smashed on the floor. Tereska, her rage by then dissipated, confessed she had done it: how she had managed to lift the damn thing, she herself couldn't understand. It wasn't that McCarthy had been on the air again; it had been some murderous children's program, but it was all the same.

Later, with her own money, she went out and replaced the set. What could a person do in America?

I sat in the office of a television producer at NBC, a crew-cut type in charge of an "experimental" project for "quality" playlets; did I have any ideas? Meanwhile there were telephone interruptions. He was in the midst of casting; one call apparently came from an actors' agent, for the producer repeated a well-known name with a touch of surprise that the man would work for so low a price. Then, "I'll call you back." At once he dialed on an inside phone, and I heard him say the actor's name. And: "Too bad, I thought he'd been cleared." And wearily, paying no attention to me, as though going through a routine with which everyone must be familiar, the producer called back the agent and said, "Sorry, but on second thought he doesn't really fit the part."

That was how it worked.

Eventually the sample script I wrote was turned down; it "didn't really fit the program."

Was I on the list? How could one know?

And suppose I were called and put under oath. Had I ever been a member of the American Communist Party? There I had no problem. But then they asked if you knew any Communists.

At times it would seem to me that I had known nothing but Communists. Right out of college there were two good friends I went with on a cattle-boat to Europe—even now I suppose I had best change their names, so let us call them Joe and Hal. In the Depression, both quite openly became members of the party. Hal was beaten up by fascists. To get material for a scene in *Citizens,* I had attended a cell meeting in Joe's house.

50

And then there were the members of the International Brigade whom Mabel had known while running the lab in the Brigade hospital in Spain. Several of them had for years afterward kept in touch with us. And the Hollywood Ten—didn't I know at least half of them?

Indeed on my arrival in Hollywood to look for work after my *Esquire* troubles, I had been invited for a talk by a writer I had not known before; I sensed myself being put through a kind of ideological examination. The limitations of the fellow traveler. Some time later I was asked to join in establishing a literary magazine. It was to be purely literary, an outlet for the curbed creative urges of the many authors out on the West Coast, an organ in the high tradition of the "little magazines" of discovery. Purely nonpolitical. I joined the editorial board. We had pleasant meetings in each other's homes, feeling like real literary folk again as we discussed the merits, the signs of talent, in submitted material. *The Clipper* began to have a bit of a reputation. Then one day an article written by a member of the editorial board came up. The subject was "Peace Mobilization."

The Nazi-Soviet pact had been signed, Poland had been divided, America was not yet in the war, but certain heavy industries that needed a lengthy period for shifting to war production were, obviously with the encouragement of President Roosevelt, making the changeover. Against this, a "Peace Mobilization" campaign was under way, conducted through slogans, mass meetings, and leadership that fell into the Soviet pattern. This was to be one of the shorter zigs in the dialectic zigzag—it was to reverse itself on the day Hitler attacked the Soviet Union—but in the interim, confronted with the Peace Mobilization panegyric that was to be the leading article in our coming issue, I reminded my confreres that *The Clipper* had been established strictly as a literary, nonpolitical periodical. Ah, but this was a warmongering crisis from which we could not turn away! Outvoted, I resigned. A few days later one of my closer friends on the board had lunch with me. We talked freely. I told him I had been aware that several of the board were party members, but after all, it had been specifically agreed— He smiled, an odd, somewhat commiserating smile, as toward a child's naïveté. "Meyer, just you and one other were not."

For the very reason that the magazine was so insignificant, the rigid conformity to political policy, even here, could still surprise me.

Nor was this magazine of minuscule influence to be missed by the red-hunters in their turn. *The Clipper*—soon enough defunct—along with the names of its editorial board, including mine, was cited in the California state investigations that preceded the McCarthy attacks.

I kept seeing the names of my former co-editors in the press. Such and such, a two-thousand-, three-thousand-dollar-a-week Hollywood writer, had listed the names of the members of his cell, back in the thirties. Many big names. He was doing this out of conviction, the witness would be quoted as saying, because he now felt the whole movement, secret and conspiratorial, was morally wrong, and a danger to democracy, and that he had been a deluded fool.

The rat!—we then heard all around us—Just so he could be cleared to work again at his three thousand a week!

There came the most startling confession of all, not only in the news columns but blazoned in an ad on the theater page, a statement by Elia Kazan. In his testimony, Kazan listed the names of his former comrades. Big names. His ad contained a passionate declaration. He was doing this out of sheer conviction. Reformed.

What would I do, if I should be called?

There was one thing you could do instead of being defiant and risking going to jail, or being compliant and naming names. Lawyers had worked it out, and this third choice was the new byword—"Taking the Fifth." When asked the key question as to party membership, one could invoke the Fifth Amendment to the Constitution, which provided that one need not answer if the reply might be self-incriminating.

But "taking the Fifth" itself implied guilt. Even if you yourself did not view being a Communist with guilt, the public did, and the communications industry had to, so that a person "taking the Fifth" in those hysterical years was automatically on the blacklist. Yet various individuals declared that they "took the Fifth" not as a confession, but as a protest. They might or might not be members of the party, but of first importance to them was liberty of conscience and political privacy.

Would I be one of those?

A whole range and variety of replies began to appear. The timing of "taking the Fifth" had importance. Some witnesses openly declared their party membership up to a certain date only. "Were you a Communist Party member in 1935?" "Yes." "In 1936?" "Yes." And so on up the calendar until perhaps 1950, when the witness would suddenly invoke the Fifth. There were even cases of "A week ago?"—Defiantly, "Yes." "Today?" Fifth Amendment. I was unable to follow the finer shading of such admissions. However, the temper against McCarthyism was growing—the tide was turning, though the plague was to take several years to subside. Lillian Hellman, who had been named as a Communist Party member by one of the "sincere" Hollywood turncoats, was summoned. She prepared an emotional statement to be read before the inquisitorial committee, taking care to have it widely disseminated in the press; it declared that she would answer questions about herself, but under no circumstances would she involve others. Miss Hellman became a cultural heroine. Arthur Miller wrote his play about early American witch-hunts.

The frenzy was analogous, yes, and the protest was essential. But the question in our time was not so much whether we lived in a demonic world, as whether we lived in a conspiratorial world. Can anyone today doubt this? One may be dubious as to the extent to which conspiracy is effective in determining events. One may hold that spying, rumor-mongering, underground activities form only a lesser portion in social and political control. But who today denies the presence of conspiracy? From every side, in every form?

Yet already, then a counter-frenzy to the witch-hunt had come into being. It was already dangerous in liberal circles to question the completeness of Miller's analogy. A reverse-McCarthyism was being created.

There may be no such thing as objective truth, but in my kind of writers' world there is a belief in the search for truth. To seek the truth in politicized areas poses a constant dilemma, for one finds one cannot really deny the conspiratorial structures in the world their circumstances of moral legitimacy. Revolutions begin in conspiracy, and only time, perhaps, can show which is the "good" and which is the "bad" revolution. McCarthy's method was to arouse the fear of the unknown and raise it to such dimensions as to make it seem determinative for our very society, for our lives. Thus, his "Communist conspiracy."

To see a magazine ad for the Rosicrucian society need not convince one that the Rosicrucians secretly run the world. To be told that every president of the United States was a member of the Masons need not convince us that the Masonic order runs the nation. To know that the Joint Distribution Committee operates a relief agency for Jews in many countries does not mean there is an international conspiracy of the Elders of Zion to rule all mankind.

In our time we are submerged in the conspiratorial concept. Television has become an almost continuous exposition, with scientific trappings, of superspy groups manipulating mankind, not only from earthly power centers but also from outer space. Today's "entertainment" is built on the same half-credence as the response to McCarthyism. The average person may feel he is as yet far from being affected in his own life—but after all, conspiracy exists even in a little office clique that seems to exclude him. If such things continue—where then, for each person, and for the world, is the healthy limit, where the edge of paranoia?

That conspiracy was an instrument, and in a sense a legitimate one, of the few against the many, the weak against the powerful, I could agree. In our time, perhaps more than ever before, it is the sling of David. Had I not filmed an entire conspiratorial operation, the underground escape of the Jews from Europe? This was a "good" use of conspiracy, undertaken to save people, like the underground stations in the escape of slaves. Such conspiracy had an ethic. Well, so did revolution. I believed in the right of revolution. Of every revolution? Of every means? Terror, betrayals, blackmail? No, I did not believe the end always justified the means.—So—you leave the dirty work to others?

Since McCarthyism was based on the exaggeration of this fear of the secretive and unknown in us, on the evoking of what might in medieval terms be called the evil spirits, wasn't Miller's response in terms of witch-hunt correct?

Then what was my reservation? A curious, underneath feeling that, since hard-core Stalinists, too, were engaged in manipulating public opinion, then, while I had every sympathy for their struggle against McCarthyism, I had to preserve my own wariness as to their aims. Particularly in the area of Jewishness.

Is it possible even today when "McCarthyism is dead" to write with candor about the Communist movement in America? I don't mean about specific party activities: there have been innumerable confessions, exposures, and books of revelation by disillusioned party members, some from among the top leadership. What I would like to convey is the effect of the "movement" on someone like myself who considers him-

55

self an equalitarian, a radical of sorts, but is considered by the "movement" people as a "dangerous" emotional liberal, and in my case is tagged even more venomously as a "nationalist Zionist." (Incidentally, while devoted—not blindly—to Israel, I have, in order to maintain my sense of freedom as a writer, never been an organized Zionist.)

Today the good-hearted humanist, once a fellow traveler, doesn't have room to maneuver: one has to be either savagely "for" or "against." One is a no-good unless lined up with the Maoists, the Trotskyites, the Neo-Stalinists, or at least the amorphous New Left. In earlier days, even if I was regarded as a misguided Zionist, those of my fellow writers who were part of the Hollywood Communist clique welcomed me as a liberal-radical friend. With the Scottsboro case and other causes, with the dominance of the proletarian school of writing, dedicated Communists were somehow our spearhead heroes, even when they were earning enormous salaries writing slick movies. The experience of the Depression, traumatizing all our lives, the sense of all civilization in constriction and fear, gave heroic stature to the self-pronounced revolutionists, as their action culminated in the struggle for Loyalist Spain. Liberals had perhaps a sense of moral inferiority before those who went to fight, but still no outcast shame. We mere fellow travelers admired the courage of those who had gone all the way to accepting "party discipline," even when we thought in the end that their party was disastrously wrong.

The danger in their discipline we had only begun to see, some at the moment of the Hitler-Stalin pact, some after the war. Today, even only in terms of the Hollywood writer-revolutionaries, it is clear that the very same ability to adjust one's sense of truth to a "higher value" for the sake of party discipline was what made it possible for these writers to adapt themselves so successfully to the requirements of Hollywood producers. Censorship and adaptability can work for any master. It is striking that of the number of gifted writers who

56

were part of this Hollywood group, not one thenceforward seriously developed his talent.

In my Hollywood days I felt there were even a few who had hitched onto the movement so as to be in with a powerful clique and to make successful careers. In a somewhat shameful way I could not help but sense a twinge of satisfaction when some talentless careerist who had gained Hollywood status out of his political allegiance was summoned. At least, I told myself, I had known what it was all about. I had been protected from swallowing whole an ideology that contained an enormous defect—the command of total subservience. It was my intense absorption in the Jewish fate that had been the most important separating factor between myself and my friends in the movement.

But as one who had been to Spain, as one who had led the Chicago protests against the police killings of ten steel-mill strikers, most of them shot in the back, I would certainly not "name names" if I were called. Perhaps ironically, I'd have to be one of those who "took the Fifth."

But I was never called. And even more ironically, it was to be a reflex of McCarthyism, reverse McCarthyism, even more miasmic, even more prolonged, that became "the trouble" for me.

It was in the atmosphere of McCarthyism that the ramifications of the trouble over the Diary developed. As publication date at last approached, Otto Frank wrote me to get in touch at Doubleday with a young woman named Barbara Zimmerman who had been assigned to edit the book, and who had developed a warm correspondence with him.

At her Doubleday desk I met a low-voiced, unobtrusive girl of the age Anne would have attained, and who, it was clear from her first words, identified passionately with the Diary. This was her first real assignment, Barbara told me, and she

57

was uneasy about the firm's attitude. The big bosses at Doubleday estimated that the book might sell a few thousand copies at best, mostly to libraries; they had taken it on, it seemed, rather as a gesture toward the Jews. Advertising and promotion were not to be expected. Could I think of any way to bring the book to public attention? Already, Barbara said, she had had the idea of getting Eleanor Roosevelt's name on an introduction—she had herself written the foreword and Mrs. Roosevelt had agreed to sign it! What else could we do? It became as though Barbara and I were founding a benevolent conspiracy to keep the Diary from sliding into oblivion as merely another title on Doubleday's enormous list.

I explained to her about the Jewish organizational world and the Anglo-Jewish press, which I undertook to activate, but more urgent was the question of securing general reviews, particularly a prominent review in the all-important Sunday *Times*. Everything would depend on the choice of reviewer. That, as the public never seems to realize, is how things are managed.

We now set ourselves to this game for the sake of Anne Frank's Diary. The problem was that neither I nor Barbara— at the time—had much influence.

I could write reviews in half a dozen Anglo-Jewish weeklies, I could contact community leaders from Hadassah to the rabbinate. But there remained still the key question of the *Times*. Could we get a "big name" to ask to review the Diary? John Hersey? In the end, though I was hardly so big a name, Barbara thought it might be safest for me to ask for the book myself.

The *Times* sent me the Diary, but the slip called for only a few hundred words. That meant the rear pages. In the limited few paragraphs, I tried to convey the importance of the book, the need to make the public humanly aware of the Holocaust. Then I added a letter to the editor of the Sunday *Times Book*

Review, urging that he read the Diary himself to judge whether it was not worth a far more extensive treatment. At the time, the overall Sunday *Magazine* editor was the redoubtable Lester Markel, for whom I had written some pieces as far back as the twenties; his daughter Helen read the Diary and she also urged fuller treatment.

A call came. I was to "go all the way." Write as much as I wanted! This could mean the front page of the book magazine! Gleefully I told the news to my fellow-conspirator, Barbara.

And so it turned out. On the Monday after the review appeared, the Diary was a best seller.

Anne Frank alone, obviously, is the source of the Diary's success. Yet never have I received, over a single piece of writing, the measure of response that came to this book review. A year later I was still receiving letters about it, some from as far away as Australia.

Many other enthusiastic reviews appeared. I was called upon for radio, for television; blowups of the *Times* review were placarded in bookshop windows; Barbara and I gloated.

That same Monday Broadway producers began to call Doubleday, inquiring about the dramatic rights. Some were among the very ones who had told me the Diary was unadaptable for the stage. Now, however, it was a "property."

A Doubleday executive called me. Could I tell him who controlled the stage rights to the Diary?

Otto Frank himself, I said. But he had asked me to represent him.

Was I the agent?

Why, no. I had long wanted to do the play, and he had authorized me to find a producer, subject of course to his approval.

Did I have a contract?

Otto Frank had put all this in a letter.

Ah.

The next person to call from Doubleday said, "This is Ken McCormick."

The editor-in-chief. A writer may never find himself intimidated by governors or even presidents, by tycoons or even movie stars, for he knows he has the power to write about them. But editors have the power to pass on his writing.

Not that Ken McCormick was in any way intimidating; he was genial, he said he had long been an admirer of my work, and he was most appreciative of all I had done for the Diary. Now, as to those calls that were coming in regarding the dramatic rights—from the biggest producers on Broadway—didn't I think Doubleday would be in a better position to handle this complicated, commercial side, and get a better deal for Mr. Frank, than I—a writer?

Certainly, I agreed, all I wanted was to write the play. I had long ago suggested to Otto Frank that he get an agent, but he had insisted he wanted someone he knew, like myself, to represent him.

Oh. And was I—uh—to receive the agency commission?

Of course not.

Fine! Then would I send a wire to Mr. Frank—Doubleday would pay for it—advising him to take Doubleday as his agent for the play?

An enormous firm like that, wanting a 10 percent agency fee? Already I had a foreboding. Was it a maneuver to get the dramatization out of my hands? But why? And why shouldn't I accept the situation at face value—that they could handle the commercial side far better than I?

I sent the wire, only, at the last moment, adding that I should be stipulated as adaptor of the Diary.

Meanwhile I was asked to come meet a vice president of the company, Mr. Marks, who would be the one to negotiate the stage rights.

Mr. Marks inhabited an important-sized office. Short-necked, rotund, he declared himself to be a fan of *The Old Bunch;* he would be delighted to work with me. Opening a tooled-leather folder that reposed solo on his broad executive desk, Marks proceeded to read off the names of illustrious producers who had called to make offers. As royalties were standard, the deciding factor would be the prestige of the producer and the qualities of the suggested adaptor. Suggestions ranged from John Steinbeck to Clifford Odets.

Now I knew.

But had all these big-name authors expressed the desire to adapt the Diary? I asked.

Well, undoubtedly such producers would be able to deliver such authors.

Embarrassing as it was in the face of these great names, I said, I had to point out that the dramatization was my own project. At least I deserved first chance. If I failed to write a good play, a big name could still be called in.

Yes, Mr. Marks appreciated my position. Though, of course a big-name dramatist would virtually assure a Broadway success.

He closed the leather folder.

Only then did I notice that several more executives were coming into the office, as if for a meeting. I stood up to leave, but was introduced all around. It was the big brass, from the editor-in-chief to the president of Doubleday, who thanked me for my cooperation.

They got to the business. Marks reported on the production offers. Another vice president added the name of a supreme producer of musical comedies who had called him personally. As to the agent's fee, one of them suddenly said to me that Doubleday had decided I must share it with them, five and five.

I wanted no fee, I was not an agent, I repeated.

It would be embarrassing for Doubleday to accept an

agency fee if I did not, they insisted. After all, I had devoted so much time to the project and would be devoting more, since I would continue to be Otto Frank's personal representative while they were the negotiators.

Bewildered, I felt only that I must hang on, and not make enemies of these powerful people. Once my play was produced, I could drop my share of the fee. I let it ride.

Just then a secretary slipped into the room and handed a telegram to one of the executives. After a rapid reading, he turned to his colleagues; several heads bent over the cable. The recipient now addressed me. In this cable Otto Frank named Doubleday as his agent, but added that Meyer Levin was to be the dramatist—

Why, yes, that had always been understood, I said. The cable, now handed to me, said I was to write or collaborate in any adaptation "in order to guarantee the idea of the book."

With the briefest high-level glance at the editor-in-chief, the president left the room. Lamely, the discussion continued. Would a first-rate producer accept me as adaptor? Well, Mr. Marks explained, he had anticipated such a situation and asked the question of several producers. If such was the condition, almost all of them agreed.

Wouldn't it only be fair, an executive put in, to let Otto Frank know that there were now—with all deference to me— offers involving important and proven playwrights?

I had let myself in for this. I should have written the play long before and had it ready. But some strange deference had held me back. To myself I had said that I did not want to impose my version on the Diary, to freeze it into a given form, and reduce Otto Frank's chance of obtaining a producer; I wanted to write the play after consultations with the producer, so that we would be in agreement from the start.

I told the Doubleday executives that I would send Mr. Frank a complete account of all the offers, with the names of all the adaptors who had been proposed, as well as a list of those producers who were willing to try me.

Marks and I were again alone in the room. Briskly, he opened his leather-bound folder. He knew little of the Broadway world—could I go over the offers with him, and fill him in about each producer?

Inevitably, then, we came to the political question.

I have come to the writing of this portion of my book, as it falls out, on the eve of Yom Kippur, our day of self-examination. As I've already pointed out in *In Search,* this is also my birthday, and consequently I have always felt doubly the solemn import of this tradition. Today is my sixty-sixth birthday, a stage at which one has the feeling of having passed the worst temporal pressures of ambition and even partisanship, so that one can more freely seek a clearer understanding of motives and events.

For in this commandment of self-examination on this day there is also invoked the very essence, the mystique of Judaism, the entire question of the responsibility of the individual man. It was in that office on that day that the whole issue was posed in me, and perforce it had to be before someone named Marks. I was in the inevitable dilemma of the liberal, bound to be the victim of both sides. I had already had an advance taste of McCarthyism when I was fired from *Esquire.* I was already wary of partisan intervention in publishing, through the dropping of that agreement to bring out *In Search.* Since then I had met the book's almost-publisher in a relaxed, drinking atmosphere and asked him about his having been influenced to withdraw. "Was it political?" "Yes."

The politicals, it could at least be said, pursued their goal out of their own form of messianic idealism. Only, when organized Communism touched on anything concerning Jews, I was uneasy. Though I was not yet aware of Stalin's annihila-

63

tion campaign, in those very months of 1952, against Jewish writers in the Soviet Union, I had for years been at odds with my Communist friends over the Jewish issue, particularly the Zionist issue. Because of this, I was wary of getting involved with their circles on the subject of the Diary.

Among the producers who had applied for the Diary rights were two or three about whom I felt uneasy as to influences affecting the Jewish content of the Diary. They were, in terms of "worthwhile" theater, among the best on Broadway. Outstanding among them and considered the most powerful producer of the moment, was Kermit Bloomgarden—Arthur Miller's producer, and Lillian Hellman's. Probably himself unpolitical, he had nevertheless been "made" by this clique.

All through the Depression and on into the postwar era we were dominated by the literature of social criticism, and I took part in and still highly value this approach to writing, provided literature is unfettered by imposed doctrine. But to a large extent our critical reactions can be affected by our emotional adherence to causes. Writers rose to eminence whom one might have judged as being mediocre—but one hardly dared breathe this in the dominant literary circles. The clique, more apt today to be thought of as a Mafia, was powerful. Even today it is dangerous to suggest that certain of these authors, particularly the playwrights, were often merely meretricious.

My own feeling was that there had been no great American playwright since Eugene O'Neill—revolutionary enough, for that matter—in the truest sense a free spirit. I had been theatrically held by Lillian Hellman's early work, but had afterward felt disappointment about it. Arthur Miller, a genuine talent, seemed to tailor his themes to the mode of the movement. I thought *Death of a Salesman* his only play with real feeling, but even here sensed an uneasiness; as many had noticed, the characters were clearly drawn from Jews—why then hadn't Miller left them as Jewish? Would that have made the play

64

any the less universal? I scented a "play down the Jewishness" orientation in that whole circle, and hardly wanted to have to cope with it on the Diary.

Could it not be said, I argued with myself, that they had as much right to "universalist" non-Jewishness, as I had to my universalist Jewishness? But, I answered, I don't want to manipulate anything—I want to present the Diary as it is, as exactly as possible, on the stage.

Another aspect of this whole question had to be confronted. The McCarthy investigators, having finished with Hollywood, were, it was just then widely announced, about to open hearings on Broadway. Should we, in the face of this, deliberately select a producer who was likely to be involved? But if we made this a reason for avoiding such a producer, wasn't that in itself McCarthyism?

All this, quite unrestrainedly, I brought up with Mr. Marks as we went over the growing list of producer-applicants. Barbara Zimmerman usually appeared in his office during these discussions. She offered no opinion. In the end it was agreed that Otto Frank, in all fairness, should be apprised of the whole situation before he made his choice of producer. I would write to him.

One day, meanwhile, the three of us went to lunch. Again, I voiced my misgivings about possible ideological intrusion in the handling of the Jewish content of the Diary, should it be produced under doctrinaire influence. The conversation veered to a story that had appeared in the *Times* about Communists working in the book-publishing field. More witch-hunts! Suddenly Marks turned to me, saying he wondered if there was someone at Doubleday—who could it be? The moment struck me sharply. Was he baiting me? Warning me?

Dutifully, I had sent off a full report on all the producers and their proposed adaptors, adding a final plea for myself. A play by any of the big-name dramatists would first of all be the author's. With me it would be Anne's. True, I had never had a play performed on Broadway, but Otto had seen *My Father's House* and been impressed with my dramatic writing. None of the proposed writers had had any contact with the Holocaust. Finally, I told him, if he would choose one of the producers to whom I was acceptable, I would present a first draft in a month. If it was a failure, little time would have been lost, and he would be free to go to another playwright.

—But any producer could let you work for a month, then reject what you wrote and replace you with a big name!

—Of course I realized that. Only, if I wrote a bad play, I didn't want to force it on the Diary.

—And politics? You walked right into it!

—No! I tried to avoid it, didn't I? I wrote Otto Frank about the whole tangle—McCarthyism, the Jewish question and the Communists. I said I saw no reason why Anne's work should risk being tangled up in it all. I tried to make my own position clear. I said I was certainly against keeping anyone for political reasons from working or acting in a play—I certainly would not bar a producer or a director because he was a Communist—but in this particular situation with the Diary, and considering the Jewish question, my first choice would be, quality being equal, to avoid the political side. Frank wrote back that he fully agreed about this. So then I remember writing that if this whole question came up, meaning the red hunt and all that—I would know how to deal with it. Of course nothing could be further from the actuality. I didn't, and wouldn't, know how to deal with it. I had no workable sense of politics, of intrigue—I had no experience of Broadway machinations—

—And you were yourself ambivalent.

—All right.

—And it could be claimed from that letter that you were

66

yielding to McCarthyism, that you were barring producers as first choice if they could be accused by McCarthy.

—No. It was because I feared trouble over the Jewish content. . . . Exactly as was to happen.

—But, correctly or not, the other side could interpret your discrimination as McCarthyism.

—I've always seen that.

—And even now you have guilt over your attitude.

—Not guilt. Dismay, anger at the misinterpretations. And even from *their* viewpoint—in the Soviet Union the Jewish writers persecuted by Stalin have been rehabilitated! Here, I am still being punished for being "too Jewish"!

—Then why do you yourself keep up this punishment?

—No. I can't take the blame myself for all this trouble. That's too pat. Not everything is masochism. If we accept that, we end up with the attitude that the Jews themselves are to blame for the death camps. After all, the other side went after me. The fight was imposed on me. I'm keeping up the fight, that's all.

—But do it more cleverly! You've seen how clever they are! You must fight more cleverly! Tactics!

Inside I cried shit! Why must what's basic, what's right, depend on cleverness, on superior intrigues, on concealments?

As my first choice for producer I had recommended Cheryl Crawford. She had, I wrote Otto Frank, been one of the directors of the Group Theatre, the most progressive and exciting element in the American theater in the thirties. She had excellent taste, prestige and sensitivity.

On my side, there were additional reasons. Cheryl Crawford knew and respected me as a dramatist, for she had wanted the Group Theatre to produce my play *Model Tenement*—the one that had later been suppressed in Chicago. And while she was part of the progressive crowd, an old friend of mine, who knew the cliques and cabals of Broadway, assured me that she herself was not political. I would have no doctrinaire difficulties.

Otto Frank's decision came. Yes, despite all the big-name proposals, he would stand by me. He had heard from Miss Crawford and been most impressed with her letter. She had made him feel that as a woman she would bring a particular understanding to Anne. All was well, and we could proceed.

The Doubleday people were not pleased, and withdrew as agents. At least the whole embarrassment about the percentages was over with. But would they really stop trying to bring in a "name"? No matter, I assured myself: all I had to do was write a good play.

Out we went to Fire Island. The place was full of theater people; one young producer virtually sat on my doorstep so as to have the inside track "should anything go wrong with the Crawford deal."

Some distance from our cottage I found my usual type of workplace, a storage shack where I could have isolation.

The first draft came quickly. I had the play clearly in mind, the Diary virtually memorized, so that I could use Anne's own words in the dialogue. I saw the form almost as a ballet, a young girl's probing, thwarted at each impulsive moment while she strives for self-realization. In the enclosed and threatening circumstances in which she finds herself, each movement is intensified; she approaches her sister, her mother, her boy, and in each she finds an element of disillusion. And when this comes from her father as well, she sees clearly where she stands in this insane, destructive world—she at last makes her outcry, her fierce and forever echoing protest: it is not God but man who is responsible.

It's good! the producer said.

I had done it! The first draft had caught the drama. Much work remained, but the play was there.

We began discussing directors, casting. I had left the first draft overlong so Cheryl could have some voice in shaping it, and we went to work.

Just then there came a request for a radio play from the Diary, to be broadcast nationally by the Jewish Theological Seminary in a special program for the High Holy Days. I put the play's essential dialogues into radio form and rushed the script to Otto Frank for approval. He thought it fine. So my test was over. Both he and Miss Crawford approved.

The radio play went excellently, with a review in *Billboard* singling out the adaptation for praise for its sensitivity, faithfulness, effectiveness. Why should I still feel uneasy?

I had suggested to Cheryl Crawford that Otto Frank be brought over to make certain of authenticity in the production, and now he arrived. Cheryl had filled his room with flowers; Barbara Zimmerman was waiting to meet him.

That evening he came to us for dinner. I was suddenly, unreasonably, concerned about the dinginess of the flat as compared with our impressive apartment on Quai Henri IV. Perhaps he had already been reminded, since his arrival, of the enormously successful dramatists he could have picked from.

Our rapport returned, and I was ashamed of my misgivings. Already, Otto told us, he had found time to slip out for a walk on Fifth Avenue, and a touching thing had happened to him. He had gone into a bookstore, and as he stood by the counter where Anne's Diary was piled, a woman kept looking at him. Then she approached, asking whether he might not be the father of Anne Frank? She had seen his picture in the paper with an announcement of his arrival. As he said yes, the woman's eyes filled with tears. She had so loved his daughter in the book, she said, and clasped his hand.

As Otto Frank related the incident, his own eyes filled with tears.

When he left, I gave him a copy of the script to read. The next day, on the phone, he told me, "I cannot imagine how anyone could write the characters more truly." The adaptation, he was sure, couldn't be more faithful, the people more real.

I said I hoped things hadn't been brought back too painfully. He hesitated. "Only at first."

Of course, as to the theater part, he added, he was no expert and would have to leave that to the professionals.

Could something have begun?

Hardly a week later, there came a call from Miss Crawford's secretary, asking me to drop in. Amidst her clutter of furnishings from past productions, Cheryl Crawford was all at once unreal, herself a prop in a scene. Unfortunately, she said, on rereading it late last night, she had lost contact with my play. Totally lost contact. She couldn't really say what was wrong. Earlier, she had given the play to her good friend Lillian Hellman to read, and Miss Hellman had felt most strongly that the adaptation was wrong. A fresh start had to be made. Then Miss Crawford had tried again to study the play, and found she simply no longer got from it the feeling she got from the Diary. It was no use. She had to release me and seek another writer.

Dazed, I mumbled that she had perhaps read the play too many times so that it had gone stale for her. After all, her first, fresh reaction had been good. An audience would have only that first, fresh reaction.

Well, Lillian Hellman's reaction had been fresh, she said.

And what had Miss Hellman objected to?

Lillian thought my work was totally untheatrical. I simply did not write with a sense of stage. It wouldn't play.

At that time I thought of Miss Hellman only as an important, successful playwright. An authority in the theater. I had striven for an atmospheric drama, a Chekhovian effect, rather than a tightly plotted work of the kind Miss Hellman wrote.

70

And as to the playability of the scenes, I pleaded there had already been the radio presentation that had gone so well it had been repeated.

Radio was not theater, said Miss Crawford.

But what they were reading was still a sprawly first draft, purposely left long, as we had agreed, so that both she and the director could help shape it after we saw what played best. I could tighten it now, I could work on it—

Well, she conceded, if I wanted to, I could take the weekend and work only on the scenes between Anne and Peter, so as to let her see if revision would help.

I rushed off alone to Fire Island. The season was over, and I had the use of an isolated cottage. I knew the whole thing was doomed—that I could thrash around like a caught fish, but it would be to no avail; they were determined to get their big-name writer, perhaps Lillian Hellman herself. And yet I worked furiously and well. Under this desperation and pressure, I suddenly saw much more deeply into the boy, Peter, saw in the hatred he had for the quarreling of his parents the bitter, furious accusation of all youth against the whole warring, quarreling adult world. Now I showed him crying out to Anne that if he lived he wanted only to go away, to disappear, change his name, never be known as a Jew, and showed Anne exclaiming, "But Peter! That's not honest!"—There it was! The inner effect of the Holocaust, turning the Jew against his own identity! And then I had Anne rush away, writing in her diary, "He's weak! He's weak!"

Lifted out and sharpened as a character progression, I could feel the scenes between them to be gaining enormously. (These were the scenes that were to prove so shattering when the play was "illegally" and only briefly heard, many years later.) If nothing else, I knew in my bones that what I had done that weekend proved I indeed knew how to work in the dramatic form. If the play was still rejected, it could only be because of extraneous motives.

Still, a writer in the heat of composition could delude himself, could feel something was good that later would seem flat and worthless. As long as I had this doubt, I could not rely on my own judgment, and in no case must I foist a bad play on the Diary. As soon as I got back to New York, I sought out a man of the theater whose word would have to be respected, Harold Clurman.

Along with Cheryl Crawford, Harold Clurman had been one of the triumvirate directing the Group Theatre. When the Group broke apart, he had spent some time as a producer at Columbia Pictures, and it was there I had encountered him. A director for the vital and progressive Group Theatre, a scholar, a critic—who better could offer me a valid opinion?

Clurman asked me to leave the script for him at Stella Adler's—they were then still married. Miss Adler received me with her characteristic overwhelming warmth—another fan of *The Old Bunch*. And in a few days there came a most reassuring call from Clurman. He had read my work; many of the key scenes were already right, they were highly playable, the work on the whole was progressing admirably considering the short time I had been at it—I need have no misgivings, I was precisely on the right track.

During the week I had not heard from Otto Frank. I now realized that virtually from the day of his arrival a gulf had developed between myself and everyone connected with the Diary. Barbara Zimmerman no longer called from Doubleday with her constant reports and requests. Both she and Frank must already know of the trouble. All sorts of conferences must be going on, perhaps with Lillian Hellman included. I could imagine Otto Frank listening to the authoritative opinion of so notable a dramatist. Meyer Levin's script was hopeless. How could Anne's father but accept her word? What possible motive could she have except to advise him on "the best for Anne"?

But how was it that Lillian Hellman had been called in? No, it was quite natural for Cheryl Crawford to show the script to her friend. Yet the gnawing was in me. Was this sudden total condemnation a genuine opinion, or was there some other motive for getting me out? Money? Or, vaguely, like some scarecrow figure trying to make signals to me from behind a crowd, there hovered the old Jewish Question. But no. Hellman herself was Jewish. And hadn't she written an anti-Nazi play? Only, nothing about Jews. Political resistance. Heroics. Probably she simply didn't like what I had done. An extreme but honest reaction. I didn't want to believe that any genuine writer—and I gave her that status—would gratuitously cut down the work of another. There remained in me a faith—all right, naïve—in a kind of primal unity, a primal sympathy, among artists. To be a writer was difficult enough, and every writer knew it. Because of this, I felt that serious writers didn't gratuitously destroy members of the same craft.

Even when it came to political motives, there was a persistence in me of the same softness. I knew, and yet suppressed my knowledge, of merciless critical cabals in which authors like Farrell and Dos Passos had been systematically denigrated. I reminded myself that even with a fascist author like Céline, it would be hatefully agreed, "But he's done some great writing." Yet I was aware that in nations where there was political control over art, an author could be dismissed as talentless and incompetent when the real objection to him was his refusal to conform to doctrine.

With all this, I held back from believing that something inexorably political was happening to me. Was this disbelief so unusual? For two decades nearly everyone around me was to disbelieve. Most people refuse to believe, even today.

I had met, or seen, Miss Hellman only once, early in the war, when I had worked in the film section of OWI, and

73

Herman Shumlin had brought her to a screening of a documentary he had directed. Shumlin was the producer of *The Children's Hour,* which had made her famous. There were many piquant tales about the redoubtable Lillian Hellman, and, curious, I took a good look at her before the screening-room lights went out. A strong face. And I caught a few words in a decisive voice. Still, she had been passionate, selfless, in the Spanish cause.

The screening-room glimpse had remained with me to the time of Miss Crawford's injection of her name. The sense of hardness weighed more in my uneasiness than any political question. Had I not been in Spain virtually at the same time as she, wasn't I okay with them? Of course she must differ with me on Israel, on Judaism—but why should that disqualify me on a Jewish book?

Besides, Harold Clurman's word would surely count in their circles, and I repeated his opinion to Miss Crawford.

She took me to lunch at the Algonquin, said the rewritten scenes were highly improved, again discussed casting and directors. My political worries had been fantasies. It was really only a matter of the play itself. Yet the luncheon dragged. She was tense. At last, going up in the elevator to her office, Miss Crawford suddenly asked, "Would you be willing to work with Lillian Hellman?"

She had said it in such an uncertain, perturbed tone that all my apprehension swept back. I said I had no personal objection to Miss Hellman and was sure she could contribute, especially to construction. Then, my misgivings dictating the next remark, I added, "I would of course want to keep control of the content of the play."

The producer made no reply.

Waiting for further word, I kept on revising. I hadn't been able to bring myself to call Otto Frank, nor had I even told Tereska of what was taking place, except that I was making revisions. For there is a curious aspect to rejection; no matter what the reason for it, it brings a sense of shame.

—Not anger? (I was to go over this with each of my analysts, and incessantly with myself.)

—Well, when you get rejected because of using new forms, or because of original ideas, you get angry; every revolt in art has sprung from that kind of rejection. But here I had made no special innovation, so the old gnawing doubts returned, the shame of failure, of not having been good enough.

—But again and again in your life you have had rejections of works that later won high praise. Like *The Old Bunch.* Like *In Search.* Surely by this time you were adjusted to this?

—Yes, but it gets you, nevertheless. I couldn't speak of the thing to Tereska, and there was too an ironic moment just at this time when we went to see some friends. They were close friends, people whose taste I respected; he was the young film executive who had worked with me on *My Father's House*—Bill Zimmerman, no relation to Barbara —and his wife, who had worked on *The Nation.* They had begged me, so I had let them see the draft of the Diary play. When we got there, Bill and Ruth opened a bottle of champagne and toasted the script as the next Pulitzer Prize winner. How could I tell them it was rejected?

—Do you imagine Solzhenitsyn feels ashamed because his work is rejected by the publishing houses in Russia?

—But that's just it. In Russia the case is admittedly political, and the whole world protests for him. In my case it wasn't then altogether certain even to me that the rejection was political. I didn't want to believe it. This was still McCarthy-time, don't forget, and you couldn't believe such things. Right then, in the face of McCarthyism, would the comrades try to pull off something like this? Impossible! I had to tell myself that maybe it was simply bitchiness on the part of Lillian Hellman—

75

—Instead of witchiness?

—Very cute.

—Anyway, that one time you met, it was for you a case of hate at first sight.

—Look, I only raked up a disagreeable impression. All I know about her to this day is from that autobiography of hers, a real piece of self-promotion in which she reveals virtually nothing. *An Unfinished Woman.* Yes, there is a touching section about her relations with Dashiell Hammett —and he was one of those who went to prison on high principle, refusing to say whether he was a party member or not. She goes on to declare that she herself never knew —fine and noble, but I don't give a damn whether Hellman or Hammett were or had ever been party members! What difference would it make? The most important thing is what a person believes, what decides a person's actions. With certain people this is doctrine. Lillian Hellman does tell us that at one point she finally sat down and read all the heavy books and learned all those principles her friend had understood long before. Fine. Everyone should try to understand Marxist theory as well as other economic theories and philosophies, along with the fallacies in them. And if more Communists here could talk openly about being party members, we would have a more mature society. Why, a writer I'd known for years told me once that he had been assigned to keep out of the party because he could be more useful that way. All right. I don't imagine Hellman was getting orders from Moscow to see that Meyer Levin was removed as adaptor of the Diary! But if you believe in a certain set of ideas, your actions follow, regardless.

—The punchcard is in the computer? says the analyst.

—Practically all the Jews in that crowd are convinced assimilationists. Sure, they will admit, or declare, they are Jewish, even "proudly." They decry the Holocaust, and they are nostalgic about Jewish life in the past, in the *shtetl.* But there is rarely any Jewish continuation in their own lives. If they write about contemporary Jews, you cannot imagine the children of their characters having any Jewish continuation. It is a matter of final attrition, by assimilation or abandonment.

—And Israel?

—Don't we know their labels: colonialist, imperialist, etc.? As for them—Maoists, Trotskyists, neo-Stalinists, and all but a minor element of the New Left—much as they differ amongst themselves on other subjects, they're united on one point, hostility to Israel. "Zionism" has been turned into a hate word. Of course, some of them will declare that they "don't really want to see Israel destroyed, *but* . . ." So my kind of Jew is all wrong to them. That's where, even then, I felt my trouble came from—a general hostility, rather than from a specific "party order." Besides, psychologically, I couldn't lay it all to politics.

—To what else?

—As I've said, with every rejection, supposedly for lack of merit, you are stung so hard you half-believe they may be right. You need first of all to be reassured on quality. I did have Harold Clurman's reassurance, so I told myself that as with any rejection it was simply a matter of getting accepted elsewhere. Like with my books. Sure, a rejection always hurts, and to wipe out the hurt and shame you have to get accepted. Some writers will try three or four other publishers and then quit. Others continue down the entire list, and as a last resort even publish their works on their own. As I did with *In Search*. You are always borne up by the knowledge that Marcel Proust paid for his first printing. You know you should not be ashamed, but you're ashamed, and I was ashamed.

—Something like the feeling about being a Jew?

Once more I was called to Miss Crawford's office. Nothing was said about collaboration with Miss Hellman. Looking deeply pained, the producer declared that she simply had to start totally afresh with a different writer. She had told this to

77

Otto Frank. Our agreement, she reminded me, was that if my dramatization proved unsatisfactory, she could turn elsewhere.

But she had accepted it, had announced production, had had me bring over Otto Frank!

Miss Crawford looked even more pained. In the circumstances, she conceded, if I wanted to submit my work to one or two other producers, I could, and if it was accepted, she would withdraw. Almost offhandedly, she added, "I suppose you want to send it first to Kermit?"

How could I object? True, he was Lillian Hellman's producer, and true, all of my misgivings about getting drawn into the political-ideological-McCarthyist miasma confronted me again. But wasn't I already drawn in? This could actually be the test of it. Besides, with the crazy romantic vanity of authors, I kidded myself that maybe even Bloomgarden would be so taken with my play that nothing else would count. Meanwhile, I would submit a copy to Herman Shumlin. And there was the young producer from Fire Island who had wanted the play desperately. I would ask Harold Clurman if he would repeat to Otto Frank what he had said to me about the play.

Indeed he would, said Clurman, and the appointment was made for Saturday morning. But then Otto Frank called back to say, in a weary tone, that he could not meet Mr. Clurman, as he was going out to Westchester to spend the weekend with his relatives, the Strauses, at their estate; I said I would try to make another appointment, but as I hung up, I was overpowered by that despairing sense of the thing being doomed, no matter what I tried.

Bloomgarden had instantly sent back the script without comment. I could just see them all, out there on the Westchester estate, tearing to shreds that grabby Russian-Jewish nobody who had got his hooks on poor Otto in Europe. Was Lillian Hellman perhaps there too, the celebrated dramatist pronouncing her oracular decree? It was as though in the very air I could catch the reverberations of busy telephone calls going back and forth on how to handle Levin.

When I got in touch with Otto Frank on Monday to try to arrange a meeting with Clurman after all, he told me that his relatives in Westchester had insisted that he must allow the matter now to be handled in a professional manner, and had called their lawyers for him.

And so it had come to the phase of lawyers—the attorneys for Nathan Straus, who would protect Otto Frank against a scheming, greedy, incompetent writer.

There I was in the same Madison Avenue office building that contained the Doubleday establishment, feeling myself as in a squeeze between the floor of the publisher and the floor of the law firm. With Paul, Weiss, Rifkind, Wharton and Garrison, there was no hunting down corridors for an office door; emerging from the elevator, I found myself facing their floor receptionist. I didn't yet know that I was in the domain of the most powerful law firm in America, with a staff of over seventy attorneys.

Presently I was conducted to the chamber of the One Who Would Deal With Me, a commodious two-window office, so Mr. Mermin was on the firm's upper rungs. His first name, though differently spelled, was also Myer, and this somewhat disarmed me. My own kind. Maybe he'd understand. Perhaps sensing my thought, the lawyer at once assumed the human, informal role. Busy on the phone, he waved a hello and motioned me to an easy chair.

This Myer might easily have been one of the lawyer-characters in my *Old Bunch* and, inevitably, he proclaimed himself an admirer of that book. Now ensued one of those "friendly" conversations; he was interested in the stage not only as a theatergoer—in college he had been very active, performed in plays, even considered entering the field. Just between us, he wanted to tell me that I had been very careless, totally unbusinesslike, in this whole affair; he realized I was a creative individual, but after all, I had been around, I was a pro, I knew how things should be done. The way things stood, he unfortunately had to inform me that I had no legal rights whatsoever. Otto Frank's letters to me didn't really assign me any rights. Did I have a lawyer representing me?

No, I said. Mermin made a rueful smile of professional tolerance over a common foolishness. I had never believed, I said, that I could come to a point of legal dispute with Otto Frank. (Besides, and I didn't bring it up, he had written to me that he preferred not to sign a contract just yet, as he planned to move to Switzerland where taxes would be lower. A bit startled by Frank's attitude toward the Dutch, I had nevertheless written back that I understood.)

Strictly speaking, as I did not have a lawyer, it was not his place to offer me legal opinions, Mermin said, but to simplify our talk and expedite matters, he was giving me this information. I had no legal rights whatsoever. Otto Frank wanted to do his best for me. One suggestion was that since I had put in a great deal of time running around and seeing people on his behalf, I should get an agent's commission. Perhaps five percent instead of ten, as a professional agent would now have to be engaged.

Again! I explained that I had no intention of once more being put into that embarrassing light. I was a writer. My correspondence with Otto Frank provided that if I wrote a faithful adaptation of high literary quality, I should have the right of production, and to all evidence I had carried out my side of the agreement, as Otto Frank himself attested to the faithfulness, and reviews of the radio version attested to the quality, and there were the opinions of people like Harold Clurman. If producer-trouble had arisen, I had the normal right of any author to go elsewhere. If some persons had persuaded Mr. Frank that the play was bad, I was at least owed some sort of test. As Mermin well knew, there were many ways of testing a script without risking the Broadway value of the property. We could have the play read by a pick-up cast, before a few people, and get a reaction. What haunted me, I brought out, was that in justice to the work itself—for a work assumed a life of its own—I needed to know—

"I'm afraid you'll never know," the lawyer stated. His tone was final, but with a touch of regret. Like a doctor who tells you the leg must come off. Mermin had come from behind the desk and was gazing out the window, which had a high-floor panoramic view beyond the Hudson River.

There was no question of permitting even a voice reading, he declared, for one never knew what rumors could get started about a property, and it was his duty to protect his client's property, which, as I surely understood, was now potentially worth millions, on stage and screen. Still gazing out the window, the lawyer went on talking.

All that reverberated in me were those words, "You'll never know." It was the most unrelenting condition of art that I had to know. And in that moment I was already aware that I could never let go until I knew.

A very great, world-famous playwright, Mermin declared, stood ready to adapt the Diary the moment I withdrew. Though not at liberty to give me the name, he could assure me it was someone absolutely at the top and of the highest quality. Arthur Miller? Lillian Hellman herself? Perhaps Clifford Odets? Or Robert Sherwood? What vanity, what unmitigated selfishness, for an unproduced dramatist to insist on himself as against such eminence, and after his work had already been found wanting! The lawyer had almost totally unnerved me, but now he went on to say that, although I was a highly re-spected novelist, it was well known that novelists simply could not write good plays.

Sartre, Gorky, Galsworthy, Steinbeck, Wilder—! No, I

wouldn't even answer him. But I had come back to my senses.

No matter how famous his proposed adaptor, I said, it remained I who had conceived this work, the work existed, people of the highest critical standing had declared it to be excellent, and as such it had the right to be performed. At the very least, to be tested.

"Impossible!" the lawyer decreed, like an iron door closing. And unfailingly true to type, he softened his voice and advised me sincerely, almost intimately as a fellow of my own kind of background, to accept what I could get right now.

At least he didn't vocally add the "or else."

Half-running, I got to Otto Frank's hotel; he was in, and agreed to see me for a few minutes. I found him stretched out on the bed; he apologized for not rising—he wasn't feeling well. I said we'd make it another time. No, there was little time; he was leaving in a few days, since what he had come for had collapsed. There was no accusation in his voice, but it was desolate. He pulled himself from the bed and sat on a chair to listen to me.

And I was doing this to a lone survivor of Auschwitz!

I begged. Hadn't he come here because Miss Crawford was satisfied and ready to proceed with my work? I had no way of knowing all that had intervened since his arrival, but everything pointed to influences that had nothing to do with the quality of my drama, and it was this aspect alone that made me resist. If there were Broadway intrigues, political, commercial motives, obviously the only way to get rid of me would be to declare that my work was no good.

All he wanted was the best for Anne, he reiterated faintly. I had said I wanted to bring her words to the stage. Now it was I alone who stood in the way. What did I have to suggest? he asked in a lost voice. He wanted to be fair to me, but the producer had to be the judge of the play.

"Then let me have the same right any author has, to look

for another producer. Let me have a month." Impossibly short, I knew. But how could I let myself "stand in the way"?

Suddenly he blurted, "I must tell you that Mr. Bloomgarden has insisted most strongly to me that I would be insane to allow your play to be produced."

Moving feebly, he was again on the bed.

I could not allow myself to torment him any further. I would let it all drop. I rose to leave. Then, with his eyes closed, he added, "It is well known that novelists cannot write plays."

"Mr. Frank!" I burst out, "Don't you see they have nothing but such idiocies to use against me? It's me they are against, not my play."

The political question hung between us, unspoken. "A month," Otto Frank said in a half-whisper. "I will instruct the lawyer."

I had my reprieve. But I had wrung it from a sick man, a victim of the concentration camps whom I had brought into pain.

We had asked him for a farewell visit, with the understanding—I believe Tereska even stated it when she called him—that the occasion would be purely personal and our affair would not be touched upon.

The visit passed well; we were as we had been before, in Paris, and at one point Anne's father said he wanted to tell us of a coming change in his life, of which he had not yet spoken to others. When he returned to Europe, he was going to marry. Yes, she too had been through the camps.

Glad for him that his loneliness would be ended, we were deeply touched that he had chosen to tell this to us. And perhaps because of this restored personal feeling—or perhaps because I am after all a grasping person—when we were standing and saying our farewells, I made a request. It came from my already haunted feeling of powers against me—the

83

Doubleday crowd, the Hellman and Bloomgarden crowd—I'd lose. A mere four weeks and I'd lose. And that lawyer's sentence reverberated in me—"You'll never know."

All through the visit I had restrained myself from bringing up the subject, but in this last moment it burst out. "Just one small thing I want to ask of you. So I can see my work. Sometime. Somewhere on a stage. No matter what comes here—will you let me have the rights in Israel?"

He reflected for an instant, then gave me his hand in agreement and farewell. "Yes, certainly." He seemed to see it as appropriate and, I thought, to feel some relief. Thus, he would not have wronged me.

The instant he had gone, Tereska turned on me, furious. "You agreed not to bring anything up!"

All I could reply was, "I believe he understood."

The next morning we went to see him off. The cabin was crowded, and in the doorway was Mr. Marks of Doubleday. His glare was so hateful that Tereska and I said a quick farewell and left.

I took the play to a leading agent, Miriam Howell, who read it at once and declared that though a month was short, there should be no trouble in finding a producer.

I sat again with Herman Shumlin. He recalled his fearful reaction of a few years ago. Now he had read my script. "This has changed my mind," he said.

"Maybe also the success of the book?"

He chuckled. Yes. But he now saw these people. Living, on the stage. Of course I still had work to do—I quickly agreed, I was making changes every day. "It's already remarkable. Keep on." He would apply for the rights.

I rushed back to the agent. "Herman Shumlin wants it!"

Then my troubles were over, Miss Howell said.

If only Otto Frank hadn't sailed—what a happier parting this would have made! I went to the lawyers' office. "Everything is all right!" I proclaimed to Myer Mermin. "Herman Shumlin wants the play."

Mr. Mermin hardly reacted. "Yes, Herman called," he said. And added drily, "He's unacceptable."

I was shouting. In a wave of outrage, even my own trouble was submerged. How could they! Herman Shumlin was the dean of the American theater! Distinguished, honored—to refuse a man of such standing was scandalous, unthinkable! Who did they imagine they were—a firm of lawyers assuming the right to make qualitative judgments first of all on me as a writer, and now on one of America's greatest men of the theater!

"It is our responsibility to protect the property. We consider Herman Shumlin no longer capable of producing a hit," Mr. Mermin stated categorically. While I seethed, the man went on in the authoritative tone of an expert and in the jargon of Broadway. Shumlin had had several flops in a row—

"But who doesn't!"

The Shuberts had financed him *carte blanche* for two plays. "And what does Herman do, he chooses some highbrow literary piece from Italy. A total flop. And then he does the same thing again. Look, he's lost his touch. The word is out, he's through. You'll have to come up with something better. Not Herman Shumlin."

"Whoever I bring, you'll refuse! You'll find some excuse!" I was virtually screaming. People came to the door; he waved them away. "Calm down." The lawyer picked up his phone, and made a guarded call. I caught Shumlin's name, and then he turned back to me. Whom had he called? Was this another one of those blacklist checkups?

"Sorry, no go," he said.

—You mean you thought Shumlin was on a blacklist? asked Dr. Erika.

—Look, I didn't know what to think.

—Why couldn't it simply have been what the lawyer said—because of those failures? Isn't it an axiom in films and the theater that no matter how famous you are, you're as good as your last production?

—Yes. I even half-believed them. That's the trick; there is always a plausible excuse. The whole damn world has gotten to be that way. Only—to say that Herman Shumlin was no longer capable of producing a hit!—Do you know what his next production was? A play called *Inherit the Wind*. It ran for years.

—They guessed wrong. That still doesn't make it a plot against Meyer Levin.

—No. But why should I have to pay for their mistakes? And why can't they by now acknowledge them?

The analyst snorted.

—So I went back to my agent and told her they had refused Shumlin. She took it more calmly. It was true that Shumlin had had a few failures, but to bar him was ridiculous. I kept yelling I would make a scandal of it in the press, but she persuaded me to wait—she would speak with the attorneys.

—You went to the press?

—Not yet. But I had to explode somewhere. I went to see my friend, the press agent I've mentioned before— Wolfie Kaufman. He knew all the Broadway intrigues, he was even just then president of the association of theatrical press agents.

—This was the one you said was Miss Crawford's press agent?

—Yes, but I felt I could trust him. I'd known him quite a long time—since my days at *Esquire,* when I'd bought some of his stories. He'd started on a job with *Variety,* the show biz paper, and he wrote about that milieu, he knew all the gossip. I told him about Shumlin being refused.

Yeah, Shumlin had had a few flops, Wolfie said, but that wouldn't be enough to disqualify him. Everyone had flops now and again. What kind of yokel was I? Didn't I know that Herman Shumlin had been Lillian Hellman's close friend as well as her producer? They no longer saw eye to eye. Wolfie believed that among other things there had been arguments about Israel in these theater circles, and whatever it was, Lillian had gone over to Kermit Bloomgarden as her producer. Didn't I even know that Bloomgarden had got his start in the theater as Herman Shumlin's bookkeeper?

—You believed all this? You said this Wolfie was a gossip.

—It fitted. Look, how far backward is one supposed to lean? Didn't everything that happened then and afterward bear it out? What made me sick was all this Broadway intrigue over the diary of a dead Jewish girl. Over what the world should be permitted to hear on the stage out of that diary.

—Yes, that might have made you sick.

—Thanks. Call the asylum. A crazy Jewish writer is making false accusations.

Mr. Mermin had prepared a contract for me to sign. According to Otto Frank's generous wishes, I was granted a month to find an acceptable producer; if I failed, I would withdraw my play.

Appended was a list of about a dozen "acceptable" producers.

"But Mr. Frank didn't limit me to any list!"

"These are producers we consider at least of equal standing with Cheryl Crawford." Mermin's voice was hard-edged. He read on. I was to have the right of production in the Hebrew language in Israel, but not before there had been a production of the Diary on Broadway—

"He made no such condition!"

"We can't risk a flop in Israel killing interest in the property."

More. When another play was written, I could make no

87

claim of plagiarism unless that work contained material not to be found in the Diary but existing in my play.

How could I hamper the world-famous playwright who waited to undertake the task by not accepting this?

Mermin handed me the document. I glanced down the appended list. Bloomgarden. Others from the same crowd. A musical-comedy producer. This was a farce, I cried out. I wouldn't accept a restricted list.

"You have an excellent agent. Why don't you take this over to Miriam?"

As I left, I saw in the lawyer's eyes something melancholy, dark, and had a premonition: this man would succumb to the role he had to fulfill.

The agent studied the list. At least half were out of the question. Irene Selznick, for instance, had just had a total failure with a play about Jewish refugees, and was not likely to try another. Kermit Bloomgarden—was that a joke? And this one was in Europe, and that one was a friend of Kermit's and unlikely to contrary him, and another was already fully scheduled for the season. Still, there appeared to be a few serious prospects. If it was this or nothing—

"I'll go to the press!" I cried once more.

She wouldn't advise it. I'd have to let her handle the situation in her own way.

This was the world she worked in; why should she risk it all for me? Still, if she said there were a few serious possibilities—

The frantic month went by. Several producers who were not on the list made offers and were refused. I finally could not contain myself, went to the *Times* and asked to see the theater-page reporter who had called me on Fire Island for progress reports. After a time, Mr. Funk appeared and led me into a sideroom, like the little room at the *Chicago Daily News* that I had occasionally used to get rid of some crank.

88

Mr. Funk heard out my indignant complaint about barring a man of the stature of Herman Shumlin, made no comment, accepted a copy of the restricted "approved" list, with my fiery, typed statement about violating the freedom of the theater. He got up.

Nothing appeared, though every Sunday under his name there were almost embarrassingly sycophantic notes about the plans of Kermit Bloomgarden.

Of the "approved" producers, not all even read the play. One, whose partner was abroad, accepted it, but his partner, returning in the final week, could not make up his mind. On the last day, Irene Selznick's secretary called me at home to tell me how much Miss Selznick liked the dramatization and regretted—

In the night, I turned face down on the bed. I was sobbing.

My wife too lay awake. "Oh, how I wish I had never given you that book," Tereska said.

My money was exhausted. With a cameraman, I went out to do a documentary film on the work of Frank Lloyd Wright. I'd get away from the damned Diary, the black Broadway miasma. Then for the first time I ghostwrote a book, going out for longish visits to Vineland, New Jersey, the site of an early agricultural colony of immigrant Russian Jews. My subject, Dr. Arthur Goldhaft, was a doughty "original"; born of an immigrant family, he had become a veterinarian (if my boy can't be a doctor—at least, this is also a kind of doctor!) and developed poultry inoculations that had opened up the whole modern system of mechanized chicken raising, making him rich, and also a social philosopher. He hoped to save the world with cheap chicken for all. I called his book *The Golden Egg*.

But the Diary wouldn't let go of me. Notes kept appearing in the theater columns. Cheryl Crawford had engaged Carson

McCullers. What? A mere novelist! Where was the world-renowned playwright for whose sake I had been induced to give up my rights?

Rumors came. Carson McCullers had decided she couldn't do it, and Miss Crawford was approaching one playwright after another without results. A big dramatist was even said to have declared that he couldn't see how anyone could do much better than Levin's version. Presently Miss Crawford announced she was giving up the rights to the Diary because public interest had waned, and she thought a play would no longer be commercially viable.

The rights were free! And none of the producers on that famous "acceptable" list were interested. Even Kermit Bloomgarden, for months, didn't take an option. Again I was writing to Otto Frank. Why, since no one else wanted the Diary, why not let mine be done?

He must abide by his advisers.

Every night now the letters to him kept writing themselves in my head.

I must stop it. I must swallow the injustice—the world was full of injustice—I must stop thinking about it. Shut it out—

I am holding back. Add this to my paranoia if you like. A Communist under every bed. But—at this time I was writing a book review column for a weekly called the *National Jewish Post,* and one day I received for review a novel about Jewish *shtetl* life in Russia, called *A Lantern For Jeremy.* Its author was V. J. Jerome. I happened to know him slightly through his wife Alice whom I had met in the Chicago days, in connection with the steel mill strike. One night in an emergency she had come to us to get money to bail her brother out of jail. After moving to New York, Alice had married the party's leading theoretician, the editor of its journal; and now Jerome had written a novel. I went through enough of it to make me feel it would be best not to review the book. If I wrote a negative review I could, in their circles, be accused of prejudice, and if I wrote a praising review, I would be dishonest. Besides, what could it matter to Jerome if he got reviewed in the *National Jewish Post* or not?

Presently I received a phone call, not from the author but from some friend of his, asking when my review would appear. I replied vaguely. In a few days I was called again. Then came a third call, this time from someone identifying himself as the editor of *Jewish Life*. I'd seen the magazine. Strictly party-lined. (Not to be confused with a present-day magazine of the same name, published by the Union of Jewish Orthodox Congregations of America!) The caller became insistent; I replied that I was under no obligation to review every book I received. When the phone rang again, I was in bed asleep. It was the same person from *Jewish Life*. Irritated, I told him I had decided not to review Jerome's novel. He became bellicose, abusive, and finally shouted I'd regret this! Shouting back some counter-abuse, I slammed down the phone.

That was all. But as the Frank trouble deepened, the incident kept coming back to my mind. Jerome was widely spoken of as the "cultural commissar" of the party. It was he, according to testimony before the McCarthy committee, who had gone out to Hollywood in the thirties to organize the Communist unit in the film colony. At the national convention of the party in 1950 he had delivered a report entitled "Grasp the Weapon of Culture." When Lillian Hellman in her appearance before the committee had been asked whether she knew V. J. Jerome, she had refused to reply, on the ground of possible self-incrimination. The Fifth Amendment.

With all this pressing on me, I finally wrote an accusatory letter to Otto Frank. It was political hatred that was behind the campaign against me—how could he fail to see it? Hadn't I warned him long ago of the whole pattern of politics around the Jewish question, around Israel? Hadn't I warned him

91

about these very people? He had agreed that it was my duty to warn him. Doubtless they had heard and all this was their revenge on me. Surely he was aware of Miss Hellman's politics! All of us had screamed to high heaven because these people were blacklisted, but at the same time it was they who were blacklisting me!

He must reject my arguments, Otto Frank replied.

A community center in Buffalo asked to do the play. Again, letters to Otto Frank, pointing out that such a test might revive interest in the Diary. He, personally, had no objection to performances of my play, he wrote, but all was in the hands of his attorneys.

The group in Buffalo held cast readings, became enthusiastic, began rehearsals. Came a cease-and-desist letter from the New York lawyers, threatening suit for enormous damages. They gave up, and I received a large packet of scripts they had run off from stencils I had sent them—perhaps I could use them sometime; unable to get myself to throw them away, I hid them from Tereska, at the bottom of a closet.

Now the actor George Voscovic, whom I had known when he was whisked out of Prague under the noses of the Nazis, happened to read a copy that was floating around. He excitedly handed it over to a young Broadway producer who, discovering that the rights were still open, at once applied. Day after day, she could get no answer.

Suddenly there appeared news that Kermit Bloomgarden was after all taking an option on the Diary. A press story recounted that he had journeyed to Hollywood to persuade his chosen playwrights, recommended by Lillian Hellman, to undertake the dramatization. They were a husband-and-wife team of screenwriters, Albert and Frances Hackett.

"The best for Anne!"

Moreover, Wolfie told me, it was said that Lillian had purposely sought out non-Jews for the assignment.

—And you would have ruled them out?

—I never ruled out non-Jews! She was ruling out Jews!

—Perhaps their idea was simply to find what would be most popular, most commercial.

—Would Anne Frank have put commercial success above all?

—But now it was up to her father.

—He told me I stood in the way of a great playwright. If I would but step aside, a world-famous dramatist was ready to adapt the Diary.

—So you were now becoming really angry at Mr. Frank?

—Yes. The indignity of it! To throw me out for a Hollywood writing team! Now, finally, though I knew it was no use, I did go to a lawyer.

I went to see Ephraim London. Yes, he believed me about being induced to bow out to make way for a world-renowned playwright, but there was no such condition in the agreement. Those people in Rifkind's office were sharks; Myer Mermin had done his job well. I could perhaps raise the point that Mermin was aware I had no attorney—but was I prepared to tangle with them, and on a highly tenuous case? They'd make hash of me. No, even for my sake, he wouldn't touch it. He gazed at me with irritation, with sympathy, with puzzlement. "Why didn't you bring this agreement to me before you signed it?"

Ephraim London was not an ordinary lawyer but a man of intense social and philosophic concern; a nephew of the first Socialist congressman, Meyer London, he was a campaigner against censorship and suppression, and at about this time won, in the United States Supreme Court, the landmark decision that not only halted the censorship of a remarkable Rossellini film, *The Miracle,* but knocked away as unconstitutional the entire structure of film censorship boards throughout the United States. That decision, extended from films to theater and books, was the most important single action, after the case of *Lady Chatterley's Lover* and the *Ulysses* case, in opening the way to a new epoch of freedom of expression, to the erasure of taboos in literature that, in spite of its having been extended to allow pornography, has been a mind-opener for man. (Recently the pendulum has swung part-way back.)

I had come to know Ephraim through a great libertarian I had first met in the thirties, Edmond Cahn, who taught Philosophy of Law at the New York University School of Law. London had been a graduate student of Cahn's, and when problems arose in connection with Mabel's death, Cahn had sent me to his protégé. Tall, gangling, Lincolnesque, the lawyer had a rumpled face that in later years made him a double for Walter Matthau.

Why hadn't I come to him at the outset? Was it the way some people keep themselves from going to a doctor when symptoms of illness appear?

I had adopted the attitude that I would never go to law with Anne Frank's father, but getting advice didn't mean going to law—on the contrary, that could prevent it. Otto Frank himself had gone to lawyers.

For one thing, I had told myself that so impressive a law firm as Judge Rifkind's would not, in a Jewish cultural matter of this sort, treat me strictly as an adversary.

Self-entrapment. Masochism. But also something else that I somehow think has to do with being a writer. I have an innate tendency to say yes to people, and I think this is because a writer is led—or misled—by a certain all-embracing empathy. The very process of character creation is empathetic. This would appear to indicate that all writers would be subject to the "yes" syndrome, and obviously such is not the case; but I, for one, seem always to have carried this process into my life situations. Just as I have to feel with every one of my characters, so I have an impulse to feel with everyone I encounter in

94

life. If people ask me for something, my tendency is always to say yes.

So even in this situation with Otto Frank, I had yielded point after point, against my own interests.

> —Isn't there a further pattern? You give—and then you are outraged when people don't stop taking. So you scream, you fight—where have you seen that?
>
> This had already come up with Dr. A.
>
> —All right. Infantile behavior. So empathy is dangerous. Also morality?
>
> —We're in this world, not the next. Who elected you to be everyone's judge?
>
> —A writer judges. For me it goes all the way back to the Bible. The parable—it's moral judgment, in the form of a story.
>
> —Jewish righteousness.
>
> —Another crime!
>
> But my holding back from going to a lawyer had been, for me, like keeping the whole question on the level of artistic right, ethical right, rather than legalities.
>
> —And you think others are obliged to behave by these lofty notions, as well?
>
> —If they pretend to ethics, and a noble cause—then yes. And all these people did. Yes.

No, there's nothing I'd advise you to do, said Ephraim.

I did do something, I had to. I took my last few hundred dollars and put an ad in the paper. The *Times* was too expensive, so I put the ad in the *Post,* showing it to no one, not even Tereska, before it ran. Here it is:

A CHALLENGE TO KERMIT BLOOMGARDEN

Is it right for you to kill a play that others find deeply moving, and are eager to produce?

When you secured the stage rights to Anne Frank's "Diary of a

95

Young Girl" you knew I had already dramatized the book, but you appointed new adaptors. Anne's father, Otto Frank, said of my play, "I can't imagine how anyone could more truly re-create the characters."

Cheryl Crawford was to produce it but had a change of plan, common in the theater. Thereafter, three good producers made offers for my play. One said, "I'm in love with it." Mr. Frank was influenced to reject these offers. A powerful theatrical law firm gave me just thirty days to secure an acceptable producer from a restricted list. Barred from this were the producers of "Life With Father," "Junior Miss," "The Time of Your Life," "Watch on the Rhine," and many of like stature. Is such manipulation fair to my play, to the public, to the theater itself? You thereafter acquired the rights to the Diary, and shoved my play aside. The Diary is dear to many hearts—yours, mine, and the public's. There is a responsibility to see that what may be the right adaptation is not cast away.

I challenge you to hold a test reading of my play before an audience.

A PLEA TO MY READERS:

If you ever read anything of mine, "The Old Bunch," "In Search," "The Young Lovers," my war reports from Europe and Palestine, if you saw my films, "My Father's House," or "The Illegals," if you read my sequel to Anne Frank's Diary in this paper, if you have faith in me as a writer, I ask your help. Write to Mr. Frank and request this test.

My work has been with the Jewish story. I tried to dramatize the Diary as Anne would have, in her own words. The test I ask cannot hurt any eventual production from her book. To refuse shows only a fear that my play may prove right. To kill it in such case would be unjust to the Diary itself.

This question is basic: Who shall judge? I feel that my work has earned the right to be judged by you, the public.

Write or send this ad to Mr. Otto Frank, c/o Doubleday, 575 Madison Ave., N.Y., as a vote for a fair hearing before my play is killed.

MEYER LEVIN

96

Poor Levin. Sane people don't do such things.

And did I seriously believe that Kermit Bloomgarden would accept my "challenge" when from all I had heard of his character, he would only become enraged? He would laugh at my pathetic outcry as final proof that I was not only incompetent but a nut.

All this had occurred to me, but I had to publish the ad. In its pathetic plaint is my whole story, perhaps the whole story of our time, the bewildered appeal of the individual who clings to his belief in some "court of public opinion" where true justice resides. And is this utterly wrong? Is it not, still, the last resort of the strangled writers under various forms of monolithic rule, some of whom have even succeeded in reaching the outside public?

I received a few score heartening letters, and perhaps a hundred signatures. What went to Mr. Frank, I don't know.

And then?

What I had done could be ridiculed—a beep, a bleat, beneath the jet-age roar; it could make my wife shudder with fear for me. Yet, I told myself, suppose I had been able to place, not this little box, but a full-page ad, and in the *Times*? "Did you see Meyer Levin's full-page ad? There must be something behind it all!" No, but then the other side could have smothered me with counter-ads: Why on earth, they would ask, shouldn't they have accepted my play if it was any good? Without stating the real issue, the doctrinaire issue, I would remain a pesty, peevish, rejected author. And if I stated the issue, I would automatically be labeled a red-baiter, a McCarthyite!

What other move could I make? Still madly insist on going to law, even if Ephraim London said no? Though I eventually was to go to court, it would be with abhorrence, not only because I was a writer and my weapon was the pen, but because of what law has become in our society. The best lawyers tell you to swallow your hurt and avoid court. On

London's office wall hung a noted quotation from Justice Learned Hand, saying with hellish, Dantesque emphasis: Give up all hope, all ye who enter the realm of law. And it is a commonplace that our "adversary system" is not so much a search for truth as a contest as to who has the cleverest attorney, or enough money to last out every wrinkle of the legal process. Besides, my issue was one that could not be determined by law; it was really an artistic issue, and thus I was impelled to keep seeking to bring it before the public.

What was to come very close to destroying my spirit, and my mind, was the stripping away of the layers of trust that we cling to, trust in society itself.

One layer was my faith in the Jewish community structure, for though I was indeed borne up again and again by responses that came from that community itself, these were simply suffocated under the iron blanket of the establishment.

Deepest of all was my faith in the creative community, in writers and artists. My romantic belief held that no matter what the worldly considerations—profit, position, even politics—an ultimate standard, an ethos of art, remained, which would somehow assert itself against suppression. Just as from the Jewish community, heartening voices came to me from the writing community. Hundreds of authors, famous or obscure, were to respond. Eventually, they embraced an amazing diversity—Camus, Mailer, I. B. Singer, Elie Wiesel, Bruno Bettelheim, I. F. Stone, Irving Howe, John Dos Passos, Mitchell Wilson, Anais Nin. The terrifying lesson was that I could get virtually no press attention to the story. Even these voices could not be conveyed, in the proliferating control of the information media. No matter how repeatedly and decisively I was to prove the issue for that mythical "court of public opinion" we dream about, the outcry was lost. It could only be heard if "they," that compounded mythos that rules, wanted it heard. And "they" were in Kafka's Castle.

All this was to be predicted from the futility of the little ad, but such foreknowledge could not release me. I admitted to myself that I was possessed. But I had a life-axiom, again underlined by the event of my being a writer: one must follow through an experience to the end.

However, I would have to wait to see the work that was being substituted for mine. Perhaps I would be proved wrong in all my suspicions. Perhaps I would be shown that what I had done had really been inferior.

So at least there came a hiatus.

3

THE GHOSTWRITING JOB had carried me through the worst period, and now I had to go back to a novel.

We had been able to move out of the gloomy hole. A block away, facing Riverside Drive, was a building with huge, old-style apartments, rent-controlled; after slipping a ten-dollar bill to the superintendent, with promise of more, I had been going back week after week for the good word. One day he let me know of a coming vacancy. Nine rooms, each with a view of the Hudson! It would cost only a few dollars more than I was paying for the West End Avenue cave. The sky was opening.

All I needed was some sort of regular income, however minimal, that would carry me through a long writing stint. This came by a stroke of luck. Crossing the street one evening, I heard myself hailed. Didn't I remember? Abraham Cohen, from the *Menorah Journal* days. Didn't I remember the Jewish Club, atop a nearby hotel?

The scene came back—a cultural club, quite posh, in the neighborhood's more substantial days—exhibitions and debates on the perennial subject: Is there a Jewish art? Literature, philosophy, music. Yes, the Jewish Club still existed, though shrunken, in a downstairs room. Would I give them a talk?

Did I ever say no?

Meanwhile we got onto the usual "what are you doing with yourself these days?" Cohen had heard about my Anne Frank troubles, had even read my ad. As usual, only the slightest tap was needed for my whole tale to come pouring out, including my political suspicions.

"You're not wrong. I happen to know what that gang can do."

Was I writing? I explained that I needed a job that would leave me some free time to work on a novel. Cohen had a thought. A friend of his was the editor of a newspaper across the river, in New Jersey. A good Jew, an old socialist, he'd understand.

I went out to Newark. So there I was back in a newsroom, the floor throbbing to the roll of the basement presses. In a corner cubicle was a sympathetic-looking, laconic man named Philip Hochstein, who somehow reminded me of my very first editor, Henry Justin Smith of the *Chicago Daily News*. Hochstein took me to lunch; yes, he was a fan of *The Old Bunch,* and what was more, he had run my war dispatches about the liberation of the concentration camps, and about the surviving Jews.

We joked about the journalistic legend that at one time or another, on the way up or on the way down, everyone worked on the *Newark Star-Ledger*. Or back on the way up again, the editor added. He had a melancholy smile.

We would hit on some idea, he assured me; the *Star-Ledger* was the key Newhouse paper—I had not even heard of Newhouse—and if I could write a usable column to dress up his editorial page, he might get enough of the other editors in the chain to take it so as to pay me around a hundred dollars a week.

I could manage with this as a base. I'd write all six columns

102

in a couple of days and have the rest of my time free. It would be like the old *Esquire* schedule, when I crowded my job into half a week and wrote *The Old Bunch*. I was once again at the starting point, and as for the column itself, I reached back to my early time on the *Chicago Daily News,* doing a column on books, films and the theater which had been called "A Young Man's Fancy." Not so young any more, and not so fancy. How about "I Cover Culture," I suggested wryly—one day each for a play, a movie, an art show, a review of ads, a book. Could that go in Newark, and in Long Island City? Hoch smiled his melancholy smile. Would I write a few samples?

With the ever-haunting money problem at bay, I needed only a publisher. I had long ago broken with Viking Press. My agent sent me around to an editor named Robert Kuhn at McGraw-Hill, where they were looking for novelists to build up their trade department. The young editor ruminated. Chicago was my background—*The Old Bunch, Citizens,* my big books—did I have any Chicago ideas? Suddenly there came to the fore one of those subjects I had for years carried in back of my mind, as something that would one day come ripe. The Leopold-Loeb case. A crime without reason, a Nietzschean-superman exercise, the harbinger of our entire murderous era. Kuhn leaped at it. Exactly. A sensational crime story. He even recalled that there had been some remarkable detective work on the part of a reporter.

Yes, yes, on my own paper, by two friends of mine, Mulroy and Goldstein—they'd got the Pulitzer for it. But that wasn't the important aspect of the case—two other aspects had always been on my mind. It was among the earliest cases, if not the very first, in which a depth-study in psychoanalytic terms had been attempted. A psychiatric defense, with testimony by "alienists," as they were then called, had not in itself then been new, but there had never to my knowledge before been a study in virtually Freudian terms. Secondly, the boys had proclaimed themselves as Nietzschean supermen, and

103

already in Germany at that time, as we now knew, the early Nazis were invoking the same philosophy.

There was a third factor that led me into the story, though I felt no need to present it to this young editor. There are, in creativity, secret motives that may never become apparent in the work itself, which takes on its own form and may even pull away from all of the writer's motives. This third motive had an inner relevance for me, which I have already touched on: At the time of the murder there had reverberated all through our Chicago West Side, the neighborhood of Russian and Eastern European Jews, an undercurrent almost of vengeful satisfaction—these were the sons of German Jews, these two wealthy degenerates who had committed the vicious crime, and were even boasting of it! From our parents, as I have already related in the first part of this autobiography, we had heard the whisperings: Now you could see what those overproud German Jews, with their superiority and their exclusiveness, were like. Compassion, alas, failed to dispel this prejudice.

I had first become aware of the social difference between German and Russian Jews at the university, and, having gained campus status with a few short stories in the literary magazine, had found myself invited to a culture-circle of South Side German Jews which met every month in turn in one or another of their luxurious homes. I had never got over the sense of a certain condescension in some of them in accepting this precocious and talented boy from the West Side. And I had, perhaps unjustly, later scented something of this in Otto Frank. There in Kuhn's office the German Jewish theme tempted me as though I would in my own psyche be replying to Otto Frank and his powerful German-Jewish relatives, who had disdained me.

Least of all the themes eventually to be noticed in *Compulsion* was the sensitivity of the reporter-detective as a Jew of Russian extraction, pitted against the pair of thrill-killers with their superman philosophy.

Even more, when I got back into the psychiatric reports, into the depth material, I came upon incidents, remarks, that strongly hinted to me of that classic sickness, Jewish self-hatred, which I was to develop—perhaps with greater truth in fiction than in life—as a central motivating force in the crime, symbolic self-murder. One incident, when I pored over the psychiatric reports, leaped out at me. Leopold, as a little boy, had been sent for a short time to a school in a rough neighborhood, and one day had been cornered on the way home, forced to pull down his pants, and mocked as a sheenie. There flooded over me similar scenes from my own childhood among the wild Italian kids. In an empathetic flash I saw the traumatization, the hatred of being a Jew.

Perhaps the documentation did not fully justify my ideas—perhaps this is the way in which the novelist supplements the scientist. But the psychiatrists who produced the documentation had never offered a comprehensive interpretation, so the way remained open.

There was, it struck me, a significant contrast between the Leopold-Loeb murder, and the murder in *Crime and Punishment*. In that case, too, the killer was an intellectual, a student, who sanctioned his crime by his philosophy. He, too, was "superior," if not a "superman." He was his own-and-only-judge at the time of his act, above common social laws. But Raskolnikov's had been an economic rationalization: to pursue his studies he needed the money hoarded by the old crone of a moneylender, whose value to society as he saw it was nil.

The Chicago killing was rather a step toward abstraction in the philosophy of self-made law. For in this case economic and social justification was absent. Only the idea of self-license, of superiority to common social laws, was retained. All three of the boys, killers and victim, were from wealthy families. Though the murder was staged as a kidnapping for ransom, Leob and Leopold had meticulously planned to kill the victim in any case, and to collect the ransom before the body was discovered. They would use the money for a pleasure trip abroad. This, then, was a purely intellectual exercise, a "perfect crime" committed for its own sake, the *crime gratuite* of the French.

I went to Chicago for my research, stopping first at my old stand, the city room of the *Chicago Daily News*. There at the front end sat my fellow-reporter of the twenties, Clem Lane, now city editor, portly, knowing, and said to be one of the founders of Alcoholics Anonymous. After the homecoming pleasantries, I explained my mission and was escorted back to the morgue. The keeper of the files hadn't changed in twenty years: a delicately-boned man of eternal pallor, in the same gray sweater, Tom Searle. Acting as though I had never left the staff, he deposited at my elbow a mountain of clippings. First, out of curiosity, I found my own feature story of the courtroom arraignment, which centered on Nathan Leopold's father, confused, overwhelmed, muttering to the reporters, "Why come to me? What did I do? Why come to me?"

Quickly I found the pages of psychiatric data, recalling the big scoop a reporter had made by lifting these studies from the law-office of the redoubtable Clarence Darrow. As I worked through the material, someone called to me from a railed-off area—a colleague I had known slightly in the old days, now a columnist. What was I up to? This made an item for him, and the next day he called me to his phone. The item had been read by a bookdealer named Ralph Newman who was now on the line, asking my whereabouts. Newman reminded me that we had been classmates at the University, where another friend of his had been Nathan Leopold. With whom he was still in contact.

Ralph Newman had become a personality in the book world; his Abraham Lincoln Bookshop was renowned among scholars and collectors, but more to the point, all these years of Leopold's imprisonment, Ralph had been his "outside man," supplying him with books, and acting in general as his link to the exterior world. There was, Newman said, a situation that might interest me. Would I care to have a talk?

A distinguished shop, the walls covered with Lincolniana, autographs, rare memorabilia. The balcony office looked at once bookish and businesslike, as did Ralph Newman himself. What he had to tell me might enhance or alter my project, he said: Nathan Leopold was writing a book. Would I be interested in dropping mine, and working on his? Professional help was needed.

The first words had rather struck me down. Whatever my creative effort, my prospects would be enormously reduced in the face of a book by Leopold himself—should it prove to be honest. But on second thought, I could envision a collaboration of extraordinary value. If Leopold would truly reveal himself, reveal his mental processes, his inner motivations, and if I could give this form, write it with all the quality I could command, there might result a unique work of high human worth. Would Leopold go into the formation of the crime, I asked; would he describe in depth his relations with Dickie Loeb?

What Leopold had been writing was a book about prison life, Newman said, about his own experience during thirty years of incarceration. Whether he would be willing to go into the story of the crime would have to be discussed. We could explore this question with him; Newman could arrange for me to visit Leopold in prison. Knowing my work, Newman felt I would be precisely the person for the collaboration.

The proposal left me in turmoil. On the one hand, I stood to participate in the creation of a remarkable document that would increase our knowledge of man. And quite possibly earn a great deal of money. But I also stood to lose my novel, now actively working in my mind.

Besides—couldn't this intervention be a neat way of buying me off? of turning me away from writing my own book, a

107

book that would unavoidably reawaken the whole tragic scandal of the crime, about which these high-standing Chicago families were still so sensitive? Clearly they would prefer it if I could be turned toward a book about Leopold's prison life, which might indeed be of value to penology, and which, I also comprehended, would be intended to help him toward release. Understandably, that had to be his own single overriding objective. I had of course no fault to find with that objective—I had felt from the first that my projected novel might well work toward that goal—but to me that objective had to be entirely secondary.

Leaving the question to be explored by Newman, I returned to New York. The word came that Nathan wanted to see me; I filled out the prison-visit application and presently was back in Chicago, at Newman's bookshop. A chauffeured limousine arrived—the Leopold family car, Ralph explained; it was regularly supplied for his visits to the state penitentiary in Joliet.

I was to see only the administrative corridors of the vast, cold edifice before we passed through a door onto a small platform overlooking a long chamber with a table down the centerline. There were chairs on one side for the prisoners, on the other side for their visitors. From the raised entrance the guard could easily watch against any actual contact.

There was no one in the room. I took a chair midway down, so as to provide, by means of distance, a touch of privacy from the guard. Nathan Leopold appeared, almost as in a stage entrance, in the raised doorway. In his neat prison-gray shirt and trousers, a distinguished-looking man who might have stepped out of a laboratory. He was exactly my age; both of us had been college precocities. Though there had been reports of serious illness, he looked plump and well. Entirely self-possessed, he had in his bearing an air of breeding that was also noticeable in his manner of speech.

We entered into a prolonged discussion that was allowed to

continue far beyond the specified hour. To my surprise and even discomfiture, Leopold kept our talk revolving entirely around the business side of publication. Whenever I tried to turn to anything related to the crime, he smoothly changed back to questions about percentages, film rights, and syndication. Finally, in answer to a direct question, he said that in his book he did not intend to write about the crime itself.

His avoidance would only call attention to the event, which was still constantly being written about, I argued, and which I myself intended to write about—

He hoped I wouldn't.

I had no desire for any sensational retelling of the story, I said, but was interested in the psychological approach. With him alone there rested the opportunity to probe this area. Just as he had during the war volunteered his body for anti-malaria experiments, here was a case where he could volunteer his inner knowledge to humanity. Others, as well as he, had undergone the anti-malaria experiment, but in this, he alone could provide a body of material that would enlarge our understanding of human behavior. That was where my interest lay. If he would collaborate on such a book, I would drop my novel and concentrate all I had to offer as a writer in his project.

Again Leopold slipped back to the business side of writing. What about translations, foreign rights?

All of this he could of course already have learned from Ralph Newman, who was acting as his literary agent. Yet hoping to win his confidence, I went into the details.

At last he turned to his vital interest in the proposed book—the possible effect on his parole situation. To recall, to write of the crime, he feared, would have a negative effect. Better to confine himself to all he had done and learned in prison, to write about the school that he and Dick had organized before Dick was murdered, and of the library system he had introduced, and of his ideas for prison reform.

Indeed, all that must come into it, I said, particularly the effect of prison life on his thinking processes. Yet a silence on the most important area, his own psychology during the crime, would induce suspicion. After a fresh study I had been making of the psychiatric material, I was convinced that a depth presentation, in the light of today's far broader understanding of compulsive behavior, would put him in a different light, and so prove of the greatest help toward securing his parole.

In the end we agreed that I would be ready to suspend work on my own book while I examined and assessed the material he had already written. Then, if we saw things the same way, we would go ahead on his book. The question of describing the crime was left open. If, after the collaboration was done, I still felt I had to write my own book, I would be free to do so.

On the drive back to Chicago, Ralph Newman explained more fully about Leopold's parole situation. Though the judge, in passing sentence, had specifically admonished that there should never be any possibility of release for the two murderers, this obstacle had long ago been legally overcome and Leopold had been made eligible for parole hearings. Again and again over the years his case had come up, but parole had always been refused. The last time, only a year before, circumstances had appeared favorable. The governor at that time had been Adlai Stevenson; sophisticated and well aware of advances in psychiatry, Stevenson had even been ready to risk his political career, for there could be adverse public reaction to the freeing of Leopold. Through certain influences in the powerful Chicago political machine, the ground had been prepared, the parole board set up, to go along with the release of the one-time "thrill-killer." But shortly before the hearing, Governor Stevenson had resigned to run for President; the new governor, a much more routine sort of politician, had recalled only too well the history of Illinois prison-pardons in controversial cases. There was the

110

story of Governor Altgeld, another idealist, who had wrecked his career by pardoning the life-imprisoned anarchists—those who hadn't been hanged—in the Haymarket bomb-throwing case. Did I remember it? It was before my time, but at the root of Chicago's bloody history with radicalism was this event, in which several policemen, marching on an anarchist street-rally, had been killed by a bomb. The bomb-thrower had never been caught, but four anarchists—leaflet-printers and orators —had been hanged, and two others imprisoned for life. Governor Altgeld had pardoned these two men, thereby infuriating the protectors of law and order to such an extent that Altgeld had ended up in a modest office in Chicago, a lawyer again.

Yes, I rounded out the tale, and way back there, he took in Clarence Darrow as a partner. Remembering Altgeld's political fate, Newman continued as the limousine sped on, Stevenson's successor as governor had in his very first action changed the composition of the parole board. Out went Nathan's chances.

Now, after much quiet and laborious effort, there was once more a possibility of building up to a favorable hearing, especially if Nathan Leopold were seen as a chastened man who had given thirty years of his life to good works in prison and so should no longer be punished for an aberration at eighteen.

"But that is exactly what a thorough psychological study of the crime would support," I said—not that I had been particularly moved to crusade for the man I had met in prison. Yet how could one find fault with a life-prisoner's putting all his energy, all his cunning, into a campaign for freedom? I had to see him as a victim of compelling inner forces which, in combination with those of Loeb, had driven him to murder.

But could not the same compulsion revive? In physical freedom, would he not inevitably be attracted to another Loeb, and be in danger of repeating the crime?

My amateur analytic instinct said no; this was later confirmed in discussions with psychiatrists, who felt that Leopold

111

was a "blown out" case; the murderous act in itself had released him. Besides, though aggressions might be boiling under his prisoner's mask of control, it was to be noted that during a violent mass outbreak from the jail some years before, Leopold had refused to go along.

I was astonished that in all this time no psychiatric treatment had been proffered in prison, and no study made. I kept insisting to Newman that Leopold ought to compensate for his crime in the one way he could, by volunteering for a depth-study of his personality. Let him offer up the entire experience, including certain events, even possible previous murders, that had remained obscure. This alone could make the public feel he was healed.

In principle, Newman seemed to agree with me. He would take up the whole matter, he said, with the families involved.

The bookdealer, agent and "outside man" for Leopold was in New York at an important auction of Lincolniana; between bids, Newman emerged to meet me in the Parke-Bernet hallway to tell me that both families and Nathan himself had agreed—I was the exact person to do the book with Leopold. Would this include the crime? If not, as we had said, I'd still be free afterward to write my novel. But perhaps in working with Nathan, if I won his full trust, I could get him to explore the crime as well.

A few days later came an embarrassed letter from Chicago. There had been a sudden change; Leopold's prison material would now be handled in a different way. I was free to go ahead with my own book, Newman wrote, adding a standard precaution against libel.

I had no intention of libeling anyone, I replied, but as there were several gaps in the psychiatric material as printed in the newspapers, I wanted to examine the complete psychiatric reports. They seemed to have disappeared from the files in the State's Attorney's office.

Newman wrote back that he could not help me.

In Chicago I sought out the family lawyers who had all these years carried on parole efforts. Urbane, interested, not at all unsympathetic to me, a leading member of the firm described how it had been one of the founders of the firm, a cousin of the Loebs, who had pioneered the psychoanalytic approach; he had even attempted to get Sigmund Freud to come to Chicago to examine the boys. When this proved impossible, other experts had been secured, advanced for their time. But as to my request to examine the complete histories, there was a certain degree of family resistance.

In the corridor I chanced to meet a university classmate, one of our band of college literati, who was now working in this law firm. With Jack Oppenheim's help I was eventually admitted into a little side office to read the entire material. There were a few precise details of homosexual activities that had been omitted in the newspapers, as well as some references to a case of insanity such as may be found in almost any family. I now had all there was to go by.

I did some interviews, including one with a family member, who, rigid and uncertain how to treat me, nevertheless told me of the unending horror of the experience, the shame for his own children as they grew up. I assured him I did not want to hurt anyone, and that what I wrote would, I thought, help Nathan get out of prison.

For isolation while working there was always the device of borrowing someone's summer house, unused in winter. Our friends the Rosens had a place in Westport. Monday mornings I would drive out there, stopping for groceries and then shut myself away until late Thursday, when I'd drive home. Fridays, I'd scurry around getting material for my columns; Saturdays I'd write the lot, and badger my son Eli, then at the High School of Music and Art, to draw "spots" for them. Sundays I actually had free.

113

The book progressed. The basic psychiatric interviews had probed deeply into fantasy material, particularly Leopold's recurrent king-and-slave daydreams, in which he was sometimes the king, sometimes the slave—and it was the slave relationship that he had acted out with Dickie Loeb. In their secret, childlike compact, Loeb, without himself entering into the fantasy, had accepted the role of king, the agreement being that whenever he pronounced a certain code word, Leopold had unquestioningly to obey. Thus they had committed a whole series of crimes—robberies, incendiary acts, and several "major" incidents, the suspected other murders. Their relationship had become a kind of *folie à deux,* each one's aberration reinforcing the other's.

I was still striving for an illumination that would draw all this material into a pattern. Given my own absorption, I was bound to seek this in the Jewish identity problem, but again, the fact that this was my own absorption, my own tendency, probably inviting distortion, did not in itself make it poetically untrue. Even if it might be untrue of these particular individuals, Leopold and Loeb, if what I drew from the material made a form in itself—wouldn't it nevertheless be a truth?— A truth reinforced, so to speak, because it was drawn from, and fitted, a known set of events, character traits and even fantasies.

And the central king-slave fantasy, wasn't that the case of the Jew—exalted and despised?

One day, out there in the snow-covered isolation of the Westport house, the basic symbols of the act of murder aligned themselves. I experienced a literary elation, the sense of creative rightness. The burial—by stuffing the boy's body into the culvert—a return to the womb. With it, in Leopold's case, an identification with his victim, a self-murder, as I had always felt it to be, a rejection of life as he had been born into it, a rejection of being a Jew. The mutilation of the penis, a savage response to circumcision, interconnected with the early

114

traumatic incident when the neighborhood toughies had pulled his pants down, and linked also to his enslaved homosexuality. The book had come together.

But even out there in isolation, I still was not free of the Diary. The very house I worked in was a reminder, for we had met the Rosens that summer at Antibes when Tereska had given me Anne Frank's book. And then one day I chanced, in the *New York Post,* on an interview with the Hacketts, one of those puff-publicity things. They had arrived from Hollywood to help promote the opening of a film they had "scripted," a gay romantic comedy, and in the course of the questions, the reporter had asked how they were progressing on *The Diary of Anne Frank*—when would it be ready for Broadway?

They were working very hard, they said, but were having difficulties. Frankly, one of them admitted, "We don't know how to get Anne's thoughts on the stage."

The words leaped at me. This was just what I had done! It was so simple, so natural. All the thoughts she had written out—obviously these were the ideas she would have been talking about to Peter, to Margot, to her father; the thoughts had simply to be put back into dialogue in her own words and used in dramatic situations.

The whole thing was ablaze again. Unable to restrain myself, I sat down and wrote the Hacketts a fervent letter— offering my help! Trying to avoid any tone or undertone that might offend them, I explained my long and complex involvement with the Holocaust, the survivors—the profound importance the Diary had for me as a Jew. True, the play based on the Diary was now theirs to do, but my heart was still in it, and as they had encountered a difficulty, perhaps I could help. I would ask no share, no royalty, nothing whatever. It was precisely Anne's thoughts that I had put on the stage, dramatizing them in her own words—at least in this aspect no one had found my play wanting, and I was at their disposal.

115

I received no reply.

I was still getting requests from Jewish community center drama groups, telegrams from Hadassah chairwomen who recalled my radio play, asking if they could present my "Anne Frank."

Then there came Broadway talk—Otto Frank had rejected the Hackett script.

Tereska was taking the children to France for the summer. I begged her, painful as the whole subject was, to try to see Otto Frank and to persuade him to allow Jewish community groups, at least, to perform my text.

She saw him. Though personally friendly to her, she wrote, he adamantly refused.

And so it was upon me again every night—why, why on earth, why? What had turned him so completely against me? Where had I sinned? What vile things had been said about me? I began to fantasize. I would walk into Cheryl Crawford's office and force her to tell me what had really happened. I would lie in wait at the entrance to Kermit Bloomgarden's office . . .

Though I still had the trial to write, I turned the first half of my novel, tentatively called *Compulsion and Free Will,* over to my editor at McGraw-Hill. I felt I had conquered the material.

My agent, Max, called. The book was rejected.

Failed with the play. Failed with the novel. No, *The Old Bunch* had been rejected, and this had not meant I had failed as a writer. *In Search,* as well.

We would have to try the book elsewhere, I said to Max.

That would be a waste of time, he replied. What he advised was to dispose of the thing directly to a crime-story paperback house, and maybe salvage a thousand dollars for the time I had spent.

116

I'd like to make another try with a real publisher, I said, reminding him all about *The Old Bunch* and how it had eventually made my literary reputation. Perhaps now, too, there were special reasons, non-literary reasons, for the rejection, just as in that case the publisher had wanted a melting-pot story instead of a Jewish bunch. Perhaps here the families had made their influence felt. Recently a *Saturday Evening Post* writer had been publishing articles about Nathan Leopold's prison life, picturing him as a kind of saintly savant—that was the deal they had made when they had dropped me. Doubtless it had been decided this was not the time for a novel that would recall details of the crime. I asked Max if he could find out what was behind the rejection.

Not a damned thing! They just didn't think my book was any good. He would send me the editor's letter. I could try another hardcover publisher on my own if I wanted to, but he couldn't see any use.

The letter arrived. It was a page and a half long, all of it negative. The book was simply utterly bad. In my time I have received many rejections, but never anything of this kind. In the Anne Frank case I had at least had grounds to suspect that there were ulterior motives. But this had been sent to my agent and not to me, so it must be straight. It even led me to feel that I was wrong in pursuing the Anne Frank affair—if I couldn't even write an acceptable novel, I must somehow have completely lost my ability as a writer. And also my sense of judgment, never very reliable on one's own work.

There came over me such a despair as I had felt only on that wintry night when I had lost my rights to the Diary. Surely this failure was worse. For as to the Diary, I was only an adaptor, and still unproven as a playwright. Here I was destroyed as a novelist. The characters, the style, the writing—all hopelessly bad. Not a redeeming word. No editor would go to such lengths unless he was really astoundingly disappointed. When *The Old Bunch* had been turned down, at least it had been with compliments for the writing itself. In this letter I was demolished, finished. A young author might surmount such a failure, but not a man far into his career. It was the kind of letter, I told myself, that a writer would leave open on his desk when he went out and jumped into the river.

Only a grim laugh at my own self-pity prevented me from doing it.

I had nowhere to turn for emotional support. Even if Tereska had not been abroad, I would probably have hidden the damning news from her, at least until I had made a few tries elsewhere. Nor could I dare mention my trouble to my friends. There were enough rumors about me already.

I sat in the empty apartment, unable to stir. After a time a kind of anger built up. The letter was simply too extreme. I simply could not be that bad a writer. Though writers are not the best judges of their work, still, there are certain inner responses one has when a work comes off, and I had experienced this strongly with this book. The least I owed myself was to secure other editorial reactions. If I really was that bad, after the failure with the Diary and now with this, I had best stop writing.

I finally picked up the phone. The first call was to Random House, and I managed to reach Bennett Cerf himself. When I had sent him a copy of *In Search* for comment, Cerf had called me to his office and declared he would have been proud to publish the book—why hadn't I submitted it to him? Unable to resist, I told him that the manuscript had been submitted to Random House and had been turned down.

"No!" Cerf had sent a secretary to check the files. Well, such things do happen. But in the future, if I had a new book, I must get in touch directly with him.

"Good to hear from you!" And did I have a book? I said I had a novel based on the Leopold-Loeb story. There was a hesitation. Then—no, he was sorry, it was a subject he

118

wouldn't want to touch. If I had any other ideas, in the future—

Sure, I said, I'd call him first.

The fourth try was Jack Goodman at Simon and Schuster. I didn't know him, but there must have been an urgency in my telephone voice that day. Goodman said he knew my work, and as to the subject, he had no objection; would I bring over the manuscript?

After I had left it with him, I phoned my agent. "He'll hold it all summer and then turn it down," Max said wearily. Goodman held it for half the summer. I somehow kept myself working through the trial scene, which was largely documentary. Finally he called. He wanted the book. He went on to praise the writing, the characterization, the construction.

Whom should a man believe?

I went to tell Max.

My agent was busy on the phone, trying to get a magazine assignment for one of his writers. "Listen, he has to live, it's six months since you've used him—" At last, appearing to have succeeded, he hung up and turned to me.

"Max," I said, "Jack Goodman wants the book."

Max was delighted, happy to have been proved wrong. Then I asked, "Did you actually think it was as bad as that letter said?"

Truth to tell, he hadn't had a chance to read my manuscript.

Well, I said, naturally he'd receive his commission anyway, though it seemed to me we were through.

Nobly, Max refused the commission.

I had finished and turned in the book, now called *Compulsion;* the addition of "Free Will," Goodman said, made it sound like a treatise.

There would be a long wait until publication.

And the opening of *The Diary Of Anne Frank* was approaching. In the theater section of the Sunday *Times* there appeared a "Diary of the Diary" by the Hacketts, detailing their long creative struggle. When Otto Frank had turned down their first version, they had begged him to let them try anew. After several futile rewrites they had gone to Lillian Hellman, spending weekends with her on the play. Lillian's ideas had worked out fine . . .

Again, Lillian Hellman.

The pre-Broadway opening was in Philadelphia. I had to go, It was a ghostly experience—but not in the sense that Herman Shumlin had feared, of the actors on the stage seeming like apparitions. What I saw was the ghost of my own play. There on the stage, exactly as in my "unstageable" work, was the total setting of the hiding place, devised for simultaneous scenes. There was Otto Frank returning from Auschwitz and being handed the Diary, as in my radio play, and similarly, then came Anne's voice rising from the pages, merging into the enactment. True, a common device, doubtless a coincidence. But now, as the two families were about to enter the hiding place, Anne tore the compulsory yellow star off her dress. But that was not in the Diary at all. I had invented the scene for my play.

Sitting there came to be like watching my play prove itself on the stage. At moments I was elated—yes, it was good, it was just the way I had done it! Here was the scene of the arrival of Dussel, who told of the arrests and deportations that were taking place since they had been hidden here, mentioning families they knew, and immediately afterward came Anne's nightmare as she envisioned her dearest friend, Lies Goosens, calling to her for help. Exactly this way I had done it. Then why hadn't my play been staged? Couldn't Otto Frank see this was dramatically the same?

Of course there were differences, too. The slickness and coyness, as in a Hollywood script-polishing job. And the char-

120

acterization of Anne's sister Margot. Their relationship had been so important in the Diary, and so important to Anne, as we knew from later accounts, that when Margot died of typhus in Bergen-Belsen, Anne finally lost all resistance, slipping into death a few days afterward.

In what I was seeing, there was no relationship between the sisters; Margot was a nonentity, usually kept at the back of the stage washing dishes. And where was the scene—I was becoming confused between the two versions—where was the significant scene in which Anne and Margot discussed their dreams of the future, should they survive, and Margot, as in the Diary, said she wanted to become a nurse in Palestine, and Anne said she might like to go there to visit the Holy Places, but that what she really wanted was to go all over the world, to be a writer. Well, of course this was not my play but theirs. Yet the omissions were beginning to make a pattern.

These people on the stage never seemed to think about, to question, the meaning of what was happening to them as Jews. In the Diary, and in all I knew of the Holocaust, the question was constantly in the forefront. As I remembered it, Anne's fundamental outcry, her cry of faith was "It is God who has made us as we are. . . . We are Jews and we want to be . . . and perhaps it is through our suffering that the world will learn the good. . . ." Would this still come? Could this have been omitted?

Here, now, was the Chanukah scene, just as I had placed it, as the climax at the close of the second act. Anne, extremely excited, hurrying about distributing her little gifts, the excitement mounting and mounting—something seemed wrong to me. The way they had done it was more like a Christmas. Still, that wasn't the problem. The audience was touched, and after all the audience knew these people were Jews, and enormous pity was being aroused. Pity, yes—but what of understanding? Illumination?

121

Anne with Peter—all kittenish and moody and sex-provoked, yet where were their youthful outcries against the world their elders had made? Where was the final, bitter scene in which Peter declared that if he lived he would change his name and deny his identity as a Jew? And Anne virtually screaming at him, as she had written in her Diary, "But Peter! That's not honest!"

Perhaps all this simply didn't have any meaning for the Hellmans and the Hacketts. Or perhaps it did, and therefore had to be omitted.

One dramatic sequence had not been in my play at all—and not in the Diary: a scene in which Van Daan was discovered in the middle of the night stealing food from the larder, and Mrs. Frank hysterically ordered him and his family to leave the hiding place. Then all is forgotten in the sudden news of the Allied landing in Africa. Effective, yes, and dramatically justifiable, as it showed how people were driven to bestiality by what the Nazis had done to them.

But poor Van Daan was dead, among the last to be gassed at Auschwitz; there were other, equally dramatic things in the Diary that made the same point and did not leave such an atmosphere about our memory of him.

Only Otto Frank was perfect; Otto Frank and not Anne had become the center of the play. Could this have been used, there came to me in my tension, could this have been a subtle way to get him to suppress my work for theirs? How jealous could I be!

The last scene was before me. Anne and Peter stood at the window of his attic room, watching the Allied planes bombard the city. And the scene led up to Anne's reverberating cry, "In spite of everything, I still believe people are good at heart." Again I was seeing my own play! This all-meaningful line was the one I had taken out of the middle of a paragraph of reflections. And I had put Anne and Peter at the window, in the bombardment, with Anne speaking these thoughts to Peter. Exactly like this.

The audience was in tears.

My mind hammered with the train wheels. Just as train wheels seem to pound out one refrain, repeat another, come back to the first, and then unexpectedly endlessly clamor a third, so my mind ground on, leaping from one insistence to another, and back again.

First you persuade that boob Levin to step out of the way because a great world-famous playwright is taking over, the best for Anne, and he signs away his rights. Then you put the Hacketts on it, the Hacketts-Hacketts-Hacketts; of course he'd never have given up for them, but he signed, didn't he, he signed!

It wasn't only the taking of my work—that was normal in their world. I recalled the morning in Hollywood when a producer had set up a screening for me, a bygone hit, with instructions to watch for certain scenes, and see what I could use from them. Didn't Shakespeare use other people's plots? It was merely professional.

What a laugh it must have been for them when I sent my silly emotional offer to help put Anne's thoughts on the stage! They didn't need me—they already had my script. In their weekends with Lillian Hellman, their conferences with Kermit Bloomgarden, even with Otto Frank—ideas had been "kicked around" as in any story conference. Say, what about that scene where she pulls the star off her dress? That was the way writing was done in the manufacturing centers in our time. The feeling a writer got by having through his own search uncovered a form, an idea, an expression, was no longer important. All that mattered was the credit line.

Unworthy, unworthy—this was all mere personal ire—even

123

envy. It was not what they had taken from my work that was important, but what they had eliminated from the Diary. The real creator was Anne Frank, and what they had altered, and meaningfully left out, was important. The very quality of the Diary as a document of the Jewish disaster. Every Jew who had died in the Holocaust was misrepresented. But the effect of the omissions, just like the plagiarisms—as I felt they were —would be difficult to show.

And wasn't I overreacting to both? Who but I would be so sensitive to the censorlike omissions? For me, the line of censorship flowed through my whole life as a writer, from the publisher who had wanted to change the Jewish characters of *The Old Bunch* into a melting-pot mixture, to the publisher who had wanted the Jewish doctor of *Citizens* changed to a Swede, to Dave Smart of *Esquire* who had in mischievous vengeance signed my work "Patterson Murphy." So I had to set aside my personal reaction and try to pin down what they had done.

The doctrinaire motivation that I had suspected from the first entry of Lillian Hellman into the affair seemed clear to me in the play written under her tutelage. Or was it proven even now? Just because the Jewish material was minimized? The publishers who had rejected *The Old Bunch* for its Jewishness had certainly not been political. Here was one of those peculiar meeting-points between Soviet and American tendencies. While Jewish material was politically taboo in the Soviet Union, it was also—supposedly for commercial reasons—taboo in Hollywood. In magazines and books there had been a slow amelioration, and on television there was the Jewish comedy vogue of Sam Levenson. But a real Jewish character in films, or even on the stage, was then still a rarity. Thus, a Lillian Hellman, even if ideologically motivated, could take refuge in America's own commercial taboo. A kind of unadmitted anti-Semitism became "universalism." By leaving out the apparent fact that the salesman in *Death of a Salesman* was a Jew in a Jewish milieu, he became "more universal"! After all, hadn't it long been the policy of the Jewish establishment itself to keep the Jew inconspicuous in American society? Israel had changed things to a degree, but culturally there was still a lag.

In the Soviet Union, I had been told, certain Sholem Aleichem stories had been translated into Russian with the Jewish characteristics so carefully eliminated that Russians did not even know they were reading about Jews. Was this universalism? Didn't universalism spring only from the particular? And internationalism? How could there be internationalism without nationalism? Over and over. And as the wheels rolled on, there was the first refrain again—but Mr. Frank, you agreed, you insisted to me, the utmost faithfulness, the highest literary level—

—And you're still on that train, Meyer.
—And should I leap off? It never stops. It never arrives.
Oh, the bold sneering cunning of the lot of them! To have written it into the contract that I couldn't sue for plagiarism, and then unashamedly to have helped themselves to every effect they wanted from my work!
But they had overreached themselves! That scene, taking off the star—and there were others! Things not in the Diary, that I—

The play had now opened in New York, a hit, a triumph, a work of highest art. Audiences were moved. Jews brought their own emotions, wept. Schildkraut was idolized. The slick cuteness of the direction, that smirky scene where Anne put on the bra to go up to visit Peter in his room, while the two sets of parents made knowing eyes at each other—how typical! Groups from Hadassah, from suburban congregations, were swarming to benefits; from every theater page the starlet's face and Schildkraut's Otto Frank face assaulted me, and

125

the train wheels went on and on every night, and day-hours, too, in my head.

We knew, by then, of Stalin's "doctors' plot"; we were only now beginning to hear of an anti-Jewish phobia so intensive that it was forbidden in Russia to point out that the mass victims in Babi Yar were Jews.

Was it basically different, then, to prevent the hearing, on the stage, of Anne Frank's words "We are Jews because God made us so, and we want to be?" The full pattern of their omissions became clear when I had the text of their play, and could check the substitutions. "All people have suffered." The higher universalism! Who could deny that the victims of Babi Yar were simply "people"?

—But, dammit, Meyer, it's their play, not yours! They have a right—

—Do they? Do they really? The words I had her say were in the Diary. Theirs are not.

—Otto Frank approved theirs. He owns the Diary.

—Now we're at the heart of it! Even if he owns it, owns a work of art, as a property, does he have the right to let its meaning be changed?

The Diary itself, in print—was it thought any the less universal because it contained Anne's declaration of Jewish faith, and Margot's Zionist dream? Would letting Margot, on the stage, dream of a Jewish homeland destroy that universality? And if indeed it were my version on the stage—for now it was clear to me that it could have been dramatically just as effective as theirs—was it imaginable that audiences would stay away because of the inclusion of a few dozen lines about what Jews thought about God, about their identity as Jews, there in the very face of annihilation?

People believed propaganda was a matter of inculcation, slogans, down with the bosses, down with colonial imperialism. The reverse method, omission, censorship, wasn't widely understood. "You can have this book published if you will take out or change these few lines, which, as you surely can see, comrade, might be interpreted as a criticism of our leader."

What had been censored from the Diary was precisely what would have been forbidden over there. Any mention of Zionism. (Colonial imperialism.) Any exposition of Jewish faith. (Oh, you can show them clinging to a superstitious religious rite. That doesn't matter. It's even good. It shows the idiocy of such beliefs in the face of death. But this other material—their thinking about these questions—their avowals —no, that's too dangerous.)

—But Meyer, who is going to worry about what's left out? It's only a show.

Here and there an intellectual snob dared to say the show was full of *kitsch;* now and again a rabbi, almost in secret, would admit he thought it bad. But still, it was everywhere declared the hit was "doing good" for the Jews, it was arousing sympathy, many gentiles went to see it.

After a few weeks, the more serious reviews had appeared, one in *Commentary* tearing the play to pieces as false, phoney—several friends called my attention to the article— and someone also sent me the *Commonweal* review that ended with Anne furiously scribbling in her diary: "It wasn't like that at all!"

But now at last my version could be done in Israel. I would be vindicated! What a stroke—that I had kept the Israeli rights!

Orna Porat, a leading actress from the prestigious, modern-oriented Chamber Theatre, was in New York looking for plays. She took the script, read it and at once saw the contrast to the Broadway version. Would I come to Israel to work on produc-

127

tion? I would be only too happy. She would cable for the date.

The next day I read in the *Times* that the Habima theater had opened a Tel Aviv production of the Broadway success *The Diary of Anne Frank*.

Miss Porat called. How was this possible? Was I going to stop their production? They must have rehearsed in secret, as she had heard nothing whatever of such plans.

Again Ephraim London needed only a glance at the contract. "Yes, it gives you the right to production in Israel, but it doesn't say an exclusive right!"

On the subway it resumed. "But Mr. Frank! This one small thing I asked of you! You perfectly well understood—"

And that lawyer, Mermin, standing at his window predicting, "You'll never know."

Then, all night—"Mr. Frank, no, no, believe me, I don't presume. I would be ashamed to suggest that I suffer in any way as you have suffered. Only, when it started in Germany, the first thing they did was to take away from you what you had created, in your case a business, and hand it to a non-Jew. Don't you see it's the same—"

So it was my own survivor's guilt. So I had wanted this to happen to me. That was why I had failed to notice the legal loophole. I had wanted all the time to be hurt, to be punished, to be able even in a small way to identify with the Jews of Europe.

Cables, agents, lawyers; Otto Frank declared he had not given permission, he had known nothing about the Tel Aviv production. On his instruction, his lawyers were cabling Habima to impound the royalties until it could be determined whether they should be paid to me.

Mr. Frank! Can you really all this time have believed that with me it was the money, the royalties!

128

At last the sleeping pill took effect.

Otto Frank, declared his representatives, couldn't bring himself to require Habima to close down the play. He couldn't stop his daughter's words from being heard, no matter by what subterfuge the production had been put on. The Broadway play was a success in Israel, too, and it would be wrong to close it down.

Then let them change over to my text! They could even use the same set!

No. It was the Broadway success that Habima wanted. They had seen my text and found it unacceptable.

How? Through whom? By what intrigues? I had never heard from Habima. I had had offers from the Chamber Theatre and the Ohel. I would fly there and prove—

I would only make myself ridiculous, trying to force on Israel a work that had been rejected "by all Broadway"! I would only come to shame.

It was at this time, I think, that I wrote the enraged letter: "You are my Hitler."

Did I send it?

Incessantly, then, the justice obsession.

On and on in my head—worse than the wheels—a calliope.

There is a young man in Israel named Michael; when I first knew him, he was a child. Growing up, he took his turn in the army, volunteering for the paratroops, serving in many border engagements, and then in the Six-Day War. One day Michael heard a ringing in his ears. In the years that have since gone by, the sound has never stopped.

It is not so unique a malady; numbers of war veterans suffer from it. No remedy is known. You can stuff your fingers into your ears—the ringing continues. You can live in a sound-proof room—the ringing continues. The sufferer is able to work, to hear all the life around him, and music, too—but the ringing is always there. At night, when you want to get to sleep, it is the worst. But you have to live with it.

When in his modest and matter-of-fact way Michael told me about his condition, I felt I knew. I had by then had such a ringing in my head for years and years. My obsession. Michael had accepted the bleak fact that the ringing would never go away. With the justice obsession, one cannot accept this. You have to live with it and also to strive to resolve it. You, too, may manage to keep up with your work, to live your day-to-day life. But the ringing presses you into action.

Arbitration, I importuned, or a hearing before a committee of cultural leaders, or Jewish leaders, or writers, any form they would choose. Surely a man had a right to some form of hearing!

No answer.

Perhaps, the rabbinate? That time when Otto Frank was in New York, the High Holy Days had come, and he had asked me to take him to the Free Synagogue. He had met Rabbi Klein. Perhaps Rabbi Klein?

Silence.

No, I would not take it to court. To begin with, there was the political side—how could I come out with all that, in the courtroom, in public? It would sound like sheer McCarthyism! Red conspiracy over the Diary! Besides, this was essentially a Jewish thing. Virtually everyone involved was Jewish, leaving out the Hacketts, and the issue was over the Jewish content of the Diary. The right place to settle it was within the Jewish community.

There is an ancient custom. A man with a grievance may appear in the synagogue, and the prayers may not be recited until his grievance is heard.

One Friday evening I was to speak on American Jewish literature at the Park Avenue Synagogue. There before their own crowd; perhaps Myer Mermin himself was a member.

Though my talk came after the service, it was still part of the temple's Sabbath observance.

I did it. With the rabbi sitting just behind me, I told my story from the podium and cried out, "I call to a justice hearing: Kermit Bloomgarden, Lillian Hellman, Otto Frank." I was trembling.

> My analyst wheezed up his high-pitched giggle. Oh, good! Wonderful! He could just see them! The Park Avenue worshippers! And then what happened? Did they send right out and fetch the culprits, even Otto Frank from Amsterdam?
>
> Well, there had been a peculiar, hesitant silence, like that when an audience doesn't quite know whether applause is permissible. The young rabbi rose and said a few nice words about my evoking this ancient, important Jewish custom.
>
> Just to make myself heard, somehow, somewhere!

It was Dr. Sulzberger now. *Compulsion* had come out and was a best seller; at last I had some money. The trouble had entered a new phase, and I had again sought out an analyst. Feeling I ought to try someone with a different approach, I had come to Sulzberger through the recommendation of Theodor Reik, author of *Listening with the Third Ear*.

The new trouble centered on a stage version of *Compulsion* with which I meant to prove myself as a playwright at last. But for months, intrigue after intrigue enmeshed me. Dr. Sulzberger was eager to hear about every detail. He had a passion for the theater, had married a dancer.

There was no question in my mind but that the trouble stemmed from the same sources as the Anne Frank case. That cabal hadn't let up on me this whole time; I had even been terrified that when the novel came out, they would find some way to wreck it.

Could they do that? asked Sulzberger.

131

Well, not infallibly, of course, but they could create an atmosphere in publishing circles, pass the word, slip in a bad review here and there—all this could have an effect. Fortunately Jack Goodman was in with that crowd, and he had in a way protected me. Maybe from myself as much as from them. He had taken the situation seriously enough to suggest that I get out of the country for the few months before publication, because if I didn't stop talking incessantly about the comrades and the Anne Frank play, there might be reprisals.

Jack Goodman had really thought so?

Yes, and as a result I called up Arnold Gingrich at *Esquire,* though I hadn't been in touch with him for years. Told him about the trouble and asked for a couple of assignments in France to pay for my trip—

Wouldn't the publishers have advanced it?

I had used up their advance and didn't want to ask for more.

And then the book had come out, and there hadn't been any trouble?

No, but with the prospect of my doing *Compulsion* as a play, trouble had begun. Because, obviously, if I had a hit play, the claim that I was hopeless as a dramatist would be belied.

What form did the trouble take?

One producer after another would speak for the play and then suddenly back off. Finally I got going with a very peculiar Broadway operator. Oh, he'd done some excellent things, but he had an unsavory reputation. Then the trouble began with him.

But wasn't that common in the theater? What made me think it came from the same bunch?

Look, Kermit Bloomgarden had been loudly proclaiming in Sardi's that I would never get anything on Broadway.

Maybe with Bloomgarden it had become a personal feud? His animosity didn't prove it was a political cabal, did it?

132

No, of course not. But had I told him about the Jewish writers in the Soviet Union? Granted, this was going to seem far-fetched. Paranoid. But had he heard about that situation? I didn't suppose he had heard, as the story somehow didn't seem to have come through except in the Jewish press. I had got the impact of it through a kind of accident. Even after all the revelations about Stalin—the doctors' plot—I'd known nothing about the Jewish writers. But then one day I had been asked to speak at a convention of a Jewish labor organization. At the long table on the platform I found myself in the company of the real ones, the old-time leaders who talked with a strong Yiddish accent, the stubby-looking men in brownish suits, some with a Yiddish newspaper sticking out of a pocket. I didn't really fit into their world, though it had been the world of my childhood. I remembered an uncle a buttonhole-maker, an aunt a cigar-maker, and the kitchen-table gatherings with worries about the union, about going on strike. I had gone out from that world and lived my life with American newspapermen and writers and editors and Paris literati and *Esquire* glossiness and radicals in Spain and the Hollywood crowd. After all that, when I wrote about the concentration camps, the survivors, Palestine, Israel, I again became known to these labor-union Jews, and they called me back.

As the meeting opened, a *chaver* arose. There was fervor and shock and anger in his voice as he read out a series of names, and I realized he was memorializing. It took a moment for the Yiddish to flow for me, so that I could grasp what he was speaking about. The names were names all these people knew, for an awesome murmur arose at the calling of each one. Someone named Yitzhak Feffer, liquidated. Someone named Michöeles, murdered. Were they labor heroes? Someone named Bergelson, liquidated: "Who among us does not know his poems—"

I didn't know. In my American world, even with part of my life in Israel, I didn't know the living—now dead—Yiddish authors. As the memorializer went on, I began to grasp the ghastly story, something that seemed quite familiar to all these Jews, but that I hadn't heard about, that my world hadn't heard about. We had heard rumors about Stalin's sinister scheme, in his last phase, to transport all Russian Jewry to Siberia. But the tale of his systematic attack on Jewish authors and cultural leaders—why hadn't this come through to me in my outside world? In the general press?

One name after another—vanished—fate unknown—died in a labor camp—believed liquidated. Accused of making Zionist propaganda, of being agents, spies. Some of these men, the speaker reminded his listeners, had even been here in America during the war, as a Soviet antifascist delegation— of course this had been after Germany attacked Russia—to intensify Jewish labor effort in defeating the Nazis. Many in this room had met the leader of the delegation, Michöeles, that genius of the Yiddish theater. A few years after the war it had been given out that Michöeles had died in an automobile accident. Now the truth was known. That accident had been an execution. For being in contact with the West. For that very visit here, on which he had been officially sent. And after the murder of Michöeles, there had been a roundup. A trial, but even today no details were known, except that twenty-four Jewish poets had been executed in one night in August, 1952, in the basement of the Lubianka prison in Moscow.

And still more arrests and deportations. Hundreds.

As the convention rose in memory of the destroyed Jewish poets, novelists, artists, I experienced the same sensation I had felt when I entered the first death camp and found myself standing before a cordwood pile of bodies: the dead were myself. My father and mother had never left Vilna. I grew up there, became a Yiddish author . . .

"And so now you insist on identifying, you want to be-lieve that the same attack was projected on you, that Stalin reached you even here. You insist on being one of the victims."

"I know, I know about survivor's guilt. I wrote about it when I interviewed the first Jew who crawled out of hiding when we entered Paris. He had jumped out of a deportation train, leaving his wife to go on to her death. Even though they had previously agreed either one must take such a chance if it came, the survivor was ridden with guilt. I may even have made up the term."

"And if the guilt itself didn't exist, you'd have invented that, too," he chuckled.

But I wouldn't so easily be deprived. The portion of guilt was a portion of guilt, the portion of reality was reality.

"It fits, doesn't it? After all, McCarthyism or no McCarthyism, the people who are doing this to me have the same Stalinist set of ideas against Jewish particularism, Zionism, and all the rest. It shows in the omissions from the Diary after they got me kicked out. No, I'm not imagining orders from Moscow. Get Meyer Levin! Kill him on Broadway! But once you are set on an ideological course, you follow through on your own. Party or no party, to their way of thinking I'm an enemy. In fact McCarthyism gives them a perfect cover, because the minute I try to point out the meaning of what they're doing, the ideological source, they can scream red-baiter! And since hardly anybody has heard about the Jewish writers, and the whole anti-Jewish line, all my protests sound imaginary or insane."

"You think your friend Otto Frank, too, is a pro-Communist?"

I thought by then I could explain Otto Frank. As word of my complaint got around, a young woman, a Dutch refugee authoress named Dola De Jong, had called me, filling in a piece of the story. She too had tried to help Otto Frank find an American publisher, even sending my early article in *Congress Weekly* to her editor at Little,

Brown, and they, as I knew, had made an offer. Frank had cabled his acceptance. She had nearly completed her translation for Little, Brown when he had suddenly gone over to Doubleday. It was she who, to help me understand Frank, had recommended Dr. Elie Cohen's book *Human Behavior in the Concentration Camp*.

Among those who survived, Dr. Cohen pointed out, were a certain proportion who were highly apt to have identified with the power-figures of the camp. They emerged authoritative. They could not abide even the slightest questioning of any decision or opinion, of any course of action they had taken. Secretiveness was also often a characteristic.

In some—and this I myself had noted—there was a conviction of having survived by divine intent, perhaps to tell all that had happened. Their very survival was proof that their every decision, every action toward this end, had been correct, and justified, and the only way.

I seemed to be reading a portrait of Otto Frank. How had I dared ask him for a justice hearing! All he had done had to have been exactly right, for the result was that the book and play had won worldwide success.

Yes, Dr. Sulzberger knew the book. It was a real contribution. This Dr. Cohen was absolutely sound. Had the book helped me?

It had clarified Frank's behavior, yes. I had even asked myself, supposing Otto Frank was thus a kind of psychological victim—did I still have the moral right to pursue this whole affair against him? Even to going to law, as I had finally decided to do?

But all I was getting from the fight was terror and trouble. Whispering campaigns, avoidance by old friends, and this sense of being undermined on all sides. Why couldn't I drop the lawsuit, the whole affair? Maybe then they'd let me alone. Why did I have to carry on, run to this one and that one, make enemies up and down, risk my new play as well, all because of a few scenes about being a Jew omitted from their play? Why did I have to torment myself here, three times a week, getting nowhere?

"You have thought of dropping the whole thing, so that they'd stop persecuting you?"

"Then you do agree that they are persecuting me? That it's real?"

Instances—or are they delusions of persecution? Phantoms? Reality? Exaggerations? After I had heard about the Jewish writers, everything had seemed clear. I would go to Judge Rifkind himself, at Paul, Weiss, Rifkind, etc., and tell him of the anti-Jewish campaign that was behind my whole trouble. Persuading myself that if a man like Judge Rifkind learned his firm was being used to further such intrigues, my troubles would end, I had a friend call him to ask if he would see me. After all, Rifkind was virtually regarded as the head of the American Jewish community. In the war he had been advisor to General Eisenhower on Jewish affairs, and wasn't he now, hadn't he been for years, leader of the American Jewish Committee?

A diminutive, knotted-together man, the ex-judge listened to my tale of political victimization and suppression with such an air of sympathy that at several points I was affected and had to brush my eyes with a finger. It happens to me. With the Anne Frank trouble, it was happening more and more. I managed to get to the part about my chance to see my work vindicated in Israel, and the omission of the word "exclusive" that thwarted me. Suddenly his whole manner changed. Quietly and concisely he asked, "You secured this interview with me to complain about a matter being handled by a member of this firm?"

Well, yes, I babbled. Since it was really a Jewish issue—

He stood up behind his desk. He sympathized with me, he said, but as it was a matter in the firm, he could not interfere.

137

In my hunger to find the right person, the benevolent, understanding authority who straightens out everything by a simple intervention, a few words in the right place, I then even appealed to Eleanor Roosevelt. Wasn't her name signed to the introduction to the Diary?

One morning I was admitted to the quiet garden apartment in the East Sixties; the tall, fine lady of good deeds came and sat opposite me, and again I poured out my whole story: the maneuver by which I had been eliminated, the fate of the Russian writers—I really didn't want the case to come to court, for the communism issue would then inevitably come out, and I certainly had no desire to give ammunition to McCarthy. . . .

What did I want of her?

Would she intercede with Otto Frank? All I asked was that those who preferred to do my version should be allowed to do so. Now that the other side had their enormous success, why couldn't they make this small gesture? I kept getting requests from Jewish groups—shuffling amongst my papers, I found one to show her, even while telling myself I was beginning to be one of those pests who carry around bits of paper, documents, "proofs."

We finished our tea. She said she would think about the matter and let me know. Presently I heard from her. The difficulties were with Nathan Straus, who was opposed to me. I wrote back, saying I realized this made the question delicate for her, as Mr. Straus had been a close friend of her husband's, but I hoped the issue could be taken out of the area of personal reactions. A few days later I received a note saying that everything Anne Frank wrote would always be there in the Diary, and that it was the book that would live.

I made an attempt to see Nathan Straus. He refused.

Sulzberger snorted, nodded. So I had been to the justice figures. Run to papa. Run to mama. Run to the rabbi. With

138

my hurt, with my rage. "Look, they ganged up on me, they hit me! I didn't start anything, I was just a good boy, and they jumped on me and hit me!"

So then what could I do? Run to the policeman? Run get my own gang?

This is face-to-face therapy, not couch analysis. Oh, you can lie on the couch if you feel like it, letting things flow up, hoping to make the connection. A thousand times, with Dr. A, as now with Dr. Sulzberger, I had dredged up my street-terrors from childhood. Does that really help you to know what to do in the face of your grown-up world?

I went back to the rabbis.

No, it hadn't been entirely a stunt, that cry in the Park Avenue synagogue. Nor could I see it as regressive. The long-bearded rabbi-figure was hardly an authority out of my child-hood, nor had my parents "run to the rabbi" with their prob-lems. Perhaps it was from tales of the old country that "go to the rabbi" resounded, linking together justice and holiness and authority and helpfulness; perhaps I'm a *rebbe manqué*. But what was taking place, I reasoned, was an exploitation of the Jewish tragedy, mostly through the Jewish community. There-fore the problem should be solved within the Jewish commu-nity. Where was a voice? The rabbis, as I thought of them, were not the caftan-wearing graybeards of tradition but the younger, modern rabbis, the Reform and Conservative rabbis, who would be more aware, more sensitive to all the aspects of the issue. What I wanted, I kept saying, was a kind of ethical voice, a voice speaking for the Jewish community, a voice which would in a way shame the other side into granting the little that I asked, the simple right of non-commercial perfor-mance. I was ready to forgo the plagiarism question, the deceptions and legal chicanery, even the political machina-tions. Only let the work be freely heard!

I sent out a letter to the rabbis, with a petition to be signed.

139

The petition I had carefully composed so that no legal issue, no personal issue, was raised:

Although a dramatization of Anne Frank's *Diary of a Young Girl* has been seen throughout the world, an earlier adaptation by Meyer Levin, authorized by Anne's father, has been forbidden to the public because of assigned commercial rights. Comparative merits and legal issues are not in question here, but we suggest that Anne Frank's *Diary,* a legacy to humanity, be viewed as a literary work rather than as a commercial property. It is not uncommon, indeed it is stimulating, for more than one adaptation of an important book to be offered to the public. We urge that qualified productions of Mr. Levin's play be permitted in recognition, so appropriate to the *Diary,* that not only human beings but their works have a right to life.

The response was instant, overwhelming. Every morning I would rush down to the postman's ring, returning with my arms overflowing with letters, far too numerous for the mailbox.

I had had an eerily growing sense of emptiness and loneliness, a growing fear of aberration. As though all certainties were being sucked out of me—what I knew about writing, what I knew about people. Into this vacuum came the replies, the reassurances from the rabbis—by the hundreds. Some of them added letters of encouragement, cries of indignation, justice quotations from the Talmud; many affirmed that their reaction to the Broadway play had been the same as mine. Some added the congratulatory Hebrew phrase *Yashir Koach,* grow in strength! Among the signatures were renowned names from influential urban congregations, and names of leaders of rabbinical associations, and there were signatures from every state in the union. Though there exists no central Jewish authority, I had found a way to a kind of community verdict. A moral mandate, I called it, jubilating. How could such a massive, such a genuine, declaration be

140

ignored? I "still believed." I typed out a list of the signers, six single-spaced pages, and sent it, with a copy of the petition, to Otto Frank and to the Rifkind office.

There was no response.

> "Did you expect any?"
> "Yes. Honestly, this time, yes."

Then I called a press conference. At the SAJ (Society for the Advancement of Judaism) synagogue of the Reconstructionist Foundation, the center of Rabbi Mordecai Kaplan's movement, on West 86th Street, there was at that time a youngish rabbi, Jack Cohen, who had already made attempts to intercede for me with the other side. But they had refused to budge, and so Rabbi Cohen offered me the Foundation's offices for my conference. Before each seat at a long table I piled my releases, my lists; at my elbow was the stack of signed petitions.

Only one reporter appeared, but he was from *The New York Times*. Neutral looking, the typical Timesman, he took copies of everything, fingered through the stack of petitions, glancing at some of the added comments, and listened to my tale. I still carefully refrained from accusations of ideologies and politics, ascribing the motives to "Broadway intrigues" and commercialization. Again I emphasized that I asked only the right of production for those who wanted to use my version, without interfering with the Broadway play.

Several hours later I had a call from the *Times* reporter. "Mr. Levin," he said in that same neutral tone, though now it sounded controlled, "I just want you to know this. I could lose my job for telling you, but I believe you have the right to know. I wrote the story. You're an experienced newspaperman yourself, and I don't have to explain to you, outside of your personal involvement, that what you gave me is a legitimate and serious piece of news, and quite unusual. The story

141

went through the desk, but at the last moment was killed from upstairs."

I thanked him, and he hung up.

Sulzberger wheezed, nearly choking on it. Oh, that family! Oh, he knew them! He was the maverick of the *Times* family, but well he knew them! He had veered off, lived in Europe, savoring music and art, and wound up studying medicine; then he had gone into psychoanalysis. Even there he was a maverick; though a medical man, he had taken up the battle of the lay psychological wing, siding with Theodor Reik and the bunch who believed you didn't need a medical degree to be an analyst. After all, Freud himself had let them in!

Old Battler Reik with his wiry aureole of gray-white hair, stomping up and down Broadway. My former landlord, Reuben Fine, of the psychologist-analysts, had sent me to the half-deaf master, who indeed had now only his Third Ear to listen with; after a few sessions of listening to me shouting out my troubles, Reik had suggested Sulzberger.

Before resuming analysis I had finally been exploring the legal side, taking myself from one lawyer to another—all the experts on books and theater. They listened with keen interest, with bemused professional smiles; they nodded knowingly, with gleams of malicious recognition, at the way "that bunch at Paul, Weiss, Rifkind" had taken me in. They'd go so far as to say nevertheless I had a case; even though certain conditions had not been set forth in the contract—like my bowing out for a great internationally known playwright—they had been verbally promised. Oh, yes, in law that counted—and so Myer Mermin, while aware that I had no attorney, had proffered me legal advice, had he? Head-shakings. And even if Mermin had written a very tight contract, I still might be able to prove plagiarism. If the examples I cited were true. The Diary was very big money now, and damages might come to a considerable amount. And then, there was the damage to my reputation as a playwright—

—That's it. All I want is to be heard—

On the contrary, it might be wise to be cautious. If my play should prove bad, the entire action of my opponents was justified. Odd that they wouldn't let it be heard even under amateur conditions. That led one to suspect—

One of those who listened with considerable fascination was the noted Louis Nizer, who reveled in spectacular and seemingly impossible cases. He was prominent in things Jewish. —Nizer is your man, everyone had told me.

"But to prove your contention about slighting the Jewish content," he concluded reflectively, "we have to prove an absence. And that the omission really had a motive. That's the hardest thing to prove—an absence. Something that isn't there, and why." Still, I seemed to have a case and he was tempted. But he would need a twenty-five-thousand-dollar retainer for research.

Compulsion had not yet come out, and who could tell how it would fare? Pay for my column had shrunk to seventy-five dollars a week. From one to another of the expensive, celebrated lawyers, I was referred down the status-scale, until one day I found myself in the modest office of a young man named Fredman, zestful looking, with a crewcut and a football build. He was from a good school, Penn State, and well recommended. Fredman heard me out, clucking. Oh, he'd love to tangle with that Rifkind outfit, powerful though they were. (Crusading young lawyer takes on the biggest, toughest gang in the business and wins justice.) He would be willing to take the case on a contingency fee basis. Plus out-of-pocket expenses, of course. The first outlay, he grinned, would be painful for me, as he'd need a pair of tickets for the Diary— his wife would be glad of a chance to see it. Also I would have to supply him with both texts and my detailed comparisons.

After seeing their show, Fredman was bursting with zeal.

143

Oh, yes, he understood what I meant. And he smelled big money.

"Wait," I began.

"Look, the only way you can put the case is in terms of big money. That's what people understand. As far as your share goes, you can give it away, burn it, that's your affair. We may not get what we ask for, but we have to ask for a lot, to call attention to the importance of the issue."

He was right, I knew, and yet—could Otto Frank possibly be left out of it?

No. We'd have to go soft on him, but the whole case hung on his agreements with me. They were clear enough, even in the few letters I had saved.

"Could we still ask for arbitration after filing the lawsuit?"

"Stop beating your breast. We can always consent to arbitration if they come around. Let *them* ask for it. *You* ask, and all you'll get is what you got before." He made a lip-fart.

As for the Commie issue, we must avoid it, if at all possible. We could simply say the motive was money. "Bloomgarden saw big money in it, and went after Frank to discredit you and get you kicked out, simply because you had chosen another producer. That anyone can understand."

There was one aspect of the publicity around Bloomgarden's production that aroused me. An impression was being created of altruism rather than commercialism.

"They give out stories that the royalties are being donated to a Dutch village in Israel, a village for survivors from Holland. There was a signed article in the *Post.*"

He leaned back, chuckling. "Want to make a bet?"

I checked with the Israeli consulate; no one had ever heard of the existence of a Dutch village or of any such formation. I could find no confirmation of donations to any Israeli institution of royalties from the Broadway play.*

* Several years later, Mr. Frank visited Israel and made a $50,000 donation.

144

I told Fredman I was ready to go ahead.

He saw two lines of action. First I had been swindled out of my rights, and then I had been plagiarized. But before filing the lawsuit there was one document he had to have—a signed statement from Herman Shumlin that he had made an offer to produce my play.

I went directly to Shumlin. He looked pained. Did I really have to drag this into the courts? Sure, it was true that he had made an offer to Paul, Weiss, Rifkind, but—

"Do you know why they refused you?" I asked him. "They said you were incapable of ever again producing a hit."

He gazed at me and, without another word, wrote out and signed the statement.

It was then, as we became entangled in law, that the added trouble began, bringing me to Sulzberger.

No sooner had the lawsuit been filed than stories appeared, little items in the trade press—"disgruntled author suing." And little jokes were heard about Levin and his lawsuits. "Who're you suing today?" I'd be greeted. Hotly I would try to explain how I had begged for arbitration, for any kind of justice hearing—a man is entitled to a hearing—that it was they who had driven me to the courts—but with each report of legal maneuvers, the gossip increased. I was a trouble-maker, always in the courts—"But I never before brought a lawsuit in my life! And we haven't even been to court!" More jokes. And then there came a certain word. Levin was liti-gious. The word seemed to be echoing all around me. I was litigious by nature, a constant troublemaker.

Bill Zimmerman brought it to me. As my advance on *Compulsion* had run out with publication still months away, he was trying to help me with a film-dubbing job. The crumbs of the industry. Bill had proposed me to a dubbing company, and even at this level there had been an instant reaction. "He's litigious." The word struck him, since it was odd—he hadn't

145

even been certain of its meaning. Since he was responsible for assigning a great deal of the dubbing of foreign films for MGM, the company had accepted me on his personal reassurance. But then Bill heard the word again, this time, at a party. Levin was a troublemaker, litigious. The word was going around.

Fredman too had heard it. That same word. It wasn't so unusual a term in legal circles, but come to think of it, he'd heard it at a social gathering; some theater investors were there—not big ones, the kind that take a little flyer once in a while. The Diary had been talked about. Someone had asked him, wasn't I a notorious litigious character?

Then an actor's wife, one of the Fire Island crowd, repeated it to me. Yes, she remembered exactly where she had heard it. At a party. From a Broadwayite we shall call Tom Rank.

Who was Tom Rank?

Why, didn't I know? A theatrical press agent. In fact, he often worked for Kermit.

Then that was simple enough, even natural.

But it took an added turn.

A McCarthy subcommittee had come to hold hearings about reds in the theater; only lesser people were being called —the big ones had already been to Washington. In the newspapers I saw the name of the man I am calling Tom Rank, with his testimony.

Was he a member of the Communist party today? No. Had he been a member a year ago? Fifth Amendment.

I mustn't react. I mustn't make accusations. It was simply one more oddity.

Then came an additional bit of light. A study of blacklisting had been made under the auspices of the Ford Foundation, a careful, devastating piece of documentation, using long interviews in Hollywood with actors, writers, directors who had lost their work. The scholars had been careful and thorough, going back to the very roots of the red scare. And there in the

146

report I came upon a few startling pages. The blacklisting practice, they reported, might be said to have begun on the other side. Word would be spread that so-and-so was a troublemaker. Soon enough he would become unemployable, untouchable.

So this was being done to me systematically. Nothing could drive this from my mind. In every conversation, no matter with whom, no matter on what subject, I would find myself jumping over to the Diary. Every time we went to a party, to any sort of gathering, I would soon be standing in a corner, explaining: They censored out exactly what would have been cut out in Moscow—

—-Oh, come on, Meyer!

And then foolishly, knowing I was being foolish, I would plunge into the story. Beginning with Hellman. And all the way to that press agent, Tom Rank, his spreading stories about me, in the exact words of the Ford Foundation report—

A certain look would come into their eyes. But I couldn't stop. "Listen, we all know how that bunch works! Why, even half the cast—No! Listen, I'm glad they've got jobs, I'm only trying to show you it's a political thing—they smeared me, they blacklisted me exactly the way McCarthy blacklists them—!"

After all, I was talking among friends who knew my writings, my record. I was no "enemy of the Soviet Union"—I was only protesting the one aspect, the Jewish policy, on which so many agreed with me. And if anyone should be able to understand me, it should be these people, my old friends of the left! I wasn't making these charges publicly! I was saying these things amongst ourselves, in the hope of bringing that bunch back to their senses! All I wanted, all I asked for was so trivial—

I had to stop saying these things. True as they were, I had to stop. And I couldn't.

147

There was even a party where one of the Hollywood Ten was present. I admonished myself, "Don't you realize who is here! Shut up! You're making it worse!"

But an English actress had asked me why I was suing Otto Frank. I couldn't stop. Inside me something kept protesting; I wanted them to know I knew! They were the only ones that could do something about it. Let them hear! What more could they do to me, anyway?

I answered myself, You've got a book coming out! You want to make it into a play. They can wreck you again, you damned fool!

All right, all right, I would stop. I had spewed it all out, anyway, to a whole circle gathered around the actress. Now there was a dead silence around me.

We left early. As we waited for the elevator, Tereska said, "Have you gone out of your mind?" Her face was white.

These were the prepublication months when word goes around, and the fate of a book can be decided. Jack Goodman had already heard the talk about me—he had good friends in the left; he was getting worried. We went to lunch and got into a long discussion about Jewishness, Zionism, the Stalinist attack on Jewish writers, of which he had heard only vague rumors. A swift-risen bright boy, assimilated, Goodman had to have some of the basic questions in the Jewish world, even questions about Israel, explained to him.

Naturally he had been deeply upset by the Holocaust, but even in this, he believed his shock was more as a citizen of the world, though he also felt it as a Jew. As for Israel—why, yes—when I got into the story of the pioneer family I had long wanted to write about—why, yes, that would make a big, important novel. I must do it. But right now he had his little problem with *Compulsion*. If I couldn't stop myself from saying the things I was saying around town—though he fully

148

understood what made me say them—and undoubtedly I was even completely right—still, in this crucial prepublication period, I had no need to stir up more animosity, so if I couldn't stop myself, perhaps I ought to go away for a while. A hiatus. I wouldn't be running around town attacking people, and he thought he could get them to keep from attacking me. He could launch the book without handicaps.

I'd go.

That was when I called Arnold Gingrich, asking if I could do a few articles to pay my way for a short stay in Paris. Yes, he'd heard about me and my lawsuits, he understood. We'd work out a few subjects.

The book was an instant success. All at once I was a celebrity, an authority; every radio and television program wanted me to discuss the psychology of crime, and whether or not Nathan Leopold should be released on parole. I found myself virtually crusading for him.

For the first time in my life I had real money. Just turning fifty, I could at last give up the time-consuming scramble for a living while writing. For a few months I could hardly adjust to it. I kept the column going—I was afraid to spend money. And I didn't really have too much to spend, as in the contract I had limited myself to an annual stipend, thinking that if the book should be a hit, I might never have one again. Indeed, none of the books that followed in the next fifteen years earned enough to cover the time of writing.

Yet as to the obsession, the success changed nothing. All that happened on *Compulsion* would immediately be evaluated in my mind in relation to the struggle over the Diary. Though I really saw the *Compulsion* story in dramatic form, I kept telling myself that by making it into a play I would prove my case. "Mr. Levin simply couldn't write an actable play" would be their sole defense in court, and at that very time I would have my new play running on Broadway! That was one thing they couldn't interfere with! Of course, if the play failed, I would be providing proof for their side, not for myself, but this was a risk I had to take: I would stand or fall on my own work.

Jack Goodman called. Could I rush over? Orson Welles was in his office. Orson, an old friend, was mad to produce and direct *Compulsion* on the stage.

—Would he act Clarence Darrow?

He'd do that too, but the main thing would be to direct.

Welles was an idol of mine. Yes, I knew all the destructive stories about him; in my film critic days on *Esquire,* I had watched him bled and butchered by the Hollywood hacks who felt threatened by his genius. I knew the tales of how difficult he was to work with. But weren't the same things being said of me?

Right off, we were in rapport; we saw the play the same way, a modern morality play in terms of a sensational crime, but basically a puzzle on the question of free will. And the atmosphere of Chicago. Chicago in the twenties. Headlines of gang wars, of Al Capone, pulsing across the proscenium on a band of electric lights. Jazz! Chicago was Orson's town, too!

All at once, oddly, I realized that while I had come to appeal to him, Orson Welles was appealing to me. Would I hold the rights for him? He was already virtually sure he had the production money. A good friend of his in Hollywood, the writer, Francis Lederer—did I know him?—No, in my Hollywood days, Lederer had been several ranks above me in the screenwriters' hierarchy.—Anyway, Lederer was crazy to do *Compulsion,* he'd get the production money from his aunt— did I know who his aunt was? Orson watched me mischievously for the effect: Marion Davies! Wait! I needn't get upset. She was really an intelligent woman—

I had a double image of Orson Welles the genius superimposed upon Orson Welles the promoter, and thus a flash of insight into his wobbly, disastrous career. But yes, yes, I cried, I'd hold the rights for him. Still he kept promoting. It would be the play of the century. After its run, every college would be producing it, year after year—Suddenly he broke off, looking at me with uncertainty. "Shit, every top Broadway producer will be after you. You won't hold it for me. Good-bye, *Compulsion!*" And he made for the door.

"I give you my word, I want you to do it! I'll hold it for you!" I cried as he left.

Jack Goodman laughed. "That's Orson."

Goodman phoned. Orson was in Hollywood. He had the money, for sure. Would I fly out there and confer with him and Lederer?

The other thing, the unremitting thing, had been pressing me to go to Hollywood. I had convinced myself that the one person who still might beneficially intervene in the Diary trouble was Dore Schary. He was powerful and well connected in each of the three worlds involved. With his talent for giving popular material a gloss of significance, Schary had moved from the top of the screenwriter craft to the top of Hollywood itself, as production chief at Metro-Goldwyn-Mayer. Along with this, he was also highly active in Jewish affairs, and was even regarded as a quasi-religious spokesman. Thirdly, he was a Roosevelt adulator, a liberal who had shrewdly kept his balance in the Hollywood hotbed, he had always been friendly with the radical clique, and was staunchly active in the Screen Writers Guild. Doubtless, Schary would be well acquainted with the Hacketts and Hellman, too. Now that there was a new atmosphere around my name, perhaps he would intervene. I was a success—even better, in the Hollywood mythology, I had made a comeback! Should my case come to trial, best-seller author against prize-winning playwrights, there might really be attention, a scan-

151

dal—why not prevent it? Schary could perhaps persuade the other side to agree to my trivial request, a simple concession to the Jewish communities that wanted to see my "Jewish version." And with that I would drop the lawsuit.

Schary gave me an appointment. While juggling a score of studio calls, he was in the midst of dictating an inspirational message for the High Holy Days, to be delivered at some big convention, but presently he interrupted this, and asked the operator to hold his calls, and affably turned to me.

Yes, he knew about the attack on the Jewish writers in Russia. And he had heard something about my troubles. He understood my position on the Diary, but after all, the Broadway play was doing so much good, raising so much sympathy. He could assure me that the Hacketts had even gone to the most prominent Reform rabbi in Hollywood for research on Chanukah. Sure, he was glad to know my side of the story. But Lillian Hellman had had so much trouble from McCarthy. Well, if any opportunity arose, he would try to help smooth things out.

He resumed his High Holy Days message.

I would make one more try. There was an old friend of mine from the thirties whom I could ask for this favor. He had been an early Depression communist, a novelist and critic, who in those days sat amongst the clattering mimeograph machines in a dim Fourteenth Street campaign office, writing press releases to save the Scottsboro boys. Like so many others, Vic had come out to Hollywood and lingered, though always trying to get back to his own writing. From the earliest days he had given up on me as not being politically-minded, but nevertheless, Vic would say, when the barricades went up, he knew I'd be on the side of the revolution.

Driving me to his house for dinner, Vic heard about Schary and smiled. As for Lillian, plenty of party people found her a pain in the neck, but she had done a lot, suffered a lot with Dash Hammett, been blacklisted. The Hacketts were considered reliables, faithful onhangers, and they'd probably been handed the Diary as a reward. Bloomgarden? The left had made him. He did what was wanted.

Then I made my try. "Vic, isn't there someone you could talk to? To have the dogs called off? After all, from the point of view of simple expediency, there is still a big risk the whole political thing will explode in the trial, and what I ask is so little—I don't understand this absolute rigidity after all they have gained."

Vic glanced at me with a wisp of a smile. I had never understood things political. "It isn't a question of whether what you want is big or little, but of whether it is consistent or inconsistent with policy."

Perhaps at the outset he might have been able to talk to someone on a personal basis, but after that outburst I had just told him about, in front of one of the Hollywood Ten at that party in New York, I was cooked.

Besides—Vic kept his eyes fixed on the road—he himself was out.

He had dropped out once before, Vic said; that time it was over the Hitler-Stalin pact. "When McCarthy started in, I rejoined. Out of solidarity." His closest friend had gone to prison, and Vic had split his salary with his friend's family. "I had a streak of earning, just then." Afterward, the blacklist had caught up with him. Now he was writing television episodes under an assumed name, but having a very thin time.

His voice was low, weary. A burnt-out man.

He had quit the party again, he said. It was partly personal, though that shouldn't enter into it. Maybe also it was because of Hungary. Or maybe even for some of the reasons that had always kept me aloof.—The Jewish thing?—Vic shrugged, a half-assent. We rode along. Giving me a sidewise glance, Vic spoke almost wistfully. Right now he was trying to get back on

153

a novel. Covering the whole era, from the early thirties. He was going to call it *The Party*.

He'll never write it, I thought. We continued in silence for a while, and then he turned to me. "Meyer, just figure they did it to you and got away with the whole damned thing. Don't let it get you. Write your books."

"But I am writing. I wrote *Compulsion*."

He envied me. Why not enjoy my success, why keep agonizing over the Diary?

"I wish I could stop. I guess it's that old writer's disease. I can't stand suppression."

"Listen to your old uncle. No matter what you try, they won't let your version of the Diary be produced. Meyer, you don't know what they can do to you." His voice had become stern. "You shouldn't even have said the things you told me you said to Dore Schary. Give it all up. You've got your new play to worry about. Be careful." And he repeated, "You still don't know what they can do to you."

We had reached his house in the canyon. His wife was as warm and charming as ever. She was back giving piano lessons.

I went out and saw Lederer. Distinguished, casual, wearing one of those author-type loose gray cashmere pullovers. We had drinks and praised each other's work. I had really liked his script for *David and Bathsheba*. *Compulsion* was absolutely great, he said, and Orson was sure to make a tremendous comeback with the play. Orson would get in touch with me at the hotel to discuss ideas. Did I want option money? He'd write a check—No, no need, I said, at least not until he saw my first draft. We shook hands on it.

Waiting for Orson to get in touch, I gave in again, and went out to see George Stevens, the film director who was to do the Diary. Stevens called in his son—I wouldn't mind, would I?—and then listened to my story. I begged him to use his influence, I was asking so little, a token, everything could so easily be settled without going to court—Again I had to wipe the corner of my eye.

A large, beefy man, Stevens only listened, nodded, and thanked me.

All right, I was ten times over a fool.

At the end of the week Orson Welles popped into the hotel for half an hour; he'd been busy acting in some Shanghai adventure film—had to make some money. He was full of ideas, stimulating. I said I'd send him the first act as fast as I could.

Back in the borrowed house in Westport, I worked on the play; in a month I sent out the first act. They wired it was fine. I completed the whole draft, sent it. No answer.

Then Jack Goodman called. "Orson's friends are dropping out. They're worried about getting mixed up with you. They say they're afraid you'll do to them what you did to their friends the Hacketts."

"What *I* did to *them*?"

"Well, you're suing, aren't you?"

The Hacketts weren't even part of the lawsuit, which kept being protracted by legal obstructions that Fredman had to surmount one by one, each time crowing, "We're making law," as he showed me the reports in the *Law Journal* of his successful motions and counter-motions. For me these maneuvers only brought a heightened obsessiveness. Refusal to arbitrate, refusal of any kind of voluntary hearing, and now, long technical efforts even to deny me my day in court. Their claim was that Mr. Frank did not do business in the United States.

"Leave him out of it," I pleaded again.

"Won't work." In order to get a trial Fredman would first have to win a court order impounding Frank's royalties at the box office.

155

The Hacketts had been left out because I felt the motivation had not come from them. Why, then, should they cause me harm with *Compulsion*? They were collecting royalties from productions all over the world, and were now on fabulous salaries writing the film. They had received the Drama Critics Prize and the Pulitzer Prize, and appeared on television, graciously proclaiming their gratitude to Lillian Hellman for her help. (Bill Zimmerman called, saying, "I told you your play would win the Pulitzer.") So Lederer was afraid I would do to him what I had done to the Hacketts!

And apparently others, too, were affected. Producers would read the *Compulsion* script, ask to see me, even discuss casting and directors, and then fade out. Time counted, for because of the early sale of film rights, the stage production would have to take place in the coming season. Already several months had been lost. Was the play bad? Had I failed? Did it mean that I had been wrong all along, that my dramatization of the Diary, too, had been bad, and that I was causing all this trouble out of wounded and mistaken vanity?

Even my agent for the Diary had decided not to handle the *Compulsion* play, deepening my double fears, either that I was incompetent, or that my untouchability was ever more widely in effect.

Then the most exciting young producer-director team of the moment, the creators of the great posthumous O'Neill hits, *The Iceman Cometh* and *Long Day's Journey Into Night*, spoke for *Compulsion*.

"You see! Hallucinations!" said my new agent, the straight-forward Monica McCall. We met with Mann and Quintero, the contracts were signed, an announcement was made in the theater columns, and Jose Quintero began at once to work with me, coming to the Riverside Drive apartment, where we closeted ourselves in my little front workroom with the cork-lined door. (Years later, Gabriel, who had then been a child,

156

told me of the awe in which he had held my office, after I nailed cork panels inside the door.)

Line after line we worked over the text. All went agreeably. Then one afternoon Quintero, on leaving, remarked that he and Mann were going to Europe. He gave me his hand softly, saying we'd keep in touch.

Completing work on his suggestions, I called his office to ask where I should send the material. The office had no address. When would he be back? They didn't know. And Mr. Mann? The same.

More weeks and no answer.

A theater item appeared. A Broadway producer had commissioned a playwright named Marchand to write *The Trial of Leopold and Loeb*. Marchand was in Chicago working at a furious pace; the play would go into rehearsal in a few weeks and be on the boards long before *Compulsion*. It would kill *Compulsion*, the producer bragged.

—And this too you took as part of the plot against you?

—No, no, but don't you see, a whole atmosphere develops—Levin is fair game—anything goes.

—It wasn't just the usual Broadway stuff? You had again found a great subject, and it could be taken away?

—It was something more, the sense of all kinds of hatreds being directed at me. From anyone, from people who didn't know me, as though it were a virtue to destroy me.

—But surely that wasn't what motivated these people with the other play? They just wanted to make money.

—I know, I know. I knew it then. I'm just saying how I felt.

With the long silence, and the new threat, even Monica was worried. She would try to reach Mann and Quintero through their lawyers.

Their lawyers were Paul, Weiss, Rifkind, etc.

157

The Castle.

No, they had no way to reach their clients.

The Diary trial at long last was approaching. Fredman had won the motion to attach the box-office funds. If I wanted *Compulsion* in performance, to prove I was a playwright, no more time could be lost.

I fell into the most degrading situation of all. Degrading, because in this desperate effort to prove myself before an audience, I tried to swim in the repulsive, murky waters of the piranhas. I threw them pieces of my work, trying to save the essential. And in the end came self-disgust, hysteria, and near-tragedy. What had happened before, in connection with the Diary, I could at least comprehend in terms of doctrinaire fanaticism. But now the dramas of *Anne Frank* and *Compulsion* and my personal life, my family life, became woven together with the underlife of Broadway, in the cliques of politicals, homosexuals, twisted half-talents, until nothing was understandable, and I labored desperately in the muck.

One day, after the fruitless weeks of trying to get in touch with the pair who had disappeared in Europe, I received a call from a producer named Michael Myerberg.—What about *Compulsion*? he asked. Regardless of the outstanding option, he would be ready to take over and go ahead. He would open before the other, threatening play.

Myerberg was a denizen of the murky waters; even I was aware that he had an unsavory business reputation in the theater. Yet along with this, he had a certain cachet as a man of daring taste; he had produced some of the most original and distinguished works in the modern theater. Thornton Wilder's *The Skin of Our Teeth* had reawakened me theatrically. (I was unaware of Wilder's bitterness over arbitrary changes made by the producer while the author was in the army.) Only a few months before, I had been excited by Myerberg's Broadway presentation of *Waiting for Godot*.

158

In the outer room of his office above Sardi's I was greeted by a male secretary, one of those all-knowing types with modulated, sympathetic voices. In the sanctum I was welcomed by a cadaverous personality with a harrowed face, and eyes that were in turn opaque and Baudelairean. The producer was off to compliments; in this play I had invented a new form for staging a complex narrative. The way I had ignored the realistic time-sequence and interwoven appearances of the defense and prosecution attorneys during the scene of the crime itself—ah, this was a *trouvaille!* The play was virtually ready for the stage, so we could go right into production, though it needed some work, of course—Yes, I hastily agreed. I had left some latitude for working with the director. Good.

Now—his eyes blinked, became obsidian; he knew my particular situation, and he was the one producer on Broadway who could help me. Kermit Bloomgarden was blowing his mouth all over Sardi's, declaring that I would never get a play of mine on stage in New York. I was an untouchable. That was why Quintero and Mann had vanished into silence. That was why they would not contest my breaking their option. But he wasn't afraid of Kermit. Before the season was over, Bloomgarden would no longer be the top producer on the street. And Myerberg launched into a catalogue of his production plans, by which it was clear that he was going to take over the crown. All this I could readily disregard as typical producer-megalomania—until Myerberg swerved to another track. He could take care of my big trouble. He knew all about the apparatus working against me, but he had once done something for the Soviet ambassador and had certain ins of his own; under his protection I need have no fear. And as for that Marchand play, it was certainly a danger, but once he announced an earlier opening for *Compulsion,* the real thing, the other project would fade out. They'd never be able to raise financial backing.

Now Myerberg began to speculate about the star—the

159

actor to play Clarence Darrow. What about Ralph Bellamy? Henry Fonda? Fredric March? And for the director—

A telephone call interrupted him. Suddenly the total manner of the man underwent a metamorphosis. Instead of the confident, artistically sensitive producer, I heard a half-maniac shrieking curses and threats at someone on the other end of the line, who, I gathered, was trying to collect a rental fee for a film projector that Myerberg had used at some sort of fair where he was showing a puppet film he had produced. If he heard once more on the street that he was being called a deadbeat, Myerberg screamed, he would drag the fellow into court for defamation!

He had worked himself into a seemingly uncontrollable fury, yet as he slammed the phone down, he turned to me and asked in the calmest of tones, had I seen his puppet film? He even knew that I had once operated a puppet theater. And so filled with a sense of fate was I that this unusual mutual interest seemed like an omen.

As for my trouble with the commies, he resumed—I had no objection to his hiring a few blacklisted actors, had I? On the contrary, I burst in, I was being terribly misrepresented—He knew, he knew. He'd put a number of their people into the cast—it was a big cast—and that would take the heat off me. Now, as to the director—

Every suggestion was fine with me. He really had taste.

Looking at me skeptically, Monica McCall sighed. Myerberg. Well, we seemed to have no choice. Better to risk it with Myerberg than to be beat out of the whole production. And so I signed.

For a few weeks things went well. Announcements appeared. Myerberg informed me he had been upstairs to the Shuberts—"I'm one of the few producers that can always be sure of a theater from them"—and they had assigned him the Belasco. Good? What could be better!

I saw another name being gold-leafed on his door—he was taking in a financial partner for the *Compulsion* production, and I was introduced to a florid, husky Mr. Gruenberg, who declared we had met before, in Israel, at the Weizmann Institute; he was a relative of Meyer Weisgal's and had worked on the "managerial side." Oddly, this gave me a feeling of trust. Mutual friends in Israel.

The anteroom was crowding up each day now with actors applying for readings. Expansively, Myerberg asked if I had any friends I'd like him to put in the cast, and I passed the word to a few, who were hired. From his window, my producer pointed across the street to a big sign over a ticket office, announcing the fall opening of *Compulsion*. Gruenberg sat in a side office, and each day, showing the pile of freshly opened mail on his desk, beamingly told me that investment money was coming in "over the transom." Unsolicited! Theater parties were already being booked. *Compulsion* was sure to be the biggest attraction of the coming season.

Fredman called. I would now have to undergo pretrial examination for the Anne Frank case. This was permitted to the opposing attorneys, in order to establish certain facts and avoid needless prolongation of the trial in the courtroom. Of course the interrogation was also used as a fishing expedition to get points on which a witness might be trapped, but I had nothing to worry about. "Just answer truthfully, and if you are unsure of your memory, just say so. I'll be there with you." The examination would take place at the offices of Paul, Weiss, Rifkind and might go on for several weeks.

When I mentioned this to Myerberg, he pounced. I had an odd feeling that he had been waiting for some such moment. No! he cried. He needed me right now. I had to work intensively with the director, in fact I was to meet the man today. It

161

hadn't been easy to get someone who would agree to work with me, but he had solved the problem, he had persuaded the top dramatic director in television! Alex Segal, a genius with actors, was eager to do a Broadway show and was ripe for one. Indeed the swift-moving television style was just right for the play, and would lend the note of originality he wanted in the staging.

Leading me down to Sardi's, he left me with the prospective director, a tight, smallish fellow, who kept the conversation to reminiscences about the Jewish neighborhoods we had lived in, interspersing bits of Yiddish. Hardly a word about the play. But with our similar backgrounds, we ought to get along. At last things were really on the way.

We reported back to Myerberg.

As I was due at the first of the pretrial interrogations, he and Segal would go over the script and make some notes for me.

The stenographer sat waiting, as Fredman and I entered the law firm's conference room, and in a moment our adversary entered, all amiability, reserving the adversary attitude for the courtroom. The lawyers behaved like colleagues, consultants, and I could even feel young Fredman's gratification at sitting with one of the big men of his profession. For, he had at once whispered to me, Silverman was the firm's top trial lawyer.

A neatly tailored, undistinguished man, Silverman never raised his voice, never prodded, led me perfunctorily from item to item. When had I first met Otto Frank? Where? Though I was uncertain of dates, I answered with a sense of ease. The worst that could happen, Fredman said when the session was over, was that they might try to trip me up in court on some date or minor fact, to show that my memory was bad, or to suggest that I was unreliable.

Once, in a short recess, I found Silverman beside me in the men's room. There came a sudden rigidity from him. Impossible to find a casual word to say to this man. From then on, I become more wary in my responses.

Suddenly Myerberg called me in. In his soft voice of concern he made a suggestion. As I was very busy and under great strain in my pretrial examinations, he wanted to eliminate all needless, rough-in preliminary work for me with the director on the script.

I was puzzled. So far there had been a few minor suggestions, and I had handled them at once, even doing a bit of rewriting here in the office.

Ah, but now things would become intensive, Myerberg said. And he had just the solution for my problem. There was a young man, indeed a protégé of his, a writer who had worked only in the dramatic medium, stage and television, and who was in unusual rapport with Segal—Segal could be difficult at times. Myerberg wanted only harmony. He had intended to employ this young protégé in any case as production assistant, so as to keep the boy going financially, for his playwriting. Indeed, Myerberg was also about to try out, in a summer theater, a drama this boy had written. Very original, showing the highest promise. It was Myerberg's thought that in this preparatory period his protégé should sit in for me with the director, and sketch up Segal's suggestions for me. I and I alone would decide what to incorporate, and I would then write the material in my own words. This way, no time would be lost—

—And you fell for it? Sulzberger eyed me sorrowfully.

I had at once been suspicious, I had twisted and turned, I had protested that there was no need, I would make the time, the pretrial interrogations were secondary and would have to fit around my work. Besides, they couldn't go on for more than another week or two.

—But these were crucial weeks, Meyerberg had coun-

163

tered. That other Leopold-Loeb play would prove trouble-some if it opened ahead of ours—

But only last week he had assured me the other play was off. What was he trying to pull on me?

Myerberg's tone changed to one of defenselessness, the tone of a friend asking you to favor his weakness. He was really fond of this young writer. Perhaps I would like to read the boy's play? We'd discuss things again in the morning.

I read the play, an unfocused series of arty, pretentious dialogues. On the stage, I could only imagine it as an utter bore.

What was it, then, what slime was I being drawn into? What was Myerberg after? Only some money for his protégé?

In the morning in the theater notes I read that Henry Fonda was the likeliest choice for the role of Clarence Darrow in the Marchand play.

In Myerberg's office sat a slender young man, the smooth type, dressed with a careless flair, handsome on the pretty side, and with wide-open unblinking eyes. He would have been suitable for the part representing Dickie Loeb. He was chatting with the male secretary, something about getting bagels for breakfast with Gloria and Sidney. This would be Gloria Vanderbilt, then married to Sidney Lumet. Myerberg emerged and introduced his protégé, Robert Thom.

"Great play," the lad said to me. "I wish it were mine."

Leading me inside, Myerberg handed me a few typed pages, a little sample, as Thom had had a session with Segal.

But why hadn't Segal called me?

The producer made a smoothing-out gesture. Segal was difficult. Robert Thom knew how to get along with him. Just give it a try.

I glanced at the sample. A few cuts in a scene. The lines put in as bridges I could rewrite. It was true some cuts were needed, the play ran long.

—But I could do this myself, I said. If Segal didn't want to work with me, we'd have to get another director.

—No, no, it was only to save time. And it would be such a great experience for Thom!

Gruenberg had come in. "Do it, do it," he half-whispered to me. Oddly, this had an effect. He was from my own world.

"At least talk to the boy," Myerberg urged.

"You know," Gruenberg murmured to me, "he's married to Janice Rule." As if the movie star's name were somehow a guarantee!

"With all your trouble," Myerberg said, gazing at me as though I ought to understand. There were connections everywhere—this lad's connections would make me more acceptable.

Again, the ritual of going down to Sardi's. The young genius who was married to Janice Rule had coffee with me. I said I would speak to him as writer to writer. Surely he understood that every line used on the stage would have to be mine. Of course, Thom said. He would just present the director's suggestions. Quite frankly, I continued, I felt I did not need any intermediary, I would find all the time needed to work with the director. Indeed, if I took him on, it would be—without any reflection on his ability—simply as a friendly gesture toward Myerberg, and I would prefer that he do virtually nothing. Yes, he certainly saw how I felt. In my place he would feel the same way. And he had the greatest respect for my work.

There it was. Writer to writer, we understood each other.

Myerberg was delighted we had got along. A wonderful boy! Sparkling, the producer now came out with what he wanted—I must assign twenty per cent of my royalties to my assistant, Robert Thom. "You'd only be paying it to the government!"

So it was money. I'd heard, I'd been warned. Could it be a kickback? With some producers it was said even actors had to agree to turn back part of their salary.

And if not?

He turned his eyes up to the ceiling. He doubted if he could go on. Things were too difficult with me. I had better go see my lawyer about his suggestion. Fredman was a reasonable man.

I called my agent.—Well, it was I who had picked Myerberg; at this point it would be difficult to get another producer, especially in view of my—eh—reputation. And the rival play. If I wanted *Compulsion* to go on, I'd have to give in.

Fredman, too. Part of that twenty per cent, it might be, would end up in the producer's pocket. Still—it was only money. I'd be paying it in income tax.

Fredman himself drew up the agreement. Not a word of the play's text could be altered without my consent. There, that was the main thing. And we took it over to Myerberg, and signed.

I saw no more of Thom. I heard nothing from the director, or even from Myerberg.

The pretrial interrogations were finished. In growing panic, I called several times only to be told by the soft, sympathetic voice of the secretary that Myerberg was out. Did I want to talk to Mr. Gruenberg?

Everything was going fine, Gruenberg said. Nothing to worry about. Thom was over at Segal's house in New Jersey working with him on the script.

At the end of the week there was a message. The suggestions for the first act were being left for me in the checkroom at Sardi's. I could pick them up and look them over during the weekend.

Tereska and I were going to see *La Strada* that night; on the way, I picked up the large manila envelope. There was half an hour before the film started, so Tereska went window-shopping while I sat in a cafeteria with the script. At the first line the blood rushed to my head.

This has to be explained. The play opens thirty years after the murder, with the reporter, the same Sid Silver who discovered the convicting evidence, now coming to interview the Leopold character in prison. As I wrote it, the confrontation was clear from the start. Instead, the prisoner was to enter, reading aloud the name on the reporter's card, "Mr. Silver?" as though he had never before heard it in his life! And the reporter was to say, "Don't you remember me? It was I who found the evidence!" Of all the absurdities. It went on, with line after line rewritten to no purpose: the action was the same, but the dialogue was changed to one cliché after another, as though on television. These Nietzschean geniuses who had talked like characters out of Oscar Wilde! Here they were screaming "You're chicken!" at each other.

Tereska came and got me, and I sat through the movie in a throbbing daze. She kept turning to me over this wonderful scene and that wonderful shot, and I would try to focus on the screen. It was like in your fever in a sickroom seeing a face coming into focus but melting away.

—Still, in your contract, you had control of your text?
—Yes. We got home and I kept calling Myerberg. No answer. I found Segal's number in the New Jersey phonebook. There was no answer there, either. Tereska had gone to bed, and I had a vision. I would get into the car and drive across the George Washington Bridge and find his house. I would wait there, and when Segal drove up, I'd grab him. I'd shake the truth out of him. Why this rewrite? Were they deliberately trying to wreck me—
—But he'd be wrecking himself.
—I'm just trying to tell you what went on in me. I even

167

saw his wife rushing out of their house to stop me. I'd use a tire-iron on him! At last I got him on the phone. I controlled my voice. I said I was sorry to disturb him, but I couldn't get Myerberg. I'd gone through this material of Thom's, and I wanted to know if these dialogue changes were Thom's ideas, or his? He shouted "Call your producer!" and hung up.

—And so you concluded that Segal and Thom were part of the cabal?

—I don't know what they were. I thought Thom might be trying to change the play enough so it couldn't be said it was mine. Levin would never get his work on Broadway! Couldn't these pointless changes be part of it? Anyway, if this stuff represented Segal's taste, the whole thing was impossible.

—Still, they can't change what you wrote unless you agree. It's in your contract.

—I don't know any more.

And I told him the worst, the most shameful.

Early that next morning Myerberg called. I must meet him at once.

I got to his office first and stood staring out the window at that damned ticketbroker's sign announcing the forthcoming production of Meyer Levin's *Compulsion*. He burst in. By what right did I call his director in the middle of the night? This was intolerable, it couldn't go on! The screaming, lashing attack continued, and I knew he was a ridiculous little dictatorial figure I should laugh at, and yet I knew I was succumbing to this insanity.

If I was going to interfere like this, while he was trying to do something great for me when no one would touch me, when I was the most hated man on Broadway, then he was finished with *Compulsion*! He had spent twenty thousand dollars so far, but he would drop the play.

—Then that's it, I found myself able to say. If that sample

script was the kind of thing he wanted, then there would be no play. And I walked out to the elevator.

He was after me. His arm was on my shoulder. The voice had dropped, the tone was now intimate, understanding. Naturally I had been upset. He himself had read that stuff and could see why I was offended. They were merely suggestions, I could ignore them all. It was my particular situation that made things difficult. One director after another had turned me down. He hadn't even realized how deep was my trouble. He was trying to protect me, and that was why it was best to have someone else instead of me to deal with Segal. But as to Thom's lines, of course I could ignore all that. But simply as a personal favor—he was so fond of the boy, he didn't want to hurt the boy's feelings—would I try to keep in a line of his here and there?

The elevator door opened while he pleaded, his voice immersed in fatalism now, a man who reveals his helplessness to you. Was this all a ruse? The elevator door closed. I hadn't got in, but I had a sinking feeling, exactly as though I were catapulting downward in some dark shaft, only within myself. Myerberg had brought me back to his office. I half-collapsed on the couch, and his voice continued. A thread of awareness kept identifying it, the pleading reasonableness that comes after the ranting. Why was I letting this happen? Again, to submit myself to some semblance of that monstrous Holocaust experience, showing myself that I too would have succumbed, that I was no better than any other terrified little Jew?

Reasonably, quietly, he was saying that we were approaching rehearsals, and it would be impossible to work if there were constant clashes. If disputes rose every time an actor found difficulty in speaking some word, and wanted it changed—

And so what he suggested was a definite way of handling

169

any little disagreements that could arise in rehearsal. An arrangement that would reassure Segal. If an actor suggested a different word, a line-change, let there be an on-the-spot arbitration agreement so no time would be lost. It was a complex play, and the schedule was tight, with no out-of-town tryouts but an opening directly in New York. Why not have someone on the spot to arbitrate any line-disputes? That would be the quickest. After all, everyone was interested in only the good of the play, and when we had our success, all that went before would be forgotten. Why didn't I try to get in touch with that lawyer of mine, Fredman, to draw up a little statement between us? Perhaps he was in his office this morning even though it was Saturday, and could draw it up. Fredman was a reasonable man you could deal with.

What was he spinning, what was he after? It sounded innocuous, but I was uneasy. I said I really saw no need to put such a thing in writing.

His tone dropped to one of true sorrow. In that case he would have to drop the play. He had made up his mind to this, thinking all night long. Unless he had such an additional assurance from me, he would have to give it up.

I said it was off. In my mind there echoed, "Goodbye, *Compulsion!*" I had a sick impulse to laugh. Orson Welles must have had an intuition.

But what was the man saying?

Undoubtedly, as my court case over the Anne Frank play was coming up, Myerberg was saying, he would be called as a witness. And in all honesty he would have to testify that he had had to drop my play because my script was not stage-worthy. Every director had refused it. He had tried to get me expert help, from a theatrical writer, but I had proved impossible!

I stumbled in a kind of mesmerized numbness to Fredman's office, a few blocks away. He was there. He listened to

170

it all. The threat. Probably that was exactly what Myerberg would do.

My agent had chosen this time to go on vacation. Fredman went back with me to Myerberg, I fell onto the couch again, while they drew up a high-sounding statement. In order to facilitate production, in such common rehearsal occurrences as an actor's request for a change of a word or a line, the director could immediately arbitrate. And because of my confidence in the producer . . .

The thing done, my lawyer went off. "There's a man you can deal with," Myerberg said, as he gazed at me with a curious, compassionate smile. And now, over the weekend, would I study the suggestions and—he repeated—do him the little personal favor he had asked? Use a few of the boy's lines?

Injustice collector. I had to find my own little Hitler. Does that help me? to say it? Does that solve anything? Again I let them ream it up my ass! Isn't that what I really wanted? Repressed homosexuality, that's what it proves! And denial only reenforces the truth!

Sure, I did it. I ate their shit. I put in some of their lines. The minimum. Appeasement. And I brought the text in to Myerberg. And then in the second act, I appeased. I even got Bob Gottlieb, my editor at Simon and Schuster since Jack Goodman died, to go over each line with Myerberg, as a witness that I had dealt satisfactorily with every request, that the script was now in order. Gottlieb came back from the last session shuddering. That man had a strange effect on him.

Rehearsals were to start. The mimeographed script was delivered to Fredman's office. I hurried there before going to the rehearsal hall. One glance was enough. It began with the prisoner reading the reporter's name, "Mr. Silver?" as though he had never heard it before in his life. And where I had taken

171

out "You're chicken!" it now read "You're chicken! Chicken! Chicken!" Every single line of Thom's was restored.

—"A great play, I wish it were mine."
And, "Levin will never get a play of his on Broadway."

Lawyers calling lawyers: "Stop the rehearsals!" "Are you prepared to put up a $200,000 bond?" "Any change in the text requires arbitration before the Dramatists Guild!" "No, Levin signed a superseding arbitration agreement, and Segal has already arbitrated each line."

—And that day when Myerberg got you to sign that agreement—yes, he manipulated you into it—but did you think he had this all planned?
—No, I think he had some crazy instinct that in some way he would do what he wanted with me, without yet knowing exactly how.
—But if the text is so bad, isn't he risking his production?
—The power of the drama is there. The lines don't change what happens on the stage. This is like with the Diary all over again. The phoney version can be a success, too.
—Then he's joined the conspiracy against you? That's his motive?
—Look, with Myerberg I think it's some kind of madness, power madness, a perversion of his own. To prove he could do anything he wanted, twist me around.
—But you chose him.
—What choice did I have? I explained it all to you. He called me at the very worst moment.
—And you fell under his spell. Something was ready in you?
—Ready in me?
Could the boy picked by sheer chance to be killed by Loeb and Leopold somehow have called the murderers to him? One can shred down one's own conditioning to the

172

last thread, one can comb over it again and again with one analyst after another, but how can one know the hidden madness of an adversary?

—The better you recognize your own conditioning, the better you can fight.

—Haven't I been fighting?

—Yes, but can't you fight more joyously? says Sulzberger. That's what I'd like to see!

I saw myself with a horsewhip marching into the rehearsal hall, straight to that limpid-eyed Thom who sat in the author's chair, and slashing him across the face. Again, again. I saw myself walking into Myerberg's office, picking up the typewriter from his secretary's desk, and hurling it at the producer's head. Police! Pictures in the *Post*! Acting out, the analyst would call it.

But what do you really do? Several of my friends, even Fredman himself, he now told me, had invested money in the production. Would I keep it from opening, destroy it, make them lose their money? A few changed words, nothing more, Myerberg was soothing them, even inviting them to rehearsals. You know Meyer is temperamental, but it's 90 percent his play.

The papers were carrying items now, about Levin in trouble with his own *Compulsion,* even while bringing Otto Frank to trial over the Diary. Tereska and I went to a cocktail reception at the Israeli consulate, and in the thick of the crowd, a tall man turned on me, shouting, "You are Meyer Levin! How can anyone sue Otto Frank!" It was the actor who portrayed Otto Frank—Joseph Schildkraut. He kept on shouting as people thrust themselves between us and pulled me away.

Anonymous phone calls had begun. Tereska would hear insults, threats. Or there would be dead silence. We had the number changed, and additional locks put on the door.

173

A telegram came. If I persisted in dragging the father of Anne Frank through the courts, I would never live to see the end of the trial.

I was seized, haunted, by the image of a knife. It had come once before, some time ago, when the prize-giving was announced for the Broadway *Diary*. The event was to be televised, and in fantasy I saw myself being admitted as part of the audience in the television studio, and when the master of ceremonies advanced toward Bloomgarden, with mellifluous compliments for the Foremost Producer of Broadway, holding open a velvet gift box in which a gold medal glowed, I would suddenly step forward, darting between them, and in front of the television cameras I would hold open my own velvet box, containing a shining, stiletto-like knife. On the handle, in gilt, would be inscribed: To the Big Knife of Broadway. The inscription had come to me, perhaps, because a play by Clifford Odets, *The Big Knife,* was being performed in revival that season.

Somehow, I had repressed the fantasy, but now it had seized me again, except that the Big Knife would be inscribed to Myerberg instead of to Bloomgarden. Suddenly one day, passing a Woolworth's, I went in and bought a forty-cent kitchen knife that had a good-sized wooden handle. I carried it home in a paper bag and hid it in my study. For my son Eli, I had got one of those electric wood-inscribers, and it lay on his desk. When no one was home I went into Eli's room and burned into the handle: "Awarded to Michael Myerberg, the Big Knife of Broadway." And underneath, "Use This, It's More Humane." Wrapping it carefully in several layers of cardboard, I mailed it to his office.

Sulzberger tilted back and uttered his laugh, something between a giggle and a chuckle. Harmless, harmless bit of acting-out. Considering the provocation I was under, a healthy reaction.

174

The story of the knife came to Tereska.

An actor whom I had got a part in the play related how the male secretary had unwrapped the package and shrieked, and Myerberg, hurrying in, had blanched at the sight of the knife. As though it had struck him. He wanted the police called. I was dangerous. I had to be put away!

A knife. My wife, too, felt the horror of my action. Not even Sulzberger could reassure her. I was destroying our life with my insane obstinacy. Over what? Over two lousy plays, she screamed at me.

The next day I found the apartment empty. In midafternoon I received a call from a friend, a lawyer. Tereska had taken the two younger children and was in hiding; she wanted a divorce. Unless I stopped all my wild futile battles.

—She'll come back, Sulzberger said.

She came back, we embraced, wept. We must not let all this evil break us up.

A few days later, in a theater column in the *Herald Tribune,* there appeared a letter from Robert Thom.

Since questions had been raised about the text of *Compulsion,* he wanted to state that the text being produced was not Meyer Levin's play at all, but a new play written by himself, based on the novel and the original court records of the case.

Alone in the apartment when I chanced on it, I found myself suddenly seized. Involuntary, raucous sounds were coming from my throat, and I could not stop them. I had a physical sense of being strapped down while my tormentors hovered about me, making ready to perform the castration. The howl that came out of my throat was the howl under their knife. In their diabolism, they had thrust my wife into the role of the castrating woman: "Give up all your fighting." No, I declared within myself, no, it would not be a castration. The gang of them were mutilating me, but my creative strength was far within me, out of their reach.

175

Still the howls came; I seized the phone and tried to reach Sulzberger, but could not. I called Bob Gottlieb and managed to suppress the howling long enough to say that something dreadful was happening to me—could he come at once. Then the howling emerged again, and I fell on the bed.

Slowly, as I lay on the bed, the wild sounds subsided. I breathed freely; I managed to reach Sulzberger, who said not to be alarmed, it was involuntary rage, it would pass; in the time of a cab ride, Gottlieb came. He had brought Fredman with him; they stood by the bed looking at me with wonderment and compassion, as at someone run over by a truck, but where was the blood? I was all right now, I assured them. Fredman said, obviously, if Thom did not retract, I'd have to enter a lawsuit, probably against the newspaper too, for printing such a damaging and outrageous lie.—Oh, what use would it be? Oh, the bastards!—Finally, reassured that I was in control of myself and that I was in touch with my analyst, they departed.

A court hearing came on the text of *Compulsion*. Refusing the Guild arbitration procedure, Myerberg had hauled me to court to keep me from interfering with the play. Meanwhile rehearsals sped on.

One imagines a courtroom, witnesses, a chance to plead one's case.

Meeting me on the broad steps of the courthouse, Fredman explained that technically I did not even have the right to be present at this kind of session. This was to be a "hearing on a motion," in which lawyers alone could speak, but perhaps the judge would not object to my presence so long as I remained absolutely silent.

We entered a large, empty courtroom and took seats. Presently in came Myerberg with his attorney, taking places as far removed from us as possible. The judge appeared, round-faced, a businessman. Gazing directly at me, he made some preliminary remarks. He recognized that an author had the right, indeed it was his duty, to fight for every word of his work. If any changes were to be made, they must be justified. He was cognizant also that I had long been engaged in the matter of *The Diary of Anne Frank,* and that the Diary case was shortly to come before the courts, but the fact that I was engaged in two such matters had no relevance here. I was a well known and respected author and entitled to every protection of the law in my art. However, a big theatrical production was a heavy investment undertaking, and the producer had every right to expect cooperation and reasonable changes from the author.

He beamed to one side and the other.

Up rose Myerberg's attorney, an orator. His client, a man of the highest artistic reputation and integrity, had gone to the uttermost lengths to help me; his client had dealt with the most celebrated authors of our time, but never in all his experience had he encountered a writer so utterly and unreasonably recalcitrant, so unwilling to make the slightest accommodation, even when the necessities of the theater plainly demanded it. It was well known that I had difficulties in adapting my writing to the theater. Everyone was trying to help me—the director, the actors, all people of vast experience in the theater, all with the highest respect for the function of the playwright—for without him obviously there would be no theater. Yet without these others, there would be no theater either.

And now it was the mystique of the theater that was invoked. There was a certain something, an indefinable sense of theater which people had or didn't have. The director of *Compulsion* had it in the highest degree. And therefore I had agreed to make him the arbiter on the text. A novelist could sit in his studio and write each word as he wanted it, but a play-

177

wright had to cooperate with other artists, equally as qualified as he was. I had never been able to get a play produced, being notoriously impossible to deal with, and Myerberg was the sole producer who would risk working with me. Yet even Myerberg was now exhausted and at the end of his remarkable forebearance. Because of Myerberg's high reputation, investors had risked their money; each day of delay in disputes with me would cost thousands of dollars. Foreseeing this, he had got me to sign the special arbitration agreement that superseded the clumsy, protracted method of Guild arbitration. Under our agreement, Segal was named as arbitrator of dialogue, and he had already arbitrated. The court was therefore asked to enjoin me from interference with the production.

All this was orated with the highest passion and sincerity.

Fredman rose. Never had he heard such misrepresentations—

The judge kept gazing at me with that sympathetic smile for the temperamental artist.

The words were pounding behind my closed lips: How Myerberg had pressured me into signing whatever he wanted, with his threat of testifying at the Frank case . . . why didn't Fredman say that?

Invoking legalities, my lawyer finished. The judge rose and retired to make his decision. We could go to lunch.

In an hour everyone was back. The judge read out his decree. The special arbitration agreement indeed superseded Guild arbitration.

Myerberg rose, victorious, directing at me his venomous and yet sorrowful gaze.

However, the judge went on, there clearly had been no arbitration process, and he was therefore ready to have the textual changes argued in his presence at the earliest possible time.

Each change had to be justified. The presumption was with the author.

178

Then I was safe! Beginning with that first-line absurdity, "Mr. Silver?"

By the time I reached home, the *Post* had already appeared with a story: "Levin Loses in Court." Someone had telephoned Tereska.

I entered the apartment to find her rigid. I began to explain about the coming arbitration before the judge, to tell her that every textual change had to be justified . . . Her eyes became more and more wild. She fled to the bedroom. A few moments later, uneasy, I went to explain to her again. She was nowhere in the apartment. On the kitchen table I found a scribbled note.

The rest of that night I can't write about directly. I did once try to write it out of myself, in *The Fanatic,* a novel that parallels the Anne Frank experience. I can only insert here what I wrote of that night. The events are the same.

The Fanatic is about the fate of the work of a young poet who was destroyed in the Holocaust. His writings had been left with his beloved Anika. Maury, an American Army rabbi, but also a writer, has married Anika and brought her to New York. He has given up the rabbinate to write plays and has dramatized the dead poet's work. Trouble has arisen over this, and over a new play of Maury's. Yes, I had pictured myself as a rabbi.

Tereska had not, like Anika, been in the concentration camps, but had escaped from France when the Nazis were already at the Spanish border. The terror and hysteria that arose in her on this night is in what I wrote of Anika. What happened to us was exactly the same.

The scene in *The Fanatic* takes place at Yom Kippur. The whole series of events was a Yom Kippur to me:

Anika places the bag of groceries in the go-cart with Carola, but from the newsstand a headline catches her eye: "WRITER

THREATENS PRODUCER." And a huge photograph of the actors assembled around Jess Weaver, who holds the glittering knife on his open palm. "JUDGE RESTRAINS RABBI PLAYWRIGHT."

So he has lost . . .

Sick, sick, sick, the postcard shrieks at her from a drugstore window, sick, sick, sick, this entire world, sick in Europe with the murderers rife, sick in the strong life-giving America, sick.

She has reached the house, the hallway, and the telephone is ringing . . .

"Tell that sonofabitch to look in the papers, we got him! He's a dead pigeon, you hear? Finish!"

It is the voice of a madman, but that already has become normal. Only madness is normal. She sees their faces sometimes on the television screen when all the intervening shades are burned out and the faces are streaks of heavy dark lines with luminous holes for eyes.

She is still holding the silent telephone when Maury arrives. He is cheerful. He is even able to laugh at the newspaper photograph! "Don't worry, darling, I'm not giving up!" He takes the phone from her hand, calling his lawyer.

His lawyer! Injunctions, appeals—fight it! Anika runs into the kitchenette, closing the door, tight, tight.

Kruger will work all night—he will be in court in the morning. Maury wants to explain to her, there is still a way . . . she is not in the kitchen. On a piece of paper torn off the grocery bag, he reads, "Maury, I can't stand any more. Stop all your fighting, or you will have an orphan in the morning."

He cries out "Anika!" Hastily, he peers into the bedroom, the closet—there is nowhere to hide in this small box of walls—he runs to the elevator, waiting while it interminably rises.

"No," says the elevator man. "No, she didn't come down."

The stairs? Down—or up? Bounding up the stairway, five flights higher, storming through the iron fire-door onto the roof, he calls her name. It is growing dark now. The livid sign from across the river screams to him, *Spry, Fry, Spry.* A song from childhood echoes, *I spy, I spy—*

If he goes to the edge and looks down—the little broken doll body, like the disarticulated bodies in the pit in Bergen-Belsen? Fire engines, sirens, "Missed Death in Auschwitz to Find It on Riverside Drive." No, only the lighted streetlights far below, calm.

Maury runs again, downstairs now. How is it, a man can run like this, up and down this stairway maze, passing floors of people, people in their cubicles watching their televisions, unaware of their neighbor's frantic fear, so close to them? How is it, in these buildings filled with terrors and fears, nothing ever pierces through the walls, only the radio waves, the television?

It is raining, and he is in his shirt sleeves, exactly as in a movie. Because of the rain, the street is deserted, silent; all the Jews, the Yom Kippur Jews, have hurried on this one night to overflow the synagogues; all is silent except for the constant tire-hiss on the lower driveway. No, if she let herself be hit, there would already be a traffic knot. No. It must be the river. The Hudson, the Danube.

And just then he sees her. Down the slope, on the gravel path, in a space of darkness between two street-lamps. She is standing and watching him.

He approaches, but as he nears, Anika tautens, backs away. He halts.

"Anika, what's got into you? Come home!"

"No," she says under her breath.

He moves a step closer, and she moves downward a step.

"Anika," Maury begs, "Please, Anika, you are having some kind of an attack, you're not in control of yourself, please come home. There is no one with Carola."

The child's name holds her still, and Maury dashes down and seizes her. But in his grasp her body becomes rigid as iron.

"Carola!" She intones in a harsh voice. "Now you care for Carola! It's you—you are doing this to us! You! Because you have to fight the whole world, because you have to be right! What happens to Carola, what happens to me, is nothing, so long as you can say the whole world is wrong and only you are right. And for what? For two damned plays in a theater, for your vanity. You would sacrifice us all, for your vanity."

Her words strike at his arms, weaken his arms that are holding her.

"Come home, come home, Anika," he begs, but suddenly, twisting out of her coat, leaving it in his hands, she has wrenched herself

181

from his grip, whirling with wild strength and grace, and under his very eyes she has disappeared.

Maury stumbles down the grass incline; there are no further streetlights down there. The rain has increased from a drizzle, and he stands there in his white shirt, the rain dripping down his hair, down his face, down his shirt, and he feels it cannot be, this melodrama cannot exist, and he calls her name, "Anika, Anika," running from bush to bush, certain she is standing somewhere peering at him.

"Anika, I beg you, Anika!"

And why is there no one here, not a soul? Even in this rain there should be someone to help.

"Anika!" He hangs her coat on a bush. "Anika, at least take your coat!" Perhaps this cunning will bring her, and he moves back into the darkness, but she doesn't approach.

Nothing moves. There is only the constant hiss of the cars, above and beyond him now . . .

It comes to him that this is the moment of *Kol Nidre,* the air must be filled with it: "All vows and oaths, *kol nidre v'esarey, v'chamarey* . . . with which we have bound ourselves . . . so as to estrange ourselves from those who have offended us, or to give pain to those who have angered us—they shall be absolved . . . these vows shall not be vows . . . these bonds shall not be bonds . . ."

He will give, he will give up, he will let the play go, he will call Kruger and say, cancel the appeal. God, I will give it to you, I will give up the play, the case, everything, God, let her be!

Anika hears her name. She is crouched in the dark screen of rain, further, higher along the cement river wall, watching the black water. The water can hardly be seen, but it is there, flowing, and as it pulses, sometimes a sheen of blackness glimmers to her, as though from a sinuous muscle-movement under the black skin.

It is the downdrag that has never really let her go, never since Vienna; it has always kept its lurking hold on her. But she is afraid, afraid the water will be cold, and she tries to remember, was it cold in the Danube? And she vaguely hears her name, and she waits to make sure no one will catch her.

Maury clambers up again as far as the driveway, and hurrying

182

along the pavement he notices, cut into the side of the embankment, something he has never seen before though he has passed there many times. It is a grating, an iron gate in the side of the slope. He pulls and it opens. Perhaps she is hiding somewhere in there?

Inside, there is a chill smell of concrete, and dimly he makes out a vast hollow space. He stands on a ledge, and far below he hears a long rumbling as of wind in a closed mine. Iron stairs lead downward. But it could not be the subway down there, the subway is blocks away. Then Maury recalls—a railway passes below, here; this is a railway tunnel.

Could she have come down these stairs?

Partway down he halts and calls, "Anika! Anika, I beg you, answer me! Anika—" The reverberation comes, the syllables of her name distorted into a windy howl. His mind notes this, and again Maury curses his self-dramatization . . . Slowly, Maury descends.

A rumbling from the far-off reaches him, not the subway rumbling when a train approaches, but an elemental, organic howling, a force imprisoned. Suddenly a train hammers into his presence, as if to leap on him; it hammers past him, close, close—freight cars, car after car, sealed, endlessly, relentlessly, closed freight cars, and the wheels are hammering wheels, hammering down on the rails, pulverizing bones, pulverizing Anika's bones . . .

Emerging from the gate, he stands on the deserted driveway, and his vow returns to him, and he confirms it in his heart. He still must believe in God, then; he is still making compacts, bargains, exchanges with God; he has not the strength to argue, to reason with himself . . . *Oh God, oh, my God, Adonai, let her live, I'll give it all up. Accept my vow, Adonai.*

The downdrag has become stronger. Anika struggles as though she were already in the muddy bottom of the black river; she must reach up her child to the outside and safety. She is struggling with her head bent against the current, she feels she is struggling to arrive at the very source of evil so that she can block it, stop it forever with her hand, stopper it with her own self. She is there. She is touching the very heart of evil. And awesomely she knows what evil is. It is unreason.

183

She has seen the faceless face. It is unreason, the monster drawing her down is unreason. The telephone voice was unreason. Even a world of evil intent is a knowable world; even there, a being may cling onto the edge and survive. In the world of her past, evil was evil. But here, from the first moment, she has been lost in a sea of unreason. What is a good intention here turns to evil, and a good action brings knives. Now Maury has become unhinged, and she herself no longer knows what has meaning. And from this, it is better to be carried away in the darkness; others, perhaps, who can understand something of this world, will take better care of Carola.

She cannot think through, cannot answer, unreason. The down-drag tugs ever more strongly on her.

Now and now, in this instant, this last instant, someone must come to Anika, someone must intervene. She has not heard Maury's shouting, except at first long ago, as sounds from which she hid; and then all became entirely still around her, there is only the soundless river, in the soundless wind, in the soundless rain, and above her even the hissing of the tires on the road has ceased.

She stands up over the water . . .

In that dismal rain, along that deserted path, there is one other living being. A man walks there, on the edge of the river, a lonely Negro.

When the Negro quietly leaves her at the door of her building, Anika does not know clearly what has happened. An angel came, she says to herself. He spoke gently, with a sorrow of his own in his voice. He said, "What are you doing here, miss?" He said, "Don't be sad, it will be all right." He asked, "Do you live around here?" He said, "Come with me, I will take you where you live, miss, you just show me the house now."

He did not touch her, but it seemed he drew her with him, he moved her, until she stood in front of the door. And now he says, "Go on in home, you will be all right."

She turns to thank him, and he has gone.

Opening her apartment door, she calls to Carola, and she holds her and rocks her and carefully puts her into her baby bed.

There beside the crib Anika sits, among the living still . . .

Drained, exhausted, dazed, Maury turns toward his house. And

184

in this way he finds himself in the elevator, and John says, "She's home."

Maury passes through the first room and stands in the dark bedroom where she is a dark form, uncertainly visible in the chair. Anika calls his name and he sinks to his knees beside the chair and she takes his head, all as though in an enactment.

They are weeping.

In the morning, it is Yom Kippur, and Anika knows he will keep the fast; he has always kept it, no matter what his quarrel with God.

Early he telephones Kruger at home and tells him that all further legal action must be abandoned. Kruger recognizes through his voice some extraordinary intervention, perhaps another such attack as he has once witnessed.

"Maury, what's happened?"

"Something happened last night with Anika. I can't go on any more. Let them do what they want."

In the shattering of that night I had called Fredman to cancel the arbitration of the text before the judge, cancel everything. Let it go, let it all go. *Compulsion* would have to open in the smeared-over text.

I was punishing myself for Mabel's suicide. The suicide was happening again. I was the murderer; my guilt was proven—something within me was the destroyer.

I had to pay. Let my work be the sacrifice.

Thus the Myerbergs, the Thoms, like the Hellmans, the Bloomgardens, had their way. To take my name off the play would have been false, but there were changed lines for which I did not want to be thought responsible, so I required the program to state that this was the producer's version of a dramatization by Meyer Levin.

So after so many suppressions over so many years I was to have a play, even though a mutilated play, opening in a

185

theater. Tereska and others at the rehearsals kept saying, "It's really basically yours." My agent said, "What do some word changes matter? An audience sitting there doesn't know what has been changed or left out. They react to the drama, and the drama is yours."

Pains in the left shoulder and down the arm were constant now. Had I myself induced them with the desire for a physical excuse, a release, so as not to have to face any more war? Sulzberger sent me to the specialist, Dr. Masters, with his little flight of mock stairs: Walk up and down, again, again; no, there is no heart condition. But why, then, does he hand me a bottle of nitroglycerin pills, just in case?

I would not attend the opening. Oddly, a branch of the American Jewish Congress just across the river in New Jersey asked me to receive a citation on that same night. It occurred to me that this might have been arranged to make sure I would not create a scandal in the theater. Let him rave and rant in New Jersey. Arranged or not, I accepted.

Can one ever really find out? Can the chairman of the meeting tell you? Would he if he could? Perhaps he quite enthusiastically accepted someone's suggestion, without realizing the coincidence as to the date. The director, Segal, lived just around there.

Oversuspicious? Paranoiac? The analyst can only guide you in struggling with these doubts. Not for him to say; all he can do is make you better able to see what is real, what is ambiguous, in the course of events.

I completed my address, to salvos of sympathetic applause. A writer must fight for his work, protest, denounce, expose— oh yes, these few hundred liberal Jews were with me and awarded me a handsomely lettered parchment citing my struggles for freedom of expression, and the chairman himself drove me back across the bridge and deposited me in front of

186

the Ambassador theater as the first-night audience was emerging. Producer Myerberg had outdone himself in promotion: a procession of glitter was there—personalities, Marlene Dietrich among them, everyone was whispering—an enormous party at Sardi's. And the silly stubborn author who had cheated himself out of all this glory hovered there on the edge of the rubberneck crowd. Then some radio interviewer recognized him and thrust a microphone before his mouth, so Levin obliged with a passionate declaration: Yes, it is my play, but it is not exactly completely the way I wrote it. I've been pushed out of my own play as in the Anne Frank case— Thank you, thank you—The microphone is snatched away—Here comes Marlene Dietrich wearing . . . Dahling—

I saw Atkinson of the *Times* darting out, a scowl on his face, and I fought an impulse to catch at his elbow. "Mr. Atkinson, I'm Meyer Levin, I want to explain, this and the Diary, they're connected—"

The *Times* critic was gone.

The review in the *Times,* and again more strongly in the leading Sunday article, praised the drama "whoever its author" for its power and dramatic quality, but concluded with condemnation of its vulgarity, its blurring of character, its cliché dialogue. Other serious critics came to similar conclusions. Yet not one of them would mention that the author of *Compulsion* had weeks in advance made these identical protests. My letters to the critics, pointing this out, were ignored. The eerie sense of a barrier of silence was again upon me. Commonly, when authors complain of the mutilation of their work, the critics, the literary world, take up the cry. I had even sent my own text to the critics so they could check for themselves. Silence. "Whoever wrote it."

The play was running, a sort of pseudo-hit. It was to last about four months. "If you had only kept your mouth shut, it would have run for years," I was to be told by an actor who had got his job through me. "The public doesn't know the difference. It was you and your complaints."

Robert Thom got himself a Hollywood contract on the strength of his "Broadway hit," and long after productions of my own text in other cities had aroused outcries of astonishment at the Broadway mutilation, this creature kept publicizing his "authorship" of my play. In an almost artistic turn of events, after his first movie-star wife had divorced him, Thom married the girl who performed the part of Anne Frank in the Hollywood film of the Hackett play.

Just after the opening of *Compulsion,* the Anne Frank case came to trial. Filling one side of the courtroom sat Otto Frank and his entourage. He sat stiffly upright, wearing an air of outrage. On his left, a rather kindly-looking woman, the wife he had taken. On the other side, still, I thought, like a surrogate daughter, Barbara Zimmerman sat, often pressing close to whisper. In later view, when more emerged, I saw her rather as a commissar.

They would totally expose and destroy me, Tereska had heard Frank say; it would take no more than an hour. Still I could return no hatred; only a vast sadness depressed me when I looked at the tight, scornful face. I would have to pay back fifty thousand dollars, their legal expenditures so far, they were demanding as the court opened. Oh, father of Anne Frank!

In the forward railed section sat a phalanx of our opposing attorneys, with their assistants. Attendants wheeled in an enormous filing case that proved to contain—except for one highly significant item—every scrap of paper I had ever sent to Otto Frank.

As to the press—not one reporter appeared.

There was a conference around the bench. Fredman produced the telegram threatening that I would not live through the trial. The sender of the telegram was known, a respectable but unbalanced person, and arrangements were made about him.

All along I had trusted in and sought the force of public opinion; in the absence of the press, would the trial be ignored? Here was a prominent author—for *Compulsion* was still a best seller—claiming fraud and plagiarism in a drama that had won the Pulitzer Prize and the Critics Award. Was this of no news interest? Could I be wrong in all my journalistic experience? Some days later, as we walked past the open door of the downstairs press room, I heard one reporter ask another if he was going up to the Frank trial. "Wouldn't touch it with a ten-foot pole."

The judge—round-headed, small, neat—was named Samuel Coleman. Jewish, they said. But the last name? A lower-court justice, Fredman whispered to me, who was temporarily sitting in the State Supreme Court. Filling in. Ambitious for the Federal bench. Good we had stood firm for a jury trial.

Fredman had asked me to take a trial lawyer, Howard Spellman, once his teacher. As Spellman began in his quiet, almost academic voice with the questioning of prospective jurors, I felt reassured. For two days the process continued, and somehow, subtly, seemingly accidentally, Spellman maneuvered so that we were left with a jury of twelve college graduates, two of them with doctorates. An editor of the *Saturday Review* had turned up among the talesmen, but the other side had had him dismissed. Still, we had a librarian, an economist, a teacher—on the whole, a group who could grasp the issues. As we emerged from the session, one of the opposing lawyers offered Spellman a professional *well-done*.

Then I was in the witness chair.

Until I took the chair I had never known of the peculiar sensation it produces, and I was surprised that in all the courtroom literature I had read, I had not been prepared by a description of this feeling. It was as though the chair were

189

invested with a power of its own—the way a throne may be, except that this was not a projective power imparted to those who sat on it, but a power making its demand upon them. Like some magic game involving a touch-totem, as long as you sit in contact with this object, it has a power to draw from you the truth. Obviously not everyone feels this, or there would be no lying in the courtroom. Most people experience the witness chair as a strain simply because of being under attack from opposing lawyers. And even when they are under examination by their own attorneys, there remains the fear of making some blunder. But beyond all this, what I felt was an overriding sense of being within a social process; I had entered a ritual still tenuously related to the ancient days of trial by ordeal. Even during the first few days, which were given to examination by my own attorney, I felt this power on me. And when the turn of other witnesses came, I saw that it was not I alone who felt this effect. Kermit Bloomgarden, after only one session at the end of an afternoon, went home and sent notice that he had had a heart attack and would not return to the witness chair.

My lawyers and I had discussed the area of my testimony, but there had been no rehearsals. One question we had left undecided—the whole issue of political motivation. We still felt we didn't want to bring it up. If the other side brought it up, I would answer and not hold back.

In the complaint we had named Otto Frank, Kermit Bloomgarden, and Cheryl Crawford, on the basis that I had been misled and defrauded in the whole question of production of my work; there were two counts of this kind, and there was a third count of "appropriation of ideas."

The exposition completed, Spellman stepped back, as though offering me to the assault. Now began a two-week ordeal; the technique was the common one of turning the accuser into the accused. By cross-examination it was to be shown that from the first moment I had schemed to prey upon

190

Anne Frank's father, the guileless, saintly victim of the Holocaust, for money, money, money!

Out of their enormous filing case came the very first note I had written, from Antibes that summer, trying, it now appeared, to get myself a job as a translator! Was there a word of sympathy to be found in that note? No! Only business!

The judge was gazing at Otto Frank. They were the same age, it struck me.

And so it was to proceed. Silverman, top trial lawyer of Paul, Weiss, Rifkind, Wharton and Garrison, opened with ritual courtroom technique: first, a quiet word of weapon-choice with an assistant, who would go over to the file, draw out a document, and cross back to hand it over. The chief lawyer would glance at it, then draw back as far as the railing, look again at the document, and at me—a pitcher measuring his next throw. He'd hurl his question, stepping forward as with the afterforce of the pitch.

Wondering what I had written to Otto Frank five years before, I would answer from memory. On the whole I came out close enough, but one day I made a blunder. How many times, before his coming to New York, had I met Otto Frank? Twice, I said, in Paris. Twice? Was I certain? Positive? Yes, twice.

It turned out that there had been only one meeting. That long day. I had confused the morning and the afternoon into two different occasions.

Apparently I had already made this error in the pretrial examination, and thus the attorney had prepared his little trap. Oh, how he shook that lying rat Levin! Twice! It was proven to have been only once.

Then you lied just now when you said it was twice?

No, I didn't lie, I believed—

Twice, is that true or false?

Well, false, but—

You admit it! False!

191

And over this brilliant maneuver, there arose a concerted gasp from the entire Frank contingent: blood in the arena! The judge had to bang his gavel and sternly warn against demonstrations.

All the gentlemenly pretense of the pretrial sessions had fallen away, and Silverman was in there tooth and claw to destroy me, his face twisted as he flung each killer question. The whole miserable process had taken hold, the mean little traps, the trick "evidence," the entire apparatus of the adversary system where, instead of a search for truth, there is a duel of legal shaftings. Everyone who has been through a trial has felt it, and this is the citizen's resort to law! His day in court, achieved after years of effort.

Thus Silverman pounded and pounded on my "lie": "Everything you testified to before was a lie, wasn't it? Yes or no!"

Spellman stepped in, with the judge's permission, and asked me, "You just got mixed up, isn't that it?"

"Yes," I said. That one was over with.

Silverman let it drop, and attacked from another direction. I was the author of the novel *Compulsion*?

I was.

This novel had been dramatized?

Yes, it was currently running on Broadway.

Wasn't it true that I had been unable to dramatize it and that another writer had had to be called in to make the play actable?

No! I burst out.

Was I sure of this?

Now was the moment to shout it all out, the whole dirty scheme to discredit me, even with my own play, the whole doctrinaire gang of them—Hellman starting it, and Bloomgarden swearing I would never get a play of mine on Broadway; but even as the words formed, it was as though I, as a juryman, could hear them: Why, the fellow is insane! A wild McCarthyite! Communists under every bed! And because of this crazy red-baiter, poor Otto Frank has had to be dragged into the courtroom.

I turned to the judge and asked, might I explain this matter more fully? He nodded.

The play was my play, just as the program stated, I said. As often happens on Broadway, it had been tampered with, and the producer had, largely because of the approach of this trial, been able to force me into a position where lines written in by his assistant had remained. There were lines that were so vulgar and out of character that I could not let it be assumed that I had written them, could not allow my name to remain over them, and therefore I had insisted that the term "producer's version" be added.

I had managed to say all this directly to the jurors, with calm.

Silverman dropped that line of questioning.

But the real issue? The question of Jewish content in the Diary as the root of all these troubles—Why hadn't I gone on?

In another session, the way seemed open. At last the technique of the filing cabinet rebounded badly. They had introduced, in trying to show how I went to all lengths to keep my claws on the Diary, my letter to the Hacketts offering help. But once they had presented the letter in evidence, the entire text could be read, with its passionate history of my absorption in the Jewish fate. And even my declaration that I wanted no royalties, but wanted only to see that the full meaning of the Holocaust reached the public.

From there, I could have pressed on. Again I was inhibited. Let it stand as it was, without the political issue.

And I too blundered. When my lawyer introduced a letter that had passed between Miss Crawford and Otto Frank, showing how even before I began my work they were contemplating my elimination, I became utterly confused. Presently Justice Coleman read out his decision that the complaints dealing with fraud would be dismissed because of lack of sufficient evidence, and only the third claim, that of appropriation of ideas, would continue to be heard, for decision by the jury.

With that issue, I felt more at home.

In the courtroom, two new persons appeared—a small woman in mink, accompanied by a spare-looking man. The Hacketts had been brought as surprise witnesses to finish me off, and to defend their professional honor.

While we used the term "appropriation of ideas," in effect this could only mean a form of plagiarism. I had no real desire to see the Hacketts branded as plagiarists, just as I had had no desire to connect Otto Frank with deception. I only wanted to have the suppression lifted from my work, and even at this late date kept offering, through my agent, to withdraw all my charges if they would permit non-commercial performance of my play.

At least we were out of the area of legalisms and were moving into the literary realm. There was a technical fascination: when two dramatizations proceeded from the same source-work, could there be any proof of plagiarism? Mermin's contract had limited plagiarism claims to material that was in my play but not in the Diary. I had found a number of instances, such as the stripping of the yellow star, but it seemed to me that the very process of dramatization, even when two writers chose the same lines to put on the stage, could be copied. For the staging itself was "not in the Diary." Out of an infinite number of possible staging methods, how was it that both plays used the identical open-stage form, the identical rhythm of scenes, particularly after my work had been rejected as "unstageable"?

With Hackett taking the stand first, Silverman led him through all of his achievements and qualifications; he had started as an actor, but had become a writer, collaborating with his wife. We heard of their great labors on the Diary, the many versions they had written—eight, was it?

Good; we could demand the scripts in evidence.

And had he ever seen the Levin dramatization?

Never. Indeed he and his wife had from the first been most careful to avoid it. And as they were even now engaged in writing the film script, they still did not want to know what was in it.

Respectfully, Spellman approached for his turn. Point after point of similarity in staging was established. Then scenes. The stripping of the yellow star? A coincidence—any writer might have hit on it. They had never seen my script.

Ah, but had they not conferred with Mr. Bloomgarden, who was familiar with my script?

They had.

And it was customary for producers to suggest ideas, even scenes?

No, Kermit had made no suggestions.

After taking the train all the way to Hollywood? And in all those many conferences?

No.

And they had conferred with Otto Frank who had seen the Levin script?

They had visited Mr. Frank in the hiding place itself, but he had made no suggestions.

And they had conferred with Miss Hellman, who had read the Levin play?

Yes, but she had made no specific suggestions—

Indeed? Here was their own publicity piece, "The Diary of the Diary," from the *New York Sunday Times* . . . Weekend with Lillian . . . Lillian's ideas working out beautifully—

Well, they were just general ideas, nothing specific.

And substantial scenes from my play had been nationally broadcast in a radio version—

195

The judge intervened. He would accept that they had had access to my material, without further questioning to establish this point.

He had also become rather intrigued, it seemed, by the problem of what happened when different adaptors chose the same lines to use on the stage. Would they necessarily do it the same way?

Spellman came to the crux of it. Here was a line from the Diary, a line that had come to be accepted as the essence of the Diary, a line that, in the book itself, was simply part of a paragraph of general reflections, thoughts, not part of a conversation or scene at all. He read the line: "In spite of everything, I still believe that people are really good at heart."

To hear it read aloud in that courtroom of hatred, and worse, in that atmosphere of squabbling! I wanted to rise up and shout: How can this go on! I wanted to cry out to Otto Frank: For God's sake, listen to her, listen to her words! What made you harden your heart against me? Stop this horror! All I ever asked was to let her words be heard, not only these, but others, just as meaningful, that have been suppressed!

I turned and gazed at them, the whole row of them, Barbara Zimmerman whispering to him, Frank rigidly impassive. What a degradation! Was it I? Could I be the most to blame?

Now, Spellman was asking, if a writer singled out this particular line for dramatization, would he be making a contribution?

Of course!

But there were many possibilities for dramatizing that line. Anne could say these words, as might have been most obvious, to her father. Or her sister. Or to everyone together. If the writer chose to dramatize it by having the girl say it to the boy, Anne to Peter, would that be a significant contribution?

Indeed!

And, if he further dramatized it by staging it at the climax of the play, with the force of a curtain line?

196

Hackett was leaning forward in the chair, eagerly. That was what was meant by dramatization!

And if the girl said it to the boy in the intimacy of his room, while they leaned out the window watching a bombardment, in such a moment, with all its added irony—to have her say, "I still believe that people are good at heart—"

"That's the whole play!" Hackett cried out.

"Indeed it is. Exactly as Meyer Levin did it."

That was the whole trial, too.

I even speculated, would Hackett have fallen into the trap if he had really worked from my text? Probably someone had fed the scene to him, in one of those conferences. No matter, Spellman said, legally it was the same. They had copied the key scene.

There was other testimony. Mrs. Hackett took the stand, bristling, and defiantly repeated the blunders of her husband.

With the various drafts of their play in front of us, I could see what had happened. The first draft had been a sort of thriller, full of intrigues and action. This, even Otto Frank had rejected. Then, after "conferences with Lillian," the drafts had come closer to mine.

No! Mrs. Hackett repeated, Lillian had given them no specific advice.

Late that afternoon they put Kermit Bloomgarden on the stand. Yes, he had read the Levin play, he said, contracting his nose to show it stank. Contemptuous, insulting, overbearing. Yet, as the cross-examination began, I had a curious feeling of empathy—this man was feeling the effect of the witness chair. His growls were slower, even hesitant. At the close of the session he lurched up, glancing back at the chair as though searching for the source of bedevilment. In the morning there came hushed conferences before the bench; Bloomgarden had sent a medical report of a heart attack. Under no circumstances would he ever go back to that chair, he was said to have told his lawyers, and both sides agreed to waive the completion of his testimony.

There remained the testimony of Otto Frank. For the other side it was a matter of his presence before the jury, and a few factual items briefly confirmed. Should we question him at all?

One point would be enough, Spellman said.

Mr. Frank had kept a complete file of all my communications, even from the very first note I had sent him?

Yes, he was methodical.

And all this material had been brought to New York and was here in this steel cabinet?

Yes.

Now, the original, lengthy version of my radio play, which had been sent to him for approval, and to which the Broadway play had here been shown to have particular resemblances— was that radio play also in the cabinet?

He believed it was not.

How did such a significant document happen to have been omitted, when even my first note to him was here?

He couldn't say. He thought perhaps it had been put at the bottom of an old trunk, somewhere.

Spellman thanked him, and glanced at the jury.

Had we been cruel?

There came the summations, Silverman first. Money, money, money, that was what I had been after. Let him rave on, the jury was not that stupid. Yet, I could still wonder at such things; it was impossible that this important attorney (later to be made a judge) did not know the real motives in the affair of the Diary. Of all the sickening upturnings in the long, brutal experience, this—though it could no longer come as a disillusion—was to remain the most haunting.

I was certain his fulminations had lost the case for them,

but even if I won, my work would still remain suppressed. That night I sought out Monica McCall at her apartment; she was a friend of the president of the Dramatists Guild, who was in turn a friend of the Hacketts. I begged her to use all her influence to get them to accept a compromise, rather than to risk being branded by the jury for what the public would only see as plagiarism. Let them at least allow Jewish groups to use my work—and I would drop my charges.

There was no response.

Late the next day Spellman began our summary. As to the "money" charges, they scarcely needed rebuttal; he had only to refer to my letters on the subject to Frank and the Hacketts. Why, then, were these people so adamant in refusing any hearing for my drama? Obviously, as every one in the jury must have concluded for himself, if the work was as bad as Mr. Bloomgarden claimed, they could have long ago been rid of me by letting it be tried out. And again, if it was so bad, why had they imitated it to such an extent?

The hour was late; he would have to conclude in the morning.

It was on coming home from the courtroom that I received the news of Meyer Steinberg's death. I called my sister. A third heart attack. The funeral was tomorrow.

I called the lawyers. No, I could not leave, it was required that I, as the plaintiff, be in the courtroom during the charge to the jury, nor could we request an adjournment at this moment; it would have a dreadful psychological effect. I stayed.

I sat there unhearing. What sort of beast was I? What had I brought on here, what was the meaning of all this—a play, another play, what did it matter before the fate of Anne Frank, before the Holocaust, before all death? I heard only occasional echoes—again Anne's cry in that courtroom, "In spite of everything, I still believe—" And the judge's instructions and the jury filing out.

I hurried to the airport.

The funeral was over.

We were all in Bess's kitchen when the phone rang, and my nephew said it was for me from New York.

It was Fredman with the jury's verdict in our favor.

It was then that my sister Bess said to me, "I know it was my Meyer that did it. He went straight to heaven and asked for justice for you."

Fifteen years later in an analyst's office the tears came.

4

DURING THOSE FIFTEEN YEARS the obsession never left me, not for a day, not for a night, nor can I say that it has left me now, in this second attempt to write it out of myself, though people about me seem to recognize that it is under far better control. I no longer feel compelled to go into the whole affair every time *The Diary of a Young Girl* happens to be mentioned in a conversation; sometimes I even take the initiative in changing the subject. But when something specific happens, I act on it as best I can. And these happenings take place—they have never in all this time ceased to take place; requests continue to arrive for my version of the Diary—only last night there was one from a religious trade school here in B'nai Brak in Israel. I tell them the legal situation and tell them that if they want to go ahead and perform the play in defiance of suppression, I will pay any resulting legal costs, and some of them do go ahead. Invariably, if an advance notice gets to Paul, Weiss, Rifkind, etc., attempts are made to intimidate such groups. Even now.

It is not only I who cling to my obsession over the Diary but the other side as well, and the work itself clings to me; I am under obligations to it, and these have unfortunately eaten deeply into my time and my life during these years. For with a kind of passionate vindictiveness my enemies have not only made incredible efforts to keep this work suppressed, but have extended their animosity, so that I have since the trial come to feel my whole career as a writer slowly eroding under unremitting denigrating campaigns, whispering campaigns, and sometimes through plain blacklisting. To have won a clean jury verdict seems to have been my greatest sin of all.

I do not pretend that all of these increasing difficulties are a direct result of efforts only from those legally opposed to me in the Anne Frank case. Ah, no, that famous paranoia of mine could attach itself to other enemies, too. And whether they were real or fancied, and which were real and which might have been fancied, would need a lifetime of inquiry and utter candor toward me from the outer world. Tips of the iceberg kept appearing. Always, when I was ready to make a new effort to cancel these things out of my mind, a new incident would awaken the trouble.

The verdict of the jury, as announced to me that night by Fredman, was for fifty thousand dollars. In New York I learned that the jury had first decided to award me one-fourth of all royalties from the Broadway play. Since Otto Frank received half, that meant they believed my share in the work to be equal to that of the Hacketts. But the judge had required them to name a specific sum and have the matter end there, so they had said fifty thousand dollars. Not a single comment appeared as to the significance in literary terms of such an astonishing award against a prize play. News items were confined to the fifty-thousand-dollar judgment as though the case were strictly a commercial issue. The trade press, *Film Daily, Variety,* carried outraged quotes from the Hacketts' attorneys about how they had had no opportunity to defend their clients' honor.

I had from the outset declared I would give away any award above my costs, and now began to receive letters from various organizations asking for donations. Unfortunately, I had to reply, no money was as yet forthcoming—and indeed it was never to be.

But the dead silence in publications that had to do with the arts, the silence from theater and literary critics, could only serve to reawaken my suspicious, haunting sense that I was confronted not only with suppression of the play but also with a curiously concerted censorship as to the suppression issue itself. Not that I believed that the Rifkind firm, or Doubleday, or Bloomgarden, or the Jewish establishment, or all of them combined, could literally impose such a silence—but persuasion could have such an effect, particularly when it came from so many powerful sources. To which I had to add Twentieth Century–Fox, with its huge investment in the coming film. The argument would be the same as always: "The Diary is doing so much good, why tarnish the image? Perhaps Levin wasn't handled right from the start, but why let that interfere with a play that is loved all over the world, praised by everyone, a play that has done wonders against anti-Semitism? He lost out, that's all. Well, he's being paid."

And so even the publications that made a great to-do about literary freedom were silent.

Right up to the trial there had remained in me the image of the Otto Frank of the Diary, so considerate a man, and despite all his reluctance to come before arbitration, I had kept telling myself, a verdict from a jury would affect him. Here were strangers, people who were more sympathetic to him than to me, in a court atmosphere in which the judge had constantly shown sympathy to him. Before this jury, I had been mercilessly cross-examined, he had been heard, we had all testified. When the verdict came, I romantically expected that Anne Frank's father would change toward me, would concede that a mistake had been made. How could he but remember the warmth of those two years when we fought together to get the Diary published in America? How could he but remember how I had slowly made him "see" the Diary for the stage after he had written that he could not see it—and the friendly visit when he had told us of his coming marriage? I made up a speech for him in my mind. Would he not at last say, "Unfortunately we have had a dispute. Now we have been heard by a fair and impartial jury; they have decided that Meyer Levin was badly treated. As to all those other charges about the Jewish ideas being left out of the Broadway play, which fortunately did not come up in court, perhaps some of this also is true. How could I have known of all these technical matters in the theater, and how could I have believed in all these political machinations? How could I but have trusted the opinion of a world-famous playwright like Lillian Hellman and a great producer like Kermit Bloomgarden? Let us forget our quarrels and misunderstandings and make amends."

Instead, the hostility increased. As though I had somehow secured the jury verdict by a swindle! There would be appeals, and costly maneuvers, and every possible legal device would be used to cancel the verdict and restore the honor of the Hacketts and Otto Frank.

I remained the reprehensible Jew.

I had done all a man could. There had to be an end to the fight.

We would go away. The whole atmosphere had become a poison to me. If I had to go into the Times Square area, I detoured from the streets where *Compulsion* and the *Diary* were playing. I could not bring myself to go to a theater, to any theater, to any play, and this was to endure for several years.

I had to start working on something that would take me completely away from all that had happened. At long last I must start working on the saga of a pioneer family in Palestine and Israel, the story based on Yitzhak Chizik's family, that I had been putting off since the early thirties. We would move to Israel, and I would, now that I had some money from *Compulsion* to carry me through, at last get at it.

All of our books—I didn't want to sell them, so I passed the word that people could come and take what they wanted. For several days friends and strangers trooped through the apartment, picking books, carting them off. I destroyed many old manuscripts, particularly plays. Not a copy remains of the one suppressed in Chicago, *Model Tenement,* nor of several others. Nothing but grief, trouble and evil, had I ever had from the theater. It was over. Finished.

On the Mediterranean shore, a friend had rented a house for us in a village called Beit Yanai, an hour from Tel Aviv. A cottage with a beautiful garden, so renowned that troops of schoolchildren were brought to study the flora, and gaze at the peacock that came with it all.

The seashore house was the weekend home of a Hebrew University professor, and along the cliff were a few other such retreats, though none boasted such a garden. Across the road, inland, were small farms, mostly given to poultry raising. Southward was a training school for immigrant youngsters— farming, carpentry, machine-shops—a remarkable institution that had been built up over the years by Professor Dushkin and his wife, old friends from Chicago. Northward, the beach cottages tapered off to a long, wide, deserted stretch of sand, as far as the Alexander River—a good walk. Isolated on a rise above the beach stood a battered concrete hut, without doors or windows, the rusted remains of arched tin roof-sections still rattling in the wind. On the walls were bullet-pocks. This had been a British watch-post during the mandate period, guarding against the landing of illegal immigrants on this isolated coast.

205

Eventually I would get permission to rebuild that hut and use it for my workplace; indeed my last seven books, and this one, have been written at Beit Yanai.

I tried to start on my long-brewing saga of early settlers, but it would not come. Just before we had left New York, Bill Zimmerman had shown me a set of galleys of a novel named *Exodus,* about to appear, and some of the material I had intended to use was already there. I'd have to turn to another subject.

There was a film story. At the end of Israel's War of Independence I had sought out, in a small house in Rehavia, Jerusalem's "professors' quarter," the man who had first deciphered the Dead Sea Scrolls. Professor Elazar Sukenik had come early to Palestine as a Hebrew teacher. Fascinated by archeology, he had gone to America for his degree, and eventually became head of the department at the Hebrew University. Excitedly, Sukenik led me into his backyard garden to show me where he had buried the jars with the scrolls during the bombardment of Jerusalem. He told me how his eldest son, Yigael, had left his studies to take up his Haganah post, how even the family had not known that Yigael was Yigael Yadin, the chief of staff of Haganah. And then back in his study, holding a photograph of a dreamy-looking adolescent, the professor had told me how his youngest son had died in a "teacup" plane, diving on the leading ship in the Egyptian fleet that was steaming to attack Tel Aviv.

The Sukenik-Yadin story had remained with me, and already in Paris, on the way to Israel on the present trip, I had spoken to Edward G. Robinson about playing the part of the late Professor Sukenik, whom he remarkably resembled.

So turning to the story of the Dead Sea Scrolls, I went to Jerusalem to see Yigael Yadin, now in his father's post at the University. He greeted me somewhat warily, frankly telling me that he had already been warned from New York that he had best not get mixed up with Meyer Levin, that I was a trouble-maker, I sued everybody.

I managed to bring him in, to start the project, but I could never feel he was fully at ease with me in the weeks we worked together. Eventually Edward Robinson dropped out; he had changed agents and was advised not to do the part. The project died. Even in Israel, every project seemed to dissolve in my hand in the last stages; the Habima Theatre agreed to present *Compulsion*, held meetings with me, and then that too faded away. Well, why get delusions of persecution? Most theater and film projects die along the way. I had best work on a book; at least in the realm of the novel I would be on my own, free of suspicions of poisoned relationships.

If I was still blocked on the tale of the early settlers, why, I was an old campaigner against the block, I knew all the escape devices. One was to write your problem out of yourself. Head on. I would use the grueling experience of the last few years, simply transposing the Diary, the legacy from the Holocaust, into some other creation of great human value, a scientific discovery; left by a victim of the Nazis, it could, similarly, become coveted, even for political motives. I began. But I was forcing the science-story into the mold of my personal experience. It would not fit.

Just then came a letter from an Israeli woman, survivor of the camps. She wanted me to write her story. Perhaps this way I could circumvent the block. I went to see her, and began on *Eva*.

A cable came from Fredman. Judge Coleman had set aside the verdict of the jury and ordered a new trial.

Then a letter came about the strange upset, with the judge's published "reasoning." While the jury had a right to conclude and did conclude that I had suffered damage, there had been no evidence before them as to the extent of the damage. How was the jury to have been guided in fixing the amount? How could one even tell in general what an author contributed to the success of a play, the judge wrote, when the director, the actors, the scene designer, all else must be taken into account? God! Had this dolt never heard of standard author's royalties? The jury had tried to fix my share on the basis of royalties, and he had prevented them! There should be a new trial, the judge concluded, with testimony from experts on each side to help a jury determine just how much I was owed!

All praise to Paul, Weiss, Rifkind, Wharton and Garrison: How to destroy an honest jury verdict and get another crack at your opponent. Despite weeks of testimony, and all the scripts in evidence, there was "no evidence whatever as to the amount of damage," the judge declared, and this was twisted by the law firm to suggest that there was "no evidence whatever" in the whole case. In a letter sent out to this day to applicants for my play, they claim that, with no evidence, I dragged Otto Frank into the courts. After such persecution he could hardly be expected to allow my work to be performed.

And so anew, then came the nights of spinning words in my head, of outraged replies, denunciations, letters to Jewish leaders, to the press. Driving homeward, or sitting at a meal oblivious to what was said, or watching a film, the protest words spun on, directed to that pompous little judge, directed to Otto Frank, directed to Brooks Atkinson, to Edmund Wilson: no evidence whatever? But what about the texts of the plays! No testimony by experts? What about the "expert" testimony of the Hacketts!

The decision, Fredman wrote, was totally vulnerable—we must appeal; first of all, I would have to provide two thousand dollars for the printing of the trial record.

I sent the two thousand dollars.

And even if we won the appeal, there might be a new trial, costing more than the first.

I would be undertaking enormous expense and a great risk; for what? Merely for the hope of proving, under worse circumstances, since the other side now knew every detail of our case, something I had already proven.

And Tereska? We were changing our lives, we had come here so that the muck of Manhattan might be washed from our souls. What would a repetition of the ordeal do to us? Again I felt myself in that night of trauma, of the black river. Here, the pains were gone from my left shoulder and arm; I had not brought the nitroglycerin tablets, I no longer lay bound on the castration table.

And if the legal maneuvers began again, what about the book *Eva*?

No, I wouldn't walk into the trap. He must delay making any decision, I wrote Fredman, at least until I finished the book I was working on.

When I arrived in New York to confer on *Eva* with my editor, he, too, advised me: not another trial. You've made your point. After all, what the judge had questioned was the money side, the amount of the award; this had nothing to do with the moral decision of the jury. The amount could be settled.

The same advice came from my old friend, law professor and famed libertarian Edmond Cahn, who knew well the entire dismal history. I absolutely must not subject myself to another trial. I must free myself. I would appoint a committee of three; we thought of a public figure such as the president of the American Jewish Congress, Rabbi Joachim Prinz, a refugee from Berlin and a man of wide cultural interests. Perhaps he could even persuade Otto Frank to let my work be performed, as part of the settlement. Also, a writer— I named Charles Angoff. Finally, someone from the academic world, and Cahn suggested the head of Jewish studies at New York University, Professor Abraham Katch. I would give them full authority to accept any money settlement, without even consulting me, provided that the moral decision remained intact.

209

Indeed, if the other side would also appoint such a committee, we might arrive at a decent conclusion of the whole affair. The other side did not respond to this noble thought. My committee would have to deal with their lawyers.

Perhaps I would come to the end of my hauntings. For at the same time, a community theater just across the Washington Bridge was producing *Compulsion,* in my own text, unadulterated. I was at last able to work on the play in the staging. A young actor named Warren Beatty was virtually hypnotic playing the role of Artie, the charmer of the two murderers. I wouldn't remember him, Beatty told me, but once, while waiting for a reading in Myerberg's office, he had spoken to me of his enormous feeling for the part. At last he was getting to do it. Was it an omen for me? Agents came to see Beatty perform, and this proved the beginning of his meteoric career.

Alas, though actors' agents came, it proved impossible to get the critics to cross the river. I sent wires, offered to fetch them in cabs—no response. Again the paranoiac suspicion—was I taboo? Didn't these men—critics like Kenneth Tynan, then reviewing for *The New Yorker*—even have the curiosity to see for themselves what had been involved in a dramatist's struggle for the integrity of his text? Or had I been so smeared in their circles that I was untouchable? Or was it merely the heavy snowstorm, lasting through the final week of performances, that gave critics the disinclination to ride across the bridge, though it did not stop the agents?

At least one thing had been accomplished for myself. As with the Anne Frank play, there had been the tormenting "You will never know." With *Compulsion,* I now knew. It was good. Proven. The *Compulsion* haunting I could dismiss from my mind. The play continued to be performed in my text across the country, with reviewers asking in amazement why anything had ever been changed.

I was freed from *Compulsion,* but this only augmented the need to prove the same for the Diary. Myer Mermin's words, "You will never know," resounded more brutally than ever. What would not let go of me in the Anne Frank issue was not only the question of stageworthiness, but the added question of whether my version would really project a deeper meaning. Or was I still giving myself cause to cling to a sickness?

I left the disposal of the case to my committee. Returning to Israel, I began again to write it out of myself, in *The Fanatic.*

After some months there came a cable from Fredman. My committee had succeeded in settling the Anne Frank case, with full retention of the moral victory. The other side would pay, instead of the fifty thousand dollars, something like fifteen thousand to cover my legal outlay, plus a few thousand more of court costs. There would not need to be another trial.

Since I had declared I would give away anything above my legal outlay, the reduction, in effect, simply canceled the donation.

Nor did I feel it strange that there was no communication from the committee itself. I had no idea that my committee had never met.

Shortly afterward, when I came to New York for the publication of *Eva,* the settlement documents were presented to me by Fredman for signature; as I read the extended provisions, I simply didn't know what to think. Had all this been agreed to by my committee? Yes, he said. And since I had declared in advance that I would be bound by my committee's decision, I was without any choice but acceptance.

The money part was not the issue, though there had been the greatest insistence from the other side, Fredman explained to me, that not a penny should accrue to Meyer Levin, that the sum should cover legal expenditures alone, and go directly to the lawyers.

What people! But it was the rest. It was the recommendation of my own committee, the document stated, that there should be no more discussion, public or private, of this entire matter. No discussion whatever as to whether Meyer Levin's play should or should not have been produced. And this was to be part of the agreement, so that in signing it, I indicated acceptance of the recommendation.

No public or even private discussion? Unbelieving, I read the line over and over. This amounted to thought control!

Paul, Weiss, Rifkind, my lawyer said, had insisted on such a provision. Otherwise, no settlement.

This insistence came from a law firm that prided itself on its liberalism, that defended freedom of speech, one of whose founders had been a crusader—could this be serious?

Absolutely. Doubtless the insistence came from their clients.

And my own committee had accepted this?

It was not an arbitration, he reminded me, but a case of tough bargaining on the other side. After all, the moral victory stood, the sum paid was serious. And a settlement had to be a settlement. The whole purpose of it was to put an end to these ugly disputes over a document like the Diary. "Obviously if we settle, there is no longer any need for public discussion, so they want this point included and underlined."

"But it says private discussion, too!"

My good friend and defender didn't seem disturbed by this. Obviously he was tired of the whole battle; though he had gained recognition and status, he had earned virtually nothing for his enormous and protracted expenditure of time and energy, and he wanted to be shut of it all. Did I want the case over with or did I want to go on fighting forever?

Go work it out with your analyst whether you really want it over with, or are really seeking an excuse to prolong your obsession forever!

But there are basics. There are minimal principles below which comes degradation. I had said I'd accept in advance the terms my committee agreed to, yes. But a silencer! "Look, it's only recommended." "But it says I accept the recommendation. Still as a recommendation." Lawyers!

I had a thought. As I could not reject what the committee accepted, I would simply ask that a clarification be added, saying I would retain complete freedom of literary discussion.

Fredman gave me an appreciative glance. I was catching on to the ways of law. Of course such a statement would cancel out the whole silencer, and Mermin would see through it as readily as Fredman.

"Tell them I can't sign without this. It's rock bottom."

He would. But meanwhile there was more. I must agree not again to circularize the rabbis.

And this had been accepted by Rabbi Prinz? That a Jew was forbidden to approach the rabbis? Why, Prinz himself had been one of those who had signed my circulated petition.

"Well, look, Meyer, if we sign a settlement, why should you want to start agitating again?"

If my committee leader, Rabbi Joachim Prinz, president of that liberal organization, the American Jewish Congress, had agreed to such a stipulation, I'd sign out of sheer absurdity.

More! My rights to have my play produced in Israel were no longer obtainable.

The rights were in any case useless—the Habima production had killed them.

And finally, the ownership of my play was to be assigned to Otto Frank.

Simply a legal expedient, Fredman explained. The best way to lay to rest the whole plagiarism issue was for Otto Frank to own my play, precluding further claims of damage for the use of my work. Besides, he pointed out, as there was some peculiar fixation on the question of my ever profiting from performances of my play, perhaps if Frank himself owned it, he would even consent to let it be performed. One thing was certain: as long as I owned it, he would never give consent.

213

I reread the wording of the transfer of ownership to Otto Frank. "For his proper use and benefit," it said. The phrase struck me: "proper use." Could he, under this, refuse its use by the community?

Interesting, my lawyer said. I might have a real point there. If the refusals continued, it might be tested.

Let Otto Frank own my play. What was ownership but the commercial side of writing? No one but the author could ever "own" the writing itself.

They agreed to my demand for freedom of literary discussion, but wanted a quid pro quo. I was to sign a public statement attesting that Otto Frank was an honorable man, and that never in our now-settled dispute had I meant to suggest otherwise.

In return, the other side would sign a statement that never in all this trouble had there been any intention of reflecting on my ability as a dramatist.

Oh, God of hypocrisy! Thou reignest supreme!

And, almost as an afterthought, let it be stated that everyone regretted the unfavorable publicity that had accrued through this affair to the Hacketts.

I signed it all. Just as I had let myself sign the earlier agreements drawn up by Myer Mermin, and the agreements with Michael Myerberg.

Not even a Rubashov, with a last rationalization of loyalty to his cause.

Say it is bad faith. Say it is exhaustion. Say it is self-hatred. Say Meyer Levin is a shit.

Perhaps I had now so completely bound myself that I would be freed.

Began remorse and regret after somewhat recovering from torture.

Why had I not, before signing, called the members of my

committee to find out how it was they had accepted those provisions for thought control?

Excuse: I was in such disgust, I simply could not bring myself to contact them.

Certainly not Rabbi Prinz, or Professor Katch, whom I hardly knew. But weeks later I asked Charles Angoff—had he perhaps been outvoted on the agreement?

What agreement? He had never seen it. The committee had never met. He had assumed that Rabbi Prinz, as the head of it, would call them together.

Then whence had come this agreement, which I had morally bound myself in advance to accept? Why, it developed, the whole matter had been turned over by Rabbi Prinz to the legal advisor of the American Jewish Congress, Will Maslow. Mr. Maslow had carried it through as a matter of money-haggling with Paul, Weiss, Rifkind, etc., those toughies, and he had passed along as acceptable every condition they had attached.

Will Maslow, himself a big champion of civil liberties, a fighter for freedom of expression, for Jewish cultural rights, for the rights of man!

—You signed it, didn't you?

During this period I had no analyst. Could I thread my way between suspicions, delusions of persecution, to reality? Even with an analyst at my side, I had not been able to save the stage version of *Compulsion*. Now came a new series of peculiar occurrences:

For the publication of *Eva* I brought with me from Israel a short film made for the *Today* show in the Tel Aviv home of the woman whose story is told in the book. I was to appear on the show with this material, on publication day. A few days before, the whole thing was canceled.

Through a publicist working on *Eva*, I tried to find out the reason. While such a cancellation was unusual, especially for material that had been filmed to order, he said, I would just have to accept it as one of the things that happen in the media. To press for an explanation might arouse antagonism.

I happened to be sitting in the office of the same publicist when he answered a call from another author who was scheduled to appear that afternoon as a guest on a popular interview program conducted by Arlene Francis. The scheduled guest was ill and could not appear. "Will you take his place?" asked the publicist.

"Sure. But she won't accept me."

I explained. When my version of the Diary had first been canceled, Arlene Francis had been at a dinner party where I had come out with my accusations against Lillian Hellman. Later I learned that she had been greatly shocked, as they were friends.

"Aw, come on, what's that got to do with it? You're twice the name of this other guy. Your book is her kind of thing."

"Go on, phone her, you'll see."

He phoned, offered me, and was flatly refused.

Very well, it was personal. But this sort of thing had been growing, closing in on me. (With *The Settlers* I was to find myself mysteriously virtually blacklisted in the New York area.)

One had to ask whether a commentator really had a right to exercise a personal taboo. Surely I was the sort of author whom Arlene Francis's audience would welcome on her show. Did she have a professional right to taboo me on personal whim or for her own political leanings? This form of interview has grown to be an integral part of communications, of culture; it has great influence on what the public reads, and the public assumes an impartiality among the programmers. The choice of guest is supposed to be based on what is interesting to the public. That there is censorship by the commentator on the basis of his personal or political likes is not known to the

216

public, and thus this type of censorship becomes a form of manipulative power. Worse, in the hypersensitive radio and television world, word that so-and-so is controversial, or that such and such a prominent commentator won't touch him, easily spreads and becomes a taboo simply by hearsay.

Though the taboo had not yet become widespread with *Eva,* the same publicist said to me, not long afterward, "I don't know what it is, but there are shows that you definitely ought to be on, and I can't get you on."

A novel of Tereska's was being published while we were in New York; from the New York *Post,* a feature writer called to arrange an interview. The date and time were set. As her books are published under the name of Tereska Torres, my wife added, "When you get to the hotel, ask for Mrs. Meyer Levin."

There was a pause. "You're the wife of Meyer Levin, the author?"

"Why, yes."

Another pause. "I'll call you back to confirm the arrangement."

The call never came.

With my next book, *The Fanatic,* difficulties began long before publication, and this time the connection was clear. An advance publicity note appeared, saying the story dealt with a dramatist's fight for the integrity of a play about the Holocaust. At once my publishers received a notice from Paul, Weiss, Rifkind, Wharton and Garrison demanding that publication of the book be canceled. I was therefore informed that the novel would have to be postponed while legal experts, who had already gone over the manuscript, once more scrutinized the parallels to the Anne Frank case for possible libel. After half a year of postponement, Ephraim London at last recommended publication. I came to New York for consultations. If

217

the Rifkind office should sue, London declared, there was an adequate defense of truth. But he was sure there would be no lawsuit. "They certainly won't want to call attention to the book." On the contrary, he warned me, some of my enemies would most likely make efforts to get the book buried. They'd plant killing reviews. "If you have any way of protecting yourself on reviews, in places that count, you'd better get busy."

I belonged to no clique, I had no influence. The one time I had made an effort in this direction had been for the Diary. I tried to protect my book by at least having Charles Angoff request *The Fanatic* for review from the Sunday *Times*.

He received the book, but shortly afterward it was called back; he was told that a mistake had been made, the book had already been assigned.

The Sunday *Times* review appeared, damning *The Fanatic* with faint praise. Elsewhere, in reviews from New Haven to Los Angeles, I found disparaging phrases being repeated as though they had come from a single source. Obsession again. I was going around with a pocket filled with clippings which I would pull out to prove my point.

The Eichmann trial was about to take place, and I asked my agent to get me an assignment to cover it. Writers and journalists were arriving in Israel by the score. Here I was, right on the spot, with expert background knowledge. My agent could find nothing for me. At the last moment, simply to secure accreditation, I offered to write some articles for *Congress Weekly,* the journal of the American Jewish Congress. How was it that with dozens of journalists being sent in who knew little about the Holocaust, I couldn't get a real assignment?

When I met Martha Gellhorn, an old friend, walking through Jerusalem to the trial sessions, I could not keep myself from pointing this out, from relating my troubles, pouring out the whole Anne Frank story, with my suspicions that poisonous tales were now affecting my whole career. Though I realized that by these complaints I was myself spreading such tales, I couldn't hold back, couldn't prevent myself from going into every detail.

Martha seemed relieved as we reached the hall.

It happened with other old friends too. No, absolutely, I must stop talking like this. This was how it worked on you.

Haunted, I decided on a head-on attack in my characteristic manner, and sent out a letter to a number of editors and producers, explaining my situation: As a result of the Anne Frank case, a character-assassination campaign seemed to be going on against me, using the terms "litigious," "trouble-maker," "red-baiter." A few friendly replies came, one from Arnold Gingrich. Yes, they had heard the tales. Unfortunately such things were difficult to counteract.

To further blacken the picture there arose the *Compulsion* lawsuit. Nathan Leopold had been paroled; and virtually his first act had been to file a multimillion-dollar action against me and everyone who had had anything to do with *Compulsion,* claiming invasion of privacy and a sort of ownership of the material of the crime.

A man I had helped! Strangely, in the vagaries of popular image-making, everything was reversed. Nathan Leopold was a sufferer, a kind of savant-saint who was devoting himself to good works in a remote hospital in Puerto Rico, and I—I was some sort of exploiter. Hadn't I persecuted Otto Frank? Here I was anew in a lawsuit. Litigious Levin.

Would I ever get rid of this smear? As writers commonly do when things go badly, I decided to change agents. There was a hot young crewcut man named Herbert Jaffe. Yes, he was interested in the author of *Compulsion.* We had lunch. How was my lawsuit going against Leopold? he began.

I groaned.

No, it was Leopold who was suing me, I explained. I

launched into my tale. Levin, lawsuits, "litigious," and the whole political source.

He held up his hand to stop me. "You don't have to explain. I may even know some of this better than you." To my surprise, Jaffe remarked, "You met me before, some years ago, but you couldn't have noticed. It was my first job out of college, and I was working in a small P.R. agency, films and books. They had a novel of yours, *My Father's House.*"

"Oh, sure. Billy Friedberg's agency. So you worked there? I went to him with my last five hundred dollars—I didn't want to miss a chance of having that book make it. A disaster. Not even a single radio interview or a line in a column!" I waved it off. He was looking at me with a peculiar fixity.

I went on, professionally. "We had a drink when it was over. Billy said he had knocked himself out, but it was just one of those things—nothing worked."

The gaze was now marked with a wondering smile. "But why did you come to Billy? Didn't you know—"

"He was a friend of mine from the OWI"— Suddenly I realized. I had always known Billy was political. It made no difference to me—but why had I come to him with a novel that he could only have seen as Zionist?

"I was ashamed of what the outfit did to you," Jaffe said. "Of course I was fresh out of college and still pretty naïve."

So it went that far back. Even before Anne Frank.

Was everything political? Long ago I had heard that wise slogan propounded: Everything is political. Even the most innocuous material could be used politically. Unwittingly, I was political. Everything Jewish was political.

Even the Anne Frank case hadn't taught me. What I as a writer and what the general reading public thought of as human stories, the experience of people's lives, were examined by politicals first of all in the light of their doctrines. I had always known this on the surface, but had not yet realized how deep and strict was the rule.

220

To a V. J. Jerome I must long before the Diary have been on the "dangerous" list. I had been utterly blind about their doctrinaire view of *My Father's House*. And *Eva*? Wasn't *Eva*, to them, the story of a Jewish girl who survived Auschwitz, and went to work for the Soviet Union, only to reject that world when her lover, a Jew, was murdered by anti-Semites? Worse, she then decided to go to Israel. So I was again guilty. As with *In Search*. And at about that same time I had published a tale heard from someone who had been in a Siberian labor camp; there he had met a young lad from an assimilated Jewish family, who as a student had become interested in library material on Jewish history. For drawing out these restricted books he had been arrested. "If you ever reach the outside world, let it be known," he had begged, "that a Jew is punished here for wanting to know about Jews." Surely this had been one of the earliest stories of the situation of Soviet Jewry, and this too must have marked me.

During a Paris stopover I encountered Albert Camus on the rue du Bac. Over a coffee I was soon deep into the Anne Frank affair, and my political troubles. "Odd," he remarked, "I had wondered why the play in Paris was in the hands of that particular crowd."

I left with him a copy of my version, and of my petition. Not long afterward I read of his death. Then one day the play came back to me in the mail. He had signed the petition.

A paperback came in the mail called *Best Jewish Short Stories*, part of a series, *Best French, Best Russian*, etc. The Jewish volume was edited by Saul Bellow, and had been sent to me because it contained one of the tales of Rabbi Nachman that I had translated for my book of Hasidic stories, *The Golden Mountain*. I read Bellow's preface. Glibly he danced along, pointing out, lest anyone might take him for a Jewish nationalist, the international sources of this literature.

221

He mocked—respectfully—the not-yet-Nobel-Prize-Laureate S. Y. Agnon for having blinders on to anything outside the Hebrew writing world, and then, surprisingly, brought up the name of Meyer Levin. At least I was in lofty company. In a story of mine, Bellow said, I had written that an artist could be creative only in his own land, in his own language, free in his own tradition. Chauvinistic, xenophobic, and ultra-nationalistic ideas such as Meyer Levin's, Bellow went on, had never led to the creation of works of art.

Where could I have written this?

Then I remembered, The xenophobic, chauvinistic, ultra-nationalistic ideas were from the utterances of a character whom I had satirized in a story years ago. The whole point was obviously the very reverse of what Bellow had attributed to me. The story ended with the character's moving to Palestine and sending back to his Greenwich Village friends a crate of paintings that were totally banal and untalented.

If Bellow had read the story to the end, why had he attributed the extreme ideas of this satirized character to me, and in quotes? If he had not read to the end, he was inexcusably irresponsible.

I wrote to the publishers, sending them a copy of the original story. Hastily they wrote back, "Please don't sue!" Unfortunately the first edition was on the stands, but they would see that the point was corrected in the next edition of the book. It was.

But why had the clever Bellow gone to such lengths, resorted to such tricks, to label me a xenophobe? Everything was politics.

* * *

There came a letter from Ephraim London, advising me to stay out of any legal action for seven years, no matter how gross the injustice. He even got me to drop the long-dormant defamation case against Robert Thom for claiming authorship

222

of my play *Compulsion*. That way the lawsuit legend would die out.

It resumed with the Leopold case. Levin and his lawsuits. How could I drop the case—it was Nathan Leopold who was suing me! Leopold has succeeded in building up an image of himself as a genius who, unfortunately, had committed one mistake in his youth, but had long since atoned for it by devoting his life to helping mankind, even while imprisoned. Indeed I had contributed somewhat to this image, during my appeals for his release. When I had journeyed to Springfield to testify at his parole hearing, one of the lawyers newly enlisted in the cause had slipped into the seat facing mine on the train from Chicago. I wouldn't know his name, he said, but he knew me from high school; he had been a freshman when I was already a senior, he had adulated my writings in the school magazine and had remained a fan of mine ever since. He had wanted to write but had gone into law instead and, I gathered, hoped to become known as another Clarence Darrow.

Thus, the beginning with Elmer Gertz.

The parole hearing was held in what could have been a classroom, with the five board members on a low platform. A few dozen people, lawyers and witnesses, occupied the chairs. There was testimony from a half-brother of Leopold's, and from a college fraternity mate who had stuck by him, both emphasizing the good side of his character. Letters were read from rabbis and clergymen, including a plea from Carl Sandburg, and then my turn came. I made my amateur psychological-sociological analysis. The chairman of the board, a youngish man, called me up afterward and remarked that he had read my book and was much impressed.

The decision would be announced in due time. Meanwhile, as the *Compulsion* play was then in rehearsal, lawyer Gertz came to New York to make sure that the impact of the drama would not hurt Leopold's parole chances. He decided that, if anything, it would help. Some months later the parole board referred the case to the governor, and eventually the parole went through; it was announced that Nathan Leopold would go to Puerto Rico to work in a hospital conducted by a Christian order. I received a letter from him, thanking me for my efforts to have him freed.

And then came the lawsuit.

I was mounting the steps of a temple in a Chicago suburb where I was to speak, when two men approached, asking if I was Meyer Levin; I thought they were coming to the lecture and wanted to ask some question in advance, but as I said yes, one of them handed me a sheaf of documents. I was being served in Nathan Leopold's lawsuit, filed by my admirer Elmer Gertz, for some two million dollars against Meyer Levin et al., the "al." including some fifty-two defendants, the publisher, the film producer, even the local book distributors and theater owners who had shown the film. The charges were varied but centered on invasion of privacy and encroachment on Leopold's literary property—his crime! Scrupulously, Leopold was asking for only half of what they calculated as the total profits of *Compulsion,* since the other half would have belonged to his partner, Dickie Loeb.

For nine years, during much of which time my book was suppressed, the case was to hang over me, while squads of attorneys representing the film producer, the publishers, and various distributors, went through motions, appeals, and counter-motions in the protracted maneuvers of their profession. The issue was never to come to court—the case was eventually dismissed—but during those years it intertwined itself in my mind with the Frank case as a symbol of ingratitude and persecution. Oddly enough, there was an additional reverberation, as the name of the victim of Loeb and Leopold was Bobby Franks.

On the surface it would seem that the two "matters," as lawyers call these things, had little in common, yet to me they

224

not only had a common source in my impulse to be helpful, but a common result in subsequent misrepresentation. In the Diary affair I was being represented as a troublemaker, a man who had harassed poor Otto Frank, and in a similarly inverted way the claim of Nathan Leopold again made me out to be a devil. In those strange depths where public sentiment is determined, Leopold was now a victim, a man who had suffered thirty years of imprisonment as if in a death camp; he was a kind of culture hero—my book had helped to make him so— but also there had been an astute image-creation campaign, picturing him as a master of fourteen languages, a savant, and now a hospital volunteer in a remote monastery, a kind of Dr. Schweitzer! Added to this was a general pity for him, engendered by stories put out to help his release—he was a very sick man with at most a year to live. Whereas Meyer Levin was an exploitative writer who had first of all tried to make a fortune from Anne Frank, and then had battened on the miseries of Nathan Leopold, out of which he had become a millionaire!

And for me, just as the Frank troubles had been truly an issue of literary suppression, so the Leopold case involved a whole area of artistic freedom, the freedom to use personages and events from living history. Dostoievsky had done so in *Crime and Punishment,* Dreiser had done so in *An American Tragedy;* an entire area of literature was occupied by such works, and this lawsuit threatened to close off the use of living material. Why? We have, of course, a vast array of libel laws that protect anyone, criminal or not, from public abuse, particularly if malice is involved. Surely, in the case of *Compulsion,* there was none.

The complaint was twofold. First there was Leopold's claim of ownership, or at least half-ownership, of the crime itself. Secondly, there had been invasion of privacy. Leopold's sensibility had been outraged by one scene in my novel in which the fictitious character, Judd Steiner, corresponding to himself, had had an impulse, indeed an instruction from his

225

partner as well, to rape a girl on a date. That girl, Leopold said, was one with whom he had been in love, and he could never have entertained thoughts of violence toward her. Yet almost any young man at times entertains thoughts of rape, even of his loved one, if he is frustrated, and the episode was there in the novel to show that while his partner was psychopathically beyond control, Judd Steiner's human and moral sense could, in a crisis, assert itself and even overcome his compulsive drives. If Nathan Leopold, so long afterward, in prison, had been able to see it in this light, I do not believe he would have felt the traumatic shock that, his lawyer insisted, he had suffered from the scene. In any case I had made it very clear in my preface that such personal episodes were fictional.

But a curious incident was attached to this claim of his. In his own book, *Life and Ninety-nine Years,* which had by then appeared, Leopold had been pressed by his editors to write not only about prison life but about the crime itself, so as to outdo *Compulsion.* He had described a similar date, and in the very same atmosphere of an isolated ride in which I had put it. But I had made it up! (Of course in his description there was no impulse of violence!) I wondered, then, whether an inversion had taken place, whether Nathan Leopold had not created a memory for himself out of my fiction.

Another passage in his book insisted that on my visit to him in prison, he had implored me, even to the point of tears, not to write *Compulsion.* It was this distortion, together with the lawsuit, that led me to wonder whether his character and his philosophy had changed. The superman philosophy that he had so aggressively spouted after the arrest, the twisted Nietzschean idea of a superior mankind, an elite, unbound by ordinary human laws and moral rules—such as respect for truth—was this not still his concealed but ruling belief?

Who but a supermind would be able to manipulate society, even though it took thirty years, in such a way as to get free from a sentence imposed with double locks, so to speak: "Life plus ninety-nine years!" Wasn't there even a touch of megalomania in titling his book with those very words? I did not begrudge him his liberty, nor would I disown my campaign for it; I saw no point in his having been kept for so long in prison. But the most audacious aspect of his behavior was of course the lawsuit. Who but a superman would undertake in this way to flout the common ethics of society by attacking the very person who had done so much, as declared by his own attorney, to secure his release? Wasn't he by this action making the very same boast that he and Dickie Loeb had made as a rationale for their murder: We are above the common laws as we are above the common run of mankind? It was an attitude that was to become the plague of our time.

Finally, in his lawsuit, Nathan Leopold was daring the highest feat of all—he would at last collect the kidnap-murder ransom, and many times over! It would be handed to him by a court! What a justification for himself, and his dead friend Dickie Loeb!

He and Dickie had done the killing, they were the authors of the action, a sort of natural copyright was claimed, all accounts of the crime must pay royalties to them—or at least to Leopold for his half!

Obviously, people in our time, from criminals to heroes, have often been paid for their stories, and with the proliferation of film and television, many have been paid fortunes. I myself had been ready to share with Leopold on his book, and I had since written *Eva* in partnership—though the two instances should hardly be mentioned together—with the woman who had lived that life in the Holocaust. In all such cases, the subject supplies the material, in depth and with authenticity. But the story may also be freely told by others if the material is publicly known. Where, then, is "privacy"? Where is there "invasion of privacy"? This area of the law is filled with vagaries and confusion.

Another curious and disturbing aspect of the case was the

227

claim that fictionalization made me vulnerable. Had I written virtually the same book, using real names, as a history, I would presumably have been writing for educational purposes rather than for profit, whereas fiction was entertainment written for profit!

Nathan Leopold's lawsuit seemed to spark a whole series of astounding cases. The descendants of Al Capone filed a multimillion-dollar claim for invasion of privacy against a television station that had broadcast a portrayal of the gangster's life. Then came the case of the wife of the killer of Rasputin, who was suing a television network that had shown a dramatization of the event.

Suddenly an unease spread among writers and publishers, indeed all through the communications industry. If such cases were valid, an enormous source of material would be barred. A form of censorship threatened that was not only terrifying in a commercial sense, but that could in fact close off a perennial wellspring of art. A padlock would be clamped on the imaginative mind, where reality enters to be transformed into myth by the artist.

Among writer friends I found myself, as though I were some sort of expert, repeatedly being asked: could this or that subject be attempted? A few years later, when Truman Capote wrote a similar book while the *Compulsion* case was still pending, calling his work a non-fiction novel—I had called mine a documentary novel—the publisher made sure to secure releases from every person mentioned, even in the most insignificant connection, even a gas station attendant.

The case was much more than a harassment. If any award at all should be made, it could establish an enormously restrictive precedent.

That it involved the actual suppression of *Compulsion* for several years I learned only by accident, after the suppression was in effect. A bookdealer asked me why his orders for

228

Compulsion were not being filled. I joked about this with my publisher, "Don't you people want to sell books?"—and was told that they had tacitly withdrawn the book from the market, not because of any court order, but because one of their lawyers felt that while the case was under adjudication, some judge to whose court it came might be put off by the book's being still on sale!

Here was a book on the reading lists of various universities as literature, sociology, psychology, criminology—and it was unobtainable! I seemed destined to encounter every imaginable form of repression. In outrage, I argued that by such timidity any book could be suppressed—all one had to do was file a lawsuit. I could not help but remember that my first novel, *Reporter,* had been withdrawn at the threat of a lawsuit.

Things were not that simple, the lawyers pointed out. In the protracted *Compulsion* case, a Chicago judge had sustained Leopold's complaint against the use of his name and image in advertising, linking him to my fictional character. The judge agreed that part of the profit could rise from such use. A trial would have to be held to determine the amount that was owed. Thus the publishers, bookdealers, and film people were in a precarious situation and might even be faced with punitive damages should the book continue to be sold during this period.

At last another Chicago judge, Abraham W. Brussell, after studying the complex legal motions and counter-motions for a year and a half, together with the whole background of the fictional use of real persons, issued a lengthy analysis of the important trend in modern documentary literature toward a merging of inventive fiction with factual material. There could be no distinction, in purpose, between fiction and nonfiction, as was claimed, and there was no ownership of events; all life was open to the writer. The existing libel laws were adequate protection against abuse, and no further restrictions could be

229

imposed. Judge Brussell also dismissed the claim for compensation connected with the use of Leopold's name and image in advertising. There need be no trial.

Remarkably clear in its definition of invasion of privacy, this was surely a landmark decision in liberating writers and publishers from a growing threat. Costly and protracted, the battle provided a precedent for literary freedom.

After the long lapse, *Compulsion* appeared again. The book had been taken over by a different paperback house, and when I looked at the signature on the contract, I was startled to see the name of the editor, a man who had come over from McGraw-Hill—none other than that same Robert Kuhn who had rejected *Compulsion* at the very start, with the letter that had nearly killed me.

But at least, one suppression had been lifted.

* * *

That summer we made a car trip in the Soviet Union—the whole family. It was the best of summers; the Russians were warm and goodhearted, the countryside glowed, the cities were stimulating—we encountered no gloom. It was the time of the thaw, and for me an interlude of escape from the obsession. Tereska and the kids made great friends in Moscow's enormous outdoor swimming pool. Dominique had exhilarating discussions with young people around the university. Mikael became a photographer, and met with no restrictions except when he took a picture of a village drunk and a citizen promptly pounced on him and demanded the negative. I myself in my open-neck shirt was highly flattered when the *maître d'hôtel* stopped me at the entrance to the bar in the Hotel National in Moscow and said, "Tovarich, this place is only for foreigners."

And also, I met a fairly wide assortment of Jews.

230

We drove straight east from Paris, virtually not stopping through Germany, and in Poland I at long last saw Auschwitz. Somehow in all my tracing and filming of the Jewish fate, during and just after the war, I had not come to this ultimate point. Though I had imagined I knew Auschwitz from the minute details Ida Lehv had given me when I wrote her story in *Eva,* and also from Ka-tzetnick's *House of Dolls* and a dozen other books, it remained what none of us can ever know.

Group-visit buses took people to a compound of brick barracks, the part that had been the Auschwitz camp itself, where countless prisoners, mainly Poles, as well as some of the Jews, had been "processed." We joined the tour. Tortured in this hole, shot against that wall, marched in and out of this gate to the factories, slave labor. Yet this was not the worst. In the literature of Jewish survivors the area is called Auschwitz-Birkenau, and it was at the Birkenau spur, a few miles away, that the death-processing took place.

Their tour didn't stop in Birkenau. We found ourselves walking alone through the lanes of destroyed barracks, and over the flattened remnants of brick rubble on the enclave where the chimneys had stood. A few long sheds were still intact, cleaned now and barren inside. On the area perimeter, a tourist bus rolled by for a glance at this most concentrated of killing grounds, but this after all was primarily a Jewish affair.

The railway spur ended at an unloading platform as at any processing plant. Here the families, families like ours, arriving, had been administratively divided, as it might have seemed to them, the men separated from the women and children, still not certain it was the moment of final parting. Here, the two streams passed before Dr. Mengele or his wand-waving assistants, to labor, or to the "showers."

The walk was short to where the shower-building had stood. Right up against the edge of the area we walked, and beyond

231

the edge a peasant was working in his thriving field of cucumbers, the soil still fat from heavy deposits of fertilizing ashes.

We drove straight onward, on a good wide road to Brest, the way Napoleon's armies had gone, the way Hitler's armies had gone. And on this road, fleeing before Hitler, tens of thousands of Polish Jews had managed to save themselves in the Soviet Union before the border was sealed off.

A nice ride in peacetime, and at the border checkpoint we waited only an hour or so, chatting pleasantly with French and Danish tourists who were also making the USSR car-trip, some with elaborate camping equipment.

Then, all rubber-stamped and briefed, with a map of the main road network that was permitted to motor tourists, with a list of our overnight car-camp stops, and our city-hotel stops, we drove into Brest for our first night.

Hardly had we settled into our vast room in a comfortable oldish hotel when a knock came—surely an interrogation or a KGB inspection? (Who knows, say the sophisticates, perhaps that's exactly what it was.) A nice middle-aged lady said she had noticed the Jewish name, Levin, on the register. She was employed in the hotel, and if we didn't mind, she was eager to hear about Jewish life. Though she had nothing to complain of in her own life as it had worked out, she said, with a smiling little Jewish sigh, there sometimes comes a yearning to hear a Jewish word. She was one of those who had fled into Russia from Poland at the outbreak of the war, she and her family. A young girl then, she had been sent with the family and a whole group of Jews to a refugee camp in Siberia. They had worked, yes, life had been hard, but no harder for them than for the Russians; after the war her parents had gone back, and from Poland they had emigrated to Australia. Meanwhile she had fallen in love with a Russian—no, not Jewish, she added with that curious inflection that always has in it a defiant touch of "I don't regret it, I'm not apologizing." But we could under-

232

stand—a Jew has a hankering sometimes to hear about Jews. She had children. Her smile broadening, she took out a photograph of her eldest, a round-faced, very serious-looking teenage girl with glasses. "She's first in mathematics," the mother proudly declared. "A *Yiddische kopf*."

That was really about all. Regarding ourselves she didn't pry, though I told her a bit about American Jewry and also about Israel. The woman went off, with another Jewish sigh, and good wishes for our journey. Tereska said to me, "Well, so you worried about how you were going to manage to meet any Jews! So Jews in the Soviet Union are terrified of talking to foreigners!"

The next morning we drove to Smolensk, still straight on the broad flat invasion route. At the tourist office we asked for a guide to show us the city, and were assigned a university student specializing in English. He took the boys for a ride on the miniature railway in the Park of Culture, then showed us the new apartment blocks built over the wartime rubble, and the historical church.

Levin with his mania had, then, to observe that Smolensk had once been a fairly important center for Jewish study and culture; was there a Jewish community left? Oh, doubtless there were Jews, but they lived like everybody else—not in any special area; there was no longer a ghetto.

Fine, I agreed. But was there a synagogue I might visit, perhaps an old one? Preserved, like the church?

Ah, synagogue—yes, there had been a synagogue, our guide believed, but it had been moved. He even took the trouble to inquire at the Intourist office but with no luck. No one seemed to know where the synagogue might be found.

We drove to our car-camp. A mixture of motel and camping ground, it was attractively laid out, with clean, charming huts among the trees. No Holiday Inn, no swimming pool, but group showers and toilets as in a kibbutz. Bedding and blankets were available, as we had been informed, for a few pennies' overnight rental, and there was a modest restaurant as well as a food-supply shop with cooking facilities.

Exploring the Ping-Pong and volleyball areas, the kids instantly picked up friends, young Russians who wanted to try their English, and we discovered that these car-camps were filled not with foreign tourists but perhaps 80 percent with Russians. Who were the Soviet car owners? Engineers, a few doctors—Jewish, one turned out—from Moscow. And there were groups of vacationers and students who didn't have cars but came by bus.

From a neighboring hut emerged a tall, distinguished-looking man, speaking a fairly good English; he teased us a while to guess his profession, and finally declared, "I am a clergyman." The "pope" of a Moscow church, he insisted we visit him when we reached the city, and there his wife was to overwhelm us with a magnificent dinner; seven years later, when Mikael returned with a student group, the friendship continued.

As for my Jews—while we stood watching the Ping-Pong game, a man of about my own age, an engineer in mass-housing construction, told me of his life. He was doing well enough—look, he had a car, and a good apartment in Moscow. True, it sometimes seemed to him that were he not a Jew he might by now have advanced higher in his field, that he had been bypassed for lesser men. But how could one judge such things? He had been a lieutenant in the war, he had fought not far from here, in that very Smolensk where I had been this morning. As a young man he had lived in a Jewish cultural atmosphere—his parents were deeply interested in the Yiddish theater and literature, though not particularly religious. He, not at all. Well, he had intermarried. A grown son. When the time came, his son had opted to have the classification "Jew" omitted from his identity papers. As I knew, the children of mixed marriages had this choice when they reached sixteen

234

and received their own papers. Over 90 percent, he would guess, chose not to be stamped as Jews.

It will all die out, he said with a tinge of nostalgic regret. After us, after our generation, it will all die out. Perhaps it was not so important. Sentimental memories. The food. The Jewish customs at home. The holidays. Childhood. Then he added, under his breath, "I confess to you, sometimes I feel there is no meaning in my life."

In Moscow we did all the standard things—joined the line at Lenin's tomb, shopped in the crowded department stores and in the special foreign currency stores. We were intrigued by a mildly satirical comedy about bureaucracy, we saw the visiting Leningrad Ballet in the beautiful new theater in the Kremlin area, modern amidst the spires, more elegant than Radio City Music Hall.

The film festival was in progress, and in the elevator a beaming beautiful woman, a star, cried out my name. Stella Adler, warm and as always overwhelming. Even here my inner switchboard turned on—Anne Frank: she must know the whole inside of the affair from Harold Clurman. I managed to keep myself from bringing it up. We had tea, and I introduced the star actress to our Tanya, the guide for our Moscow stay, who regarded me with new respect.

Tanya soon confided to us that she too was Jewish, as were many of the Intourist guides, perhaps because of the Jewish facility with languages. Black-haired, young, attractive, always ardently telling us of her Komsomol activities, one day Tanya with a curious touch of shyness said she had a question to ask us. Her mother, a designer, had told her things about Jewishness, remembered from her own youth. Was it true that Jews had a little talisman nailed to their doorposts, a talisman called a metso—-Mezuzah, I filled in. Yes, I said, observant Jews put one at every door.

Did we?

Why, no.

But hadn't we come from Israel?

I explained that not all Jews in Israel were religious. Tanya gazed at me unbelievingly.

That day I asked if she could take us to the synagogue. Honestly—Tanya was really honest with us, and already a dear friend—she didn't know where it was. But there were even tourist buses that went there, I said. Surely it was all right for her to take us. Well, she knew the general neighborhood, and directed us to it.

Since we were not observant, why seek, everywhere, for the synagogue?

Where else, how else, does a Jew interested in meeting Jews reach them when he is in a foreign land? True, in America he could look in the phone book under *Jewish* and find community centers, schools, institutions. In a large city he could pick up an English-Jewish weekly. Or he could walk around until he saw a Goldstein's Drug Store, go in and start a conversation. We had already, quite by accident, and from the very first day, encountered a few Jews in the Soviet Union, but they were quite assimilated and detached from whatever remnant there might be of a Jewish community. Like almost all the Jewish visitors to this land, even those who had little interest in Judaism at home, we were bound to take the synagogue route, though we knew that what we would encounter there would not be typical of what was happening to the general Jewish population.

Again, I admonished myself, approaching the side street that had been indicated to me, let there be no distortion in my thinking. One synagogue, or even two, for a city the size of Moscow with half a million Jews, could hardly be said to signify Jewish continuation. There were, I had been told, perhaps a dozen rabbinical students at most, in the academy here

236

that was the only one in Russia. Obviously even this pathetic remnant of religious continuation would soon die out.

As we turned into the street, a gaunt man with burning eyes seized my arm and began a tirade. All these Jews here were virtual apostates, not a true pious Jew among them! From his frayed pocket he produced a postcard, thrusting it under my eyes. It had Hebrew writing, an Israeli stamp. See, he had contacts there, look at this postcard! That proved I could rely on him; I must not listen to what others would tell me—

As we reached the synagogue with its broad flight of outer stairs, he suddenly dropped my arm and vanished. Another Jew, small, excited, hurried up to me. I mustn't listen to that informer! He was a spy, an informer, what had he asked me? Both of them, it seemed to me, were straight out of Dostoievsky.

We had come on a weekday; the synagogue was empty. A fairly familiar, solid-looking building, just the kind that the immigrants from here had built on New York's East Side, on Chicago's West Side. In the dim hallway there were a few elderly and a few very old men, who paid no attention to us, but one middle-aged whisperer, near the entrance, was trying to buy Tereska's Polaroid camera.

"With this I could go around the villages and make a good living."

"But where would you get film?"

"I'll get it, I'll get it, don't worry, only sell me the camera."

Returning on Sabbath morning, we found the shul almost filled, and after the services many of the worshipers lingered on the stairs, as at any synagogue, having a bit of talk, while several gathered around us, mentioning names of relatives in America. Did we perhaps know of them? An ordinary group of Jews, like those around a shul anywhere. The Moscow remnant of the observant. No one asked us to his house.

237

By sheer chance, while visiting the art museum we met a girl we knew in New York. She had already contacted an aunt in Moscow whom she was going to visit the next day, and she agreed to ask whether she might bring us along.

The uncle, meeting us at her hotel, insisted that we remove the tourist-badge cameras slung from our shoulders. Nor should we approach his apartment house in our own car. We must take a cab.

The apartment was almost identical to that in any housing development in Israel or to the old WPA housing in the United States, except that it was more crowded with furniture. A room plus an alcove and a shared kitchen. By a great stroke of luck, their married son had received an apartment in the same building—we went upstairs to be shown the brand new furniture. Another son lived with the parents, his bed curtained off. He worked as a mechanic but was going to night school to become an engineer. Everyone's sons and daughters seemed to be taking engineering courses. There was a grown daughter, too, in her mid-twenties; she had a closetlike cubicle of her own.

Taking us aside, the mother confided how difficult it was for a Jewish girl to get a suitable husband these days; a Jewish girl wasn't keen to marry a Russian, as they were all drunkards; meanwhile the Russian girls were stealing away all the Jewish boys because Jewish boys were known to be serious and responsible and made good husbands. See, her daughter, so attractive and already working as an engineer, was still unmarried at twenty-four.

"A new Jewish problem for you," Tereska whispered to me.

Later the son walked us to a taxi. His Yiddish was fair; we managed. What were his interests? Oh, between his job and his night studies he had little time for other interests. He was not interested in politics. As for Jewishness, he was irreligious. His friends? Well, truth to tell, he had only a small circle of friends. Did he mind if we asked whether they were Jewish, or

238

was it a mixed circle? He had never thought about this aspect, he mumbled.

I plunged. If it were possible to leave for Israel, did he think many Jews would want to go? He shrugged. Maybe some of the old folks. He had never discussed it. Departing, he was quite friendly. America, he smiled, what was being done there in electrical engineering? One day he would like to see.

We went to visit the housing engineer we had met in the car-camp. A better apartment, with its own kitchen. An opulent tea-with-cakes. He showed us his treasures, art books, some bronze figurines. We talked art and literature. It was a pleasant, cultured afternoon, like anywhere. He didn't mind at all that we drove up in our own car and parked it in front of his apartment block. He was eager for Mikael to take pictures of us together, right in front of the house.

There was one obvious source for the word on Russian Jewry, and I betook myself to the offices of the *Sovietische Heimland,* the literary magazine published in Yiddish. Its editor, Vergalis, whose name was a hate-word in passionate Jewish-survival circles, was absent, but I was received by an assistant who seemed most eager to know about American Jewish authors. As I expected, he hadn't heard of me, nor of any others except Mike Gold and, oddly, Budd Schulberg. I mentioned Irwin Shaw, Norman Mailer, Herman Wouk, Malamud, Angoff. He asked if there was anyone I wanted to meet. I replied that I would like an interview with Ilya Ehrenburg. Promptly, he put in a call to the Writers Union, but nothing ever came of it. However, when I said I hoped to get to Vilna, as my parents had come from that region, I was given the name of a poet to contact there. I departed with a few copies of *Sovietische Heimland,* and dutifully read through them. It was a careful magazine, with essays on Peretz and other past Jewish cultural figures, a piece on Yiddish as a people's literary language, a long story about a *shtetl* Jew in the days before the revolution who had a huge family and gave one of his sons into apprenticeship with a passing circus, and then the boy grew up to be an acrobat, and organized the circus workers. When the train bringing Lenin from Finland arrived in Petrograd it was he who climbed a high pole and unfurled the red flag.

In Leningrad I again took the synagogue way. Behind a magnificent old wrought-iron fence, the edifice loomed huge and ornate, with an air of dilapidated grandeur. A few upper windows were broken.

In a small office, one of the elders, after mild, generalized exchanges, suddenly broke out to me, "You know what happened two years ago? You know?" The *shamus* had allowed a tape recording to be made by someone who then took it to Israel. A few months later, that same *shamus* had been arrested and sent away for ten years. Did I want the rest of them to be sent away? Leave us alone. Everything is fine. Fine.

But passing me on the stairs, a man muttered, "Follow me, but from a distance." Then in a side street he gave me a rendezvous for the next day. "Bring me a shirt. I'll tell you everything. Write it to the world, write it."

We met the next day and sat on a bench. First he seized the shirt and stowed it under his jacket. Then there poured out involved, bitter tales; he was a tinsmith, there was discrimination on the job, he got insults, *Zhid* from the other workers. Then the usual complaints. Jews couldn't rise on the job, couldn't get into the better universities, into the medical schools—"Write it all down. Write, write, let it be known." Vaguely I had the feeling he might be telling me what he believed I wanted to hear. But he already had the shirt. "Jews—do you see any in high office in the Party? And diplomats?" It echoed, oddly, as from America in the thirties. Jews can't get into the diplomatic service, into banks, into medical

240

schools. Something more echoed from my childhood in Chicago: sheenie, yid! *Zhid*!

In the parking lot in front of our hotel the attendant, because of our foreign car license, began a conversation. Yes, a Jew. Yes, contented. Yes, Jews had their culture—the *Sovietische Heimland,* an excellent magazine, he read it regularly. Like everywhere, there were malcontents, I mustn't take them seriously. Didn't we have anti-Semitism and also much intermarriage in America?

In another car-camp a stocky, open-faced man was hosing his vehicle, singing. (Car owners are required to keep their machines spotless. Otherwise, a ticket.) I had been shamed by the family into cleaning our car as well, and as he handed me the hose, we got to talking, arriving soon enough at Levin's inevitable subject. Jews? Look at me! Party secretary in my town. A car. Anyone can rise! To the highest post! Don't listen to all that nonsense!

Every descendant of immigrants, visiting the old country, has a compelling desire to arrive at his place of origin, the town, the hamlet, the very house, if possible, from which his people came. But for their migration, he too might have been born in this place, here he might still be leading his life.

To Vilna I went alone, taking the plane. It could have been the two-engine hop from Chicago to Springfield, Illinois, cruising over the green-sectored grainland and the darker free-form patches of forest. But this flight was from Moscow to Vilna, and I strained for some emanation from the past to rise toward me, some evocation of my forebears who seventy years ago had migrated from this territory. No one from either side of the family had been left here, I had always been told. And yet the ancestral pull seemed to reach up to me, perhaps even from the days of the Gaon of Vilna, sage of sages.

241

Down there in that forest patch, maybe, stood the mansion of the legendary Polish baron who buttoned a terrified Jewish peddler inside a bearskin and made him dance with a real live bear—who, in the comical version of the tale, calmed his partner with some curses in Yiddish.

Or maybe below me was the forest of the Vilna massacre.

Did anything remain of the fabled Jewish atmosphere of this town of the Gaon, this town of Litvak swift-mindedness, of Jewish learning and theatricality?

Perhaps instinctively, I took a turn away from the modern-fronted Vilnius hotel and the big movie and the lighted shops into winding cobbled lanes. "I've come to it," something inside me said. These curtained window-doors, surely these had been shopwindows with Hebrew lettering, and perhaps a Chagall-esque shield swinging above, sign for a bookbinder, a glove-maker. Chagall's style had been evolved, a Russian at a Paris café had once told me, from the naïve picturings on such shop-signs.

I wandered into the old ghetto, the same ghetto in which the Jews had been penned for slaughter, and Jews still lived here, for I caught a snatch of Yiddish from a courtyard entrance. A tall man with a strong, stony, yet sensitive face was talking to a housewife, a shapeless woman with only a few teeth, but with the enduring bloom on her cheeks of the gushing good heart. I passed them, hesitated, returned, and said I was a fellow Jew from America and Israel.

At once I was engulfed. Four, five, more Jews appeared from nowhere. They gazed on me as though I were the legendary emissary to Jews in distress, Elijah, who had come in the guise of a tourist. Please! cried the woman. I must honor her house—what a guest! And she hustled me into the courtyard.

There it was, unchanged since Sholem Aleichem. Up crazily

242

crooked stairways we climbed three flights, while the good woman kept apologizing for making me walk so high to her dwelling.

There came an authentic wisp of baking odor, ginger-cake, the *lekach* that melts in your mouth with tea.

There was the oilcloth-covered table, and the worn leather couch, and the glass-paned cupboard with a tumbled pile of Yiddish books and papers. All this had been carried to America. I was home.

Five, six, of them were around the table; they poured out their stories, their hearts. From pockets came letters, snapshots, addresses of relatives in Israel, in America. They showed me their Yiddish newspaper, smuggled in from Poland. "There, with 30,000 Jews, they have Yiddish papers. Here, with three million, we have none!" In this city that had worn the crown for Jewish learning, they could not even have a *cheder,* a teaching-room for their children. Forbidden. Schooling was in Russian, Polish, or Lithuanian, Vilna being a city of mixed national backgrounds. "So a Jew," one of the men said drily, "has a free choice of being any of three things except a Jew."

"More tea?" My *balabusta* waved off her neighbor's complaints. A guest from Israel! Why talk about troubles here? I must tell them every detail of the homeland. What about the waters of the Jordan, that the Arabs were trying to block off? Why was Ben-Gurion still quarreling with Eshkol? They had all the news, they listened to *Kol Yisroel,* to the special broadcasts.

If by some miracle the gates were opened, I asked, would the Jews of Russia go to Israel? "I would crawl on my knees!" one said. But the man I had first talked to on the street, pointed out quietly, "Of the younger ones, who knows how many? It may already be too late. They are making their lives here. And we older ones, what do they need with us? Look around you, nearly all of us here are already on pensions."

243

Yes, in this the Russians were fair. "We receive pensions, medical care, everything fairly. In Israel we would only be a burden."

Some years later, when the miracle happened, the remaining Jews of Vilna were among the first to take the risk of asking for visas, and the greatest number of them left. Many of the younger generation, too.

I was walking back to the hotel with the first man I had met, the tall one; did I perhaps know the writer Sholem Asch, he asked? Yes, I knew the family. They were his cousins, he said. At one time he had thought of going to them in America. "Tell me," he asked, "in America can you have such a thing as a Jewish club?"

I tried to describe the hundreds of organizations, community centers, card-playing clubs, study groups, B'nai B'rith, women's clubs, Hadassah. We paced the winding street. Along here there was a remnant of the Nazi ghetto wall. And on this cleared-off lot, where a small ferris-wheel stood among some booths, there had once been a great synagogue. All along here, the finest shops.

Now my friend told me his own story: he had been in the forests with the partisans throughout the war. There his wife had died. But he had afterward brought her to the old Jewish cemetery, where the Gaon had lain for centuries. Now lately the authorities had moved the Jewish cemetery, and the Gaon's grave too, and so he had moved his wife to a new grave.

The man's loneliness weighed so heavily on me that I felt the extinction of all the Jewry of Vilna within myself, and fled into the hotel, and lay exhausted in the dusk.

In the morning the Intourist guide conducted me on the standard tour. I gazed at a whole new area of apartment blocks. I visited the old university. With our time half-ended, I asked when we would be going to the forest. But that was not on the schedule, he said. Of course many tourists did go there—it was not at all forbidden—and we went back to the Intourist office for the special permit.

This was the same route the Jews had taken, then, hardly a half-hour's truck drive into the countryside and into the woods. My guide seemed not to have been here before, and fell into silence as we followed a trodden path to the clearing, and the rim of a pit already half-filled with drifted earth. Grass had grown back after the excavation of the corpses.

A bit further on, amongst the dense trees, there was another such pit, and from there we circled back to a log hut, the museum.

On the walls were German soldiers' snapshots, the sort that could be seen in so many books about the massacres: a few uniformed men in the foreground smiling for the picture, while blurred in the background a naked woman bent, half-balanced, over the edge of the pit.

There were charts, ruled vertically and horizontally. Samples of monthly reports that had been found, from the year 1942. The vertical columns represented the disposition of prisoners: jail, labor battalions, deportation to civil or military prisons elsewhere; there was even a column marked "freed." But the final column was headed "special handling."

Horizontally, various categories of prisoners were listed: Partisans, Communists and Marxists, Saboteurs, Resistance Members, Terrorists, Spies, Jews, Helpers of Jews.

Unlike the other classifications, the Jewish line was blank all the way across, except for the "special handling" column which, for that particular month, bore the number 4,230.

Some 70,000 Jews of Vilna had been assassinated here, out of a total of 100,000 dead that included all the other prisoner classifications.

On a table lay a signature book for visitors, and I noticed the remarks of the last tourist, a woman from Brooklyn. Why isn't there more recognition, she demanded, for the fact that it was only the Jews who were slaughtered here as a group? Why

245

is it made to seem that they are just one part of what happened to everyone else?

Another sheet caught my eye. A neatly typed list of names, each with a check mark before it. They were in alphabetical order, and numbered, down to 349. One batch. Special handling. I could not help running my eye down to the L's. Yes. Someone named Levin. A common enough name, in our ancient city of Vilna.

*   *   *

In Moscow, a subway poster announced that the great Yiddish singing star Anna Gusika was making her annual appearance with her troupe.

The theater, in a Park of Culture, was a large barnlike hall with benches; the audience consisted mostly of quiet-looking elderly couples, not unlike, I told myself, those one might see in some unchanged sector of Brooklyn. In front of us sat a bright-looking well-dressed youthful pair, again, not unlike the Columbia and Barnard offspring of the Brooklynites, taking an interest in the vanishing culture of the older generation. For now in America, also, I pointed out to myself, how often, and where, would you see a Yiddish troupe?

The play, to which songs had been added, was, naturally, something by Sholem Aleichem, the approved Jewish author in the Soviet Union. "Wandering Stars," one of his lesser works, was about a pair of separated lovers, actors who wander the world, America included, and at last by chance meet again. The tale had been converted into a sort of musical centered around Anna, a tiny, electric woman who performed in the declamatory, arm-waving tradition of the Yiddish stage. Her company consisted of a pianist, a romantic lead, and a comedian.

A high point was the satiric song about the *goldeneh medina*, the golden land, America. During the sentimental

246

scenes one heard good Jewish sighs and groans from all around the dark hall. But the greatest response came at a moment one felt had been awaited, as though the audience had journeyed to hear this portion the way devotees return to hear a certain aria in an opera. At one crisis in her wanderings, Anna took the center of the stage and declaimed, "A Jew I was born and a Jew I will always remain!" Shrieks, howls, applause, filled the dark cavernous hall as from some vast pitlike repository of souls; again and again the actress tried to continue, but it was some time before the demonstration subsided. Next to me, an *altichke* in a babushka sat wiping her eyes.

During the intermission we picked up a conversation with the young couple who had been seated in front of us. They knew only a little Yiddish, but they managed to follow. This was the first time they had come to a Jewish performance, and it was out of curiosity to see the perennial Anna, who visited Moscow every year. She and her company toured the cities; there were one or two other such troupes, it seemed, still performing in Yiddish, appearing occasionally here and there.

A young man joined the conversation. Anna was the last, he declared. Did we know how old she was? Eighty! Impossible to detect—no? Anna was fantastic. She had been performing for sixty years! His father and grandfather had seen her in their youthtime! As to Yiddish theater, in his city, Kovno, there existed an amateur group. Factory workers mostly, they put on plays a few times a year. In Kovno, in Lithuania, there was still a Jewish life.

He had come to Moscow to take an examination to enter a technical school. In Kovno, he could tell us, even the young generation spoke Yiddish at home. The Bible was taught at home, and also some Hebrew. "There in Kovno I feel like a Jew, here in Moscow, no."

And he? If it became possible, would he go to Israel?

"To Israel? I would walk the whole way!"

All right, don't exaggerate, I told myself. A spark remained.

In Kiev, after being conducted to the famous monastery, we asked our guide to show us Babi Yar. There was nothing to see, really, the woman explained, just an empty field. There were plans for a memorial, but meanwhile there was nothing to see. If we insisted, we could take a taxi by ourselves; the place was just beyond the old Jewish cemetery. A shallow ravine.

Nothing. As she had said, an empty, shallow ravine, weed-grown. Behind it were rows of standard apartment buildings. In the empty area, a few children were at play.

To find the synagogue I went to a grayish section of Kiev's lower town where, back in the days of the Czars, Jews had been permitted to reside. The synagogue, reached through a shabby little yard, was barren, but with an incongruously elaborate chandelier all lit up, emphasizing the emptiness. A scant *minyan* of aged men, the quorum of ten, was beginning the evening prayer. I stood alongside one of them, and he whispered demandingly, "Did you bring anything? Prayer-books?" I said no, nothing. "We need prayerbooks, *taliesim*! A visiting Jew should bring!" Then he left off his pretense of prayer and complained, "Don't listen to what the leaders tell you! On the surface all is correct, we receive our pensions. You see all the lights lit—do you think this is usual? We get no funds for upkeep. But a visitor from America is here! Do you see any young people? If a young man comes—he soon will have his job taken away. We old ones are the last. Judaism is being choked to death—" And suddenly he began to sway. "Ignore me! Don't look at me! Say the prayers!" he hissed, under ritual phrases, and I noticed, then, the imposing figure of the community leader who had received me on

248

arrival; he came smilingly up the aisle, nodding as he passed me, as though to say, "You see, as I told you, all is well."

We drive then in a westward arc through the vast grainland, the Ukraine, golden-cropped, like Kansas. On the flat broad road we sometimes had to squeeze past enormous combines; off the road we saw groupings of vast barns, dairy buildings, of the collectives. At the crossroads there were billboards announcing crop goals, or bearing portraits of local champions in pig-raising. And what handsome bus stops, with mosaic walls!

Again and again I recognized place-names from Yiddish literature, from Hasidic tales; this was the heartland, this was the area where Jews had been permitted to live in the *shtetlach,* their townlets, in the long swath of territory called the Pale of Settlement that the Czars had taken from Poland.

We came to the Carpathian foothills; here Hasidism had been born, here had grown the folk tales that I had retold in *The Golden Mountain.* I sought out the town of Okup, where the founder of the wondrous movement, Rabbi Israel the Baal Shem Tov, had resided. So much passion for God, so much wisdom, so much joy, once centered here! A neat town with its rows of frame houses. As in all these towns, not one Jew remained.

It was from this area, too, that Yitzhak Chizik's family, after the pogroms of 1905, had left for Palestine. I was beginning to get the feel of it. I would be able to start the novel on getting home.

Passing a small lake, we stopped for a picnic lunch. Nearby were a few dozen bathers, and they laughingly urged us to go in. How friendly, how good, were these people! I must put away the past with its pogroms, I must even put away the thought of the notorious volume lately published by a scientific institute in Kiev, with its hook-nosed caricatures and its

249

"truth" about Jewish capitalists and their worldwide plot to rule mankind.

Strolling along the edge of the water, we came to another car, a Volga, its front wheels hub-deep in the lake as the owner washed the vehicle. Nearby sat his wife, watching over a rather pallid little boy with huge black eyes, who was timorously wading. "Customers for you," Tereska teased.

Indeed they were Jews on vacation from as far away as Lvov. The wife's family had come from hereabouts, and though none were left in the town, she remembered this little lake, and liked to return occasionally.

It was once an area of Hasidim, I remarked, to show my fund of knowledge. Ah, indeed. Her grandfather had been a *tsadik,* there in Okup. From as far as Kharkov, Jews had come to him. All that life was gone. Nothing was left.

Really, nothing at all? I asked.

Nothing, the husband said. The Jews were all in the cities. Didn't I know how it was with Ukrainians? Did I imagine they had changed? He gazed over toward the boisterous group of bathers.

The little boy came out of the water, examining us uncertainly with his glistening eyes. I remembered a sentimental story by Sholem Asch called "Jewish Eyes." At once, Tereska had known.

And Israel? I asked my question.

The Jew shrugged. "In Lvov it isn't bad. I live well enough."

I recalled the book by Leon Wells, whom I had met at the Eichmann trial, about the burial pit for the massacred Jews of Lvov. There he had been forced to labor in a slave *Kommando,* excavating and burning bodies. So again there were Jews in Lvov.

What was his occupation? I asked the Jew.

A manager. In the old Jewish trade—clothing manufacture.

Not a large plant. But large enough. There was a touch of cupidity in his smile.

And the car? Did it belong to the plant?

No. His own. Private.

To be able to buy a car, how did one manage?

He shrugged. Such things weren't too difficult. *Goyisheh kep* were still *goyisheh kep*. One could arrange to sell part of the goods outside. Lvov was on the border and goods could easily be disposed of.

This vast broad stairway rising from the port, here in Odessa, I lectured the children, was world-familiar through the great revolutionary film, *Potemkin*. Everyone remembered the scene of people being mowed down, and a baby carriage careening down these stairs.

But in my own mind I pictured a different scene, with small groups of *chalutzim* leaving for Palestine from Odessa; down these stairs, lugging their bundles and baggage, Yitzhak Chizik's family must have gone. And this was the city of the poet Bialik, who had left off his youthful romantic versifying to howl and thunder, after the massacre at nearby Kishinev, to weep and excoriate, in "City of Slaughter," over the timid, pallid Jews who did not raise an arm against the pogromists. This was the city where a young journalist, Jabotinsky, had joined the early self-defense units, churning out leaflets, appeals for young Jews to stand and fight when drunken hooligans once more attacked. This was the city of the giantlike bullheaded Ushishkin, whom I had interviewed in Palestine in 1929; here in Odessa he had become the leader of the "action group," impatient with political approaches, pioneers who went to the land to build it brick by brick, tree by tree.

Here, too, in that same time, young Trotsky, Lev Bronstein, son of a well-to-do Jewish farm operator, had come to study, and become a revolutionist.

251

Alongside a factory, I found the remaining relic of a synagogue, with its few elderly pious Jews. The same tales of a dying-out. Then, when we parked on the city's outskirts at a public beach, a man with two boys came along, gazing at the foreign car, venturing a word in Yiddish.

In America, he had heard, everyone, even all the workers, possessed automobiles. How many working days did the price of such a car represent? I told him, perhaps a hundred to a hundred and fifty days, and he nodded, thoughtfully.

He was eager to know about Israel; he listened regularly to *Kol Yisroel*. The boys knew about being Jews. Yes, if he could, he would go.

And his boys?

They answered for themselves. These two were eager.

What was one to conclude, then? Here and there I had encountered the yes to survival. But most young Jews I had met, and the ones Dominique talked to, had only a vestige of curiosity. How was any interest, any feeling of identity, to survive? Without teaching, without a living culture, without connection with history?

One by one, these remaining token synagogues would fall into disuse, and be closed. The rate of intermarriage would increase. The Russian Jews, as a mass, were past the point of no return.

Did it matter? To them?

Should not people have free choice as to their identity?

And what of us at home in America? So many attitudes here in the Soviet Union reminded me of Jewish youth in America. Wasn't our intermarriage rate in the colleges almost as high? Ah, but with us, the non-Jewish partner just as often chose to enter the Jewish fold, as the other way around. With us, the vast, organized and overorganized network of Jewish institutions, the whole pattern of suburban life with its three faith circles, kept, indeed sometimes rather drove, the Jew into identification. Yet among the sophisticated, among the aggressively internationalist politicals, weren't we going fast toward abandonment of Judaism? Would it not be only a matter of time—three generations instead of one—for the same process one saw here to bring about total assimilation? And I was back full circle facing the obsession. Weren't our American activists pursuing the same policy, by whatever devious means they could, of censoring out Jewish continuation? Hadn't they stifled Anne Frank's outcry, "We are Jews, and we want to be"? Hadn't they persisted in downgrading my work, because I stood out as a positivist, over the Jewish question?

Still for us in America, there was one more factor that favored Jewish continuation: the tie with Israel. Not only the money-giving, but also the increasingly serious interest in Judaic studies, in heritage, in history, in Hebrew language. An élite, perhaps, but a creative élite, even considerably left-wing, like the early settlers of Israel.

Strong enough to bring continuation? Survival?

Who could prophesy? But one irreducible ethic remained, so basic as to be organic, a rule of life: The natural process of identity had its inner right, and to choke it, to manipulate it, was—what other word could there be?—a form of mass extinction.

Yet this was what I had seen in this land.

And again I pessimistically concluded—it's too far gone.

I proved to be both right and wrong. Only a few weeks after our summer-long visit, another writer came from America, Elie Wiesel, and he passed through many of the same places, also making the vestigial synagogues his points of contact, and he doubtless spoke to some of the same people. Yet there was one sight more that he saw. On Simchas Torah in the street in front of the Moscow synagogue he saw the afflux of thousands of young people who had come to make this their once-a-year outpouring, their one affirmation, dancing by torchlight, danc-

ing the hora, singing in Russian, in Hebrew, in Yiddish, singing *Am Yisroel Chai!* The people Israel lives!

Even this, had I seen it, might not have convinced me. It
would surely have moved me, but, in my journalistic skepti-
cism I might have said, true, a few thousand are here out of a
population of half a million Jews. True, once a year they show
themselves and affirm their Jewishness, but perhaps most of
them come out of curiosity or for excitement. And even if
there is a core of young people who assert their identity as
Jews, can this really appreciably slow the process of disinte-
gration? What can feed their feeling? Religious they are not.
They only show themselves here once a year before the synagogue as the one place that symbolizes being Jewish. The
cultural studies, the ties with Israel, that can feed the Jewish
people in America, these are not permitted. And so, despite
these last sparks, I would have concluded, the fire will die
out.

Elie Wiesel had come out of the concentration camps,
himself an ember, a live coal that kindles a new fire. Out of all
that death, he, better than I, could believe in survival. And so
a few months later he published *The Jews of Silence,* which
caused a great stir in the outer world, and helped fan the
sparks in the Soviet Union.

In that particular, I was wrong.

I was wrong in my despairing sense that nothing of any
import could happen to change the situation, that the Soviet
Union would never allow anything more than the smallest
trickle to depart. I didn't—perhaps even Elie Wiesel didn't—
envision the protest movement that was to arise, with incredible risk and daring, from amongst young Soviet Jews themselves, a protest movement that within a few years was to
become a beacon for all democratic freedom movements. For,
the other freedom-seekers told themselves, if those Jews are
brave and strong enough to do it and to win concessions for

254

tens of thousands to leave, why, other resistance movements may also succeed!

Even after I had witnessed a spiritual survival from the Holocaust itself, this was still a teaching for me.

Yet in the mundane part, had I not after all judged correctly? That the greatest number were too far gone, and would not even care, much less strive, to resume the Jewish aspect of their lives.

Our last camp, on the approach to the Hungarian border, was the most beautiful, with sylvan walks along a broad river and charming little lodges. Hearing Tereska say something in French, an eager young man came over, a boy, really, not yet eighteen, it turned out. He was a student of the language and would appreciate an opportunity to converse. Handsome, vivacious, exuding warmth, indeed love for everyone, for the whole world, for all life itself, Boris stayed with us during our last few days in the Soviet Union. A member of a student group vacationing in the camp, Boris—it had to turn out—was Jewish. He had reminded me of someone. Of Yitzhak Chizik himself, when I had first met him as a student in Chicago. That sparkling love of life, that warmth. It turned out that Boris was also from Taraspol, where Yitzhak's people had come from. Could there even be a family connection? No, he had never heard of the Chiziks, though his own family had been Zionists. Oh, yes, his grandfather still regretted not having gone to Palestine. In their house, Boris's father had related to him, all the "big ones" had visited, Weizmann, Ushishkin. Boris knew their names. He knew a remarkable lot about Jewish history.

His father was a professor of mathematics in a small university. It had to be said that he had been transferred downward, probably because of his being a Jew. Boris felt no discomfort as a Jew, yet his best friends—we met a few—were gentiles.

255

For himself, the most vital interest in his life was French! Never out of Russia, he knew—and astonished us because he really knew—every street, every lane, in Paris. He was endlessly quoting French poetry—Baudelaire, Rimbaud, Verlaine. Someday, he dreamed, he would visit Paris. To that end, his whole life was planned. Next year, army service. Then he would teach French in a high school; he hoped one day to become a professor, and then to be sent to conferences in France, in Paris!

For several years Boris kept up a correspondence in French with Tereska. She sent him books. He finished his army service. He was teaching French in a high school, as planned. Soon he hoped—

The correspondence broke off. No answers came to her letters, and we thought it best for her not to write any more.

5

THOUGH I HAD BEEN IN ANALYSIS by now first with Dr. A and then with Dr. Sulzberger, though I had tried the infallible release and "written it all out of myself" in *The Fanatic,* though I had even signed away my ownership rights in my play, the fever remained. It smoldered, fed by the two unrelenting devils in the artist's psyche—doubt, and incompletion. Could my work after all have been unstageworthy? Related to this was the gnawing need to complete the work itself, on the stage.

Why had I not, in all these years, made the simple test of gathering together a few actors and holding a voice reading? Was I afraid? No, I had even advertised for such a test in that pathetic "challenge" in the *New York Post.* Why, then, hadn't I at least done it for myself? Is it part of the nature of an obsession always to leave one question unanswered, as a way of clinging to the sickness?

Then, fortuitously, all these questions were answered.

In Israel I had met Peter Frye, a director originally from Canada, who had also worked in New York, a personality on a large scale, burly and unafraid of battle. Peter had fought in

257

the International Brigade in Spain, and had been wounded; after that war was over, he had returned to New York and begun a promising career in television, only to have it cut off by the McCarthy blacklisting process. Then he had come to Israel, learned some Hebrew, and directed plays, eventually, for all three leading theaters, Habima, Chamber, and Ohel. Peter had married a talented actress, Batya Lancet, and had organized his own company, performing on Friday evenings in Tel Aviv in defiance of the Sabbath closing laws. He had trucked his players to the settlements and kibbutzim to carry avant-garde culture to the hinterland; a scrapper, he was always in a row, if not with the rabbinate, then with the critics, the government, or all three together.

We had met several times, but as I had in those years been trying to choke down my obsession, I had refrained from broaching the whole subject of the Diary to him. But one day over a coffee Peter said he wanted to hear the damn story, and the thing came out. Frye knew the Broadway scene, knew almost everyone involved; he had himself been a protégé of Harold Clurman, and he kept nodding and nodding, recognizing every maneuver, every twist. "I'd like to read the play," he said. "Why not have a voice reading?" I suggested.

So there it was at long last. Twelve, thirteen years.

It was an odd group that assembled at our house one evening for the reading. At first, things had looked promising. Many families of the American embassy staff were our neighbors in Herzlia, and among them was a lively young woman, Barbara Lawrence, wife of a career diplomat; Barbara was a theater bug. Wherever they had been stationed, she had managed to produce plays in English, and the walls of their house were covered with posters for everything from Tennessee Williams to Bernard Shaw, performed everywhere from Hong Kong to Rome. Just now she was directing the local Hebrew high school's English class in their annual Shakespeare production.

I gave Barbara the script. Wonderful! She simply had to do Petronella Van Daan. For Anne and Peter she had a couple of bright kids who would be perfect. Tereska and I happened to go down with the Lawrences that weekend to an archeological dig at the Dead Sea, and there we stumbled onto more participants, a visiting professor from a San Francisco college, with his wife, both avid regulars in a playreading circle at home. And despite all that had happened, I felt that I could read the role of Otto Frank.

An hour before the reading, we learned that the girl who was to do Anne was ill. After desperate calls to Embassy families with teenage daughters, Barbara located a young girl, sensitive and bright, who was willing to try. There was barely time to have her sight-read a few scenes before Peter Frye arrived.

Most of the assembled readers had not even gone through the script. Doubtless, I told myself, I was accepting all these handicaps so that if the result proved bad, I could tell myself that this had not been a fair test; I would be leaving an escape hatch open so my obsession might continue.

We began reading. The boy doing Peter Van Daan had constantly to be reminded of his turn. There was no flow, no rhythm.

Then the girl caught it. Suddenly she was Anne Frank. And from her, the others caught hold. The San Francisco professor sounded right as Van Daan, his wife as Mrs. Frank was perfectly in character, and Barbara Lawrence was the bouncy Petronella ready to go on stage. We were doing it! The play was coming through the way I had heard it, for thirteen years, in my head. I became so engrossed that I missed my own cues. This work was what I had always known it to be, through thirteen bitter, choked-up years. All the hatreds and horrors could have been avoided at the outset by one simple reading such as this.

"That's exactly why they wouldn't let you hold it," Peter

Frye said afterward. "They didn't want the play to prove itself."

He would think about what might yet be done. Of course the script still needed a bit of work—

Of course, of course! Wasn't that too what had driven me? The need to come to the next step, with a cast, with a stage. All along the script-margins I had made notes: cut, condense, clarify, reenforce. Or, here was a scene that I had doubted would hold—yes, it held; another didn't. Suddenly I saw the possibility of a parting moment between Otto Frank and his wife. And later in the night, as the changes and cuts and transfers and the new scene tumbled through my head, depression came, too. Yes, I had been right. The voice-reading had proved I had been right the whole time: the play would act— now at long last this was certain. But now I would be ridden even worse than before, as what I had proved for myself would have to be proven to the world, and who really cared? What was retrievable? And, in any case, Frank and Bloomgarden would never give permission for public performances.

I could feel Tereska rigid at my side. After the reading she had shared in the pleasure. It was good, and glowingly she had complimented the girl who had read Anne; afterward we had discussed how remarkably the characters had come through. True, Barbara was a professional, and the part was made for her, but that professor and his wife—excellent! And the boy too had finally caught the spirit. They could almost go right on the stage with it . . . there we fell silent. All that was raging through my mind she could sense, and she shrank away, rigid. For the whole fever would now inevitably flare up again, like a forest fire under a fresh blast of wind.

How could I stop what was an organic process in a writer? This piece of work was unfinished until done on the stage. The process had to follow itself out.

Peter had the play translated into Hebrew; a few months later he told me he was using *Anne Frank* as an exercise in his drama class at the University of Tel Aviv. They had reached the point of a walk-through. Yes, it went fine in Hebrew.

Summer had come. We left for Europe. I worked on *The Stronghold*.

On our return, Peter had something more to tell me. The head of the educational department of the Israel Defense Forces had approached him about establishing a soldiers' theater, something on a more serious plane than the skits and reviews that had been done until then. Many of the brightest and most popular Israeli entertainers had emerged from the army shows, and now it was thought that a real dramatic company should be formed to make use of such talent. In Tel Aviv there was a newly completed Soldiers House containing meeting rooms, a wedding hall, a restaurant—and an excellently equipped theater.

The proposed company, said the educational director, would perform not only there, but in training camps as well, and not only for the army, but in schools and immigrant centers, and for the general public too, presenting works of particular meaning for Israel. Did Peter have any ideas?

"I have just the thing to start with," Peter told him.

Shortly afterward Frye invited a group of high-ranking officers to attend a walk-through of the play at the University. The impression was profound, and he was authorized to form the Soldiers Theater and open with my version of *Anne Frank*.

"Now," said Peter, "I told them that you have the right to a production in Hebrew in Israel."

Did I?

I had originally reserved that right, and the legal trick by which it had been preempted still infuriated me. Stuck away somewhere amongst my folders, marked AF, was the final

261

settlement agreement in which I had turned over the ownership of my play to Otto Frank; didn't that document cancel
the right to production in Israel? Or could I consider that I
still had the right to my first never-done production? No, I was
not going to look, I was not going to consult lawyers; what on
earth could it matter as far as "rights" went—the nonprofit
production of a play by the Israeli Soldiers Theater? An iron
wall arose in me, against the simple act of looking in my files.
Even if the stipulation against production in Israel was total, I
couldn't obey it, any more than I could obey the stipulation
that there should be no discussion, public or private, of the
suppression issue. There was a morality of art, of life, that had
its own laws—Stop! I told myself. You just want to see your
play produced, and stop rationalizing. They did their Broadway play here, in the trickiest kind of violation, why hesitate
to retaliate? So I let Peter assume that I still held production
rights in Israel.

That sneaky Meyer Levin! You can never get him to honor
an agreement.

What might they do? Sue me? Good, let the whole thing
come to court, for once to be properly heard on the true issues
involved. Or would they simply try to have the play closed
down? Just as they had calculated that I would not have the
heart to silence Anne Frank, even in their version, when it
opened in Tel Aviv, so, even at this point, I persuaded myself
that Otto Frank would not prevent his daughter's words from
being heard, particularly as these really were her words.

And one phrase, I still insisted, exonerated me: I had
turned over the rights to Otto Frank for "proper use." What
use could be more proper?

Casting began.

I was risking the worst punishment of all—ridicule. Anything can kill a play. A few inept actors. A contrary mood in
the audience.

Peter was using a combination of amateurs and professionals. The young people, Anne, Peter, Margot, Miep, Henk, would be acted by army recruits picked for their talent but unlikely to have had any experience. This would be a performance before professional critics; Tel Aviv's reviewers were sharp. The world's best works had been performed here; the theater standard was high. They had all seen the other play in an impressive production by Habima. While Peter was an excellent director, he was working with youngsters who had never before been on the stage and a handful of pick-up professionals, far from the best, for the adult roles.

In the event, it was not from the amateurs that the danger came. In any production, if one uses young people to play young people, inexperience is likely. First and most vital was Anne. The fate of the entire effort, and my test, could depend on the girl. After a few tryouts there was little question but that we would risk it with an army girl named Shoshanah Rozen, daughter of immigrants from Persia. She had a quality so unaffected that every line seemed to come unprepared from her heart. No matter how often she repeated the text, it was as though each time the words rose in her for the first time, rose out of absolute feeling. (So it was to be, at every performance.) True, Shoshanah chopped with her arms a bit, she moved awkwardly, but when she cried out, "Oh, why must people build still bigger bombs—" she was every human crying out to eternity. In her scenes with her mother, all the misunderstanding and accusation of all generations was present, all the guilt of love inhibited by anger, all rebellion with its desperate need for tenderness. Shoshanah's tempo, with its repression, with its outbursts, needed not a word from the director. All the idealization in an adoring daughter's love for her father, all the indignant impatience at adult failure, even her father's failure to comprehend—oh, we had Anne. If Shoshanah could but play the work alone!

The father and mother, earnestly competent professionals, were suitable enough so that they would not break the illusion, and another professional, playing Dussel, the dentist, was building up a gem of characterization. The girl playing Margot had none of Shoshanah's gift, but a simple stolidity and earnestness that came through well enough in their sister scenes. As to the boy Peter, there was a heavy question mark. So much of the play depended on the development of his relationship to Anne, not for the puppy love and sexual suggestiveness that was the core of the Broadway entertainment, but for the central meaning, the growing spirit of youthful revolt against the world that adults had made for them. It was precisely in the progression of scenes between these two benighted, fumbling children, trying to find and to help each other in their rising world-bitterness, trying to understand and differentiate between the innate physical love-drive of their adolescence and the need to learn each other's character, that the meaning of my version was so distinct from the other. Nor, I was sure, had I lost any of the tenderness of their sense of young love; I had simply refrained from exposing them to vulgar laughter.

For Peter we had a young soldier, Dori Ben Zev, the son of a fairly well-known actor in Haifa. A quixotic, uncommunicative boy, he mostly walked through his part, reading his lines as though he were feeding cues, and never putting himself twice in the same position for a scene. Again and again we thought of replacing him. But as though teasing, he would, each time we had virtually decided he was too risky, come through with a rehearsal performance that fully matched Anne's.

The girl was a vessel, letting Anne live through her, but Dori, it became clear, was an artist, testing, trying different rhythms, different approaches, throwing away lines, mumbling. In New York he would have been at the Actors Studio, but here he might totally fall out of tune with the others. True, the Peter of the Diary was out of tune, desperately alone. In performance, all might turn out well, if the others could adapt to Dori's variability. Having no one else with his potential, we chanced it.

The real probelm was Petronella Van Daan. There was little to choose from just then in Tel Aviv, as the theaters were busy, so Peter Frye had settled on a character actress known for comic roles. In type, the actress suited the part, and she was intensely eager to play it; she understood perfectly well the pathetic side of the compulsively coquettish and sometimes shrewish mother of Peter, and amidst a more professional cast her comic personality might have been somewhat dissipated, but in this group, disaster threatened. She was the kind of comedienne who needed only to walk onto the stage to get a laugh. Each time she was about to speak, laughter came from the cast. Earnestly, the actress tried to hold down, to modulate, and as rehearsals progressed, we thought she was succeeding.

At last I had my chance to watch how the play moved, to make my adjustments just like any author working in the production phase. The principal scenes needed little alteration. Peter Frye and his wife, Batya, had contributed ideas to an acting version to which I at once agreed. For the opening, they had introduced a theatrical effect to set the mood. From the dim stage one heard a traditional mourner's melody, while the players filed on, gathering in a circle as though around a grave. During the chant of *El Maleh Rachamin* (God filled with compassion), the circle half opened, and from within, as though risen, the young girl stepped forward. "I am Shoshanah Rozen," she said, "and I will be Anne Frank."

No matter how many times I was to see this, there always came, as the girl appeared through the mourners' group, an anguished thrill, a presage of catharsis.

One change of considerable value, Peter and Batya had worked out in the text itself. The last two scenes had been condensed into one, and this I at once saw was wise, not only in terms of the length of the play, but of the rhythm. Too much atmosphere would have slowed the drama toward the end.

As the rehearsals progressed, I made further cuts, and also filled in a few points. One scene that I introduced, a scene between Margot and her mother, was perhaps in defiance of the whispering campaign that my version had been "Zionist." The entire scene had less than a dozen lines, and it touched on a possible underground escape to Palestine. But as it was offered for her alone, Margot refused.

Like any other family in the Holocaust, the Franks would most likely have heard of such an underground. In the very first pages of the Diary Anne speaks of her sweetheart, Harry Goldberg, who has been going to Zionist meetings; he gives them up in order to take her out walking. Later, she tells of discussions with Margot, who wanted, if she lived, to become a nurse in the Jewish homeland. If the Diary is to be taken as the representative drama of the entire Holocaust, surely this subject had to be given something resembling the place that it had in the psyche of an entire people under doom. At least for Israel, the scene belonged. Hadn't Anne's friends, those who survived, come to live here, as Margot had so wanted to do.

In the Hellman-Hackett version, Margot is reduced to a minor figure, hovering around the back of the stage, with little to say. And yet in the Diary Margot is a central personality, loved, admired, and also resented by her younger sister; Margot is continually held up before Anne—intelligent, beautiful, poised. Margot writes clever verses, Margot gets along with her mother, Margot is allowed to read advanced books— Anne even believes she has stolen Peter from Margot! Surely the sisters' hopes for the future—so divergent—must have been the subject of many discussions, and a scene of such a talk between them, while Anne practices dance movements, proved one of the most touching in the entire play.

Another change was made that provided a curious note on

what is "theatrical." In my first draft, written far back in 1952, there was a Chanukah celebration, ending in the singing of the holiday song. Like many writers, I make changes during every typing. At one point when I was begging for a test reading of my work, the Jewish Community Center theater in Buffalo wanted to stage it, and I began typing stencils for their use. When I reached this Chanukah scene, a theatrical idea struck me: during the singing, the audience would see a pair of ragged children who have broken into the outer hallway now creeping to the secret door, becoming startled by the voices, listening, then running away.

The Hackett play, when presented, had a similar Chanukah scene, interrupted by a break-in threat. During the New York courtroom trial the opposition lawyer had waved an early copy of my work which did not contain the break-in, and claimed that I had added the effect after seeing the Broadway play. It was Meyer Levin who was the plagiarist!

The culmination of all this took place now, with Peter Frye. Peter wanted nothing of the break-in scare. It was merely theatrical. It created factitious suspense and would detract from the genuinely moving effect of the Chanukah worship. In the end I left out the scare mostly because it echoed the Broadway play, even though I had added the touch long before that play was written. And because I felt perhaps Peter was right about its theatricality.

But what a gratification to work when only such were the problems!

We came to the opening. The theater was filled—an audience partly of soldiers on leave, partly of Tel Aviv intelligentsia, the press, and army officers. The Chief of Staff, at the last moment, had been kept away by one of the incidents presaging the Six-Day War.

The first act, as I had feared, was slow. What I had wanted

to evoke was a Chekhovian tension, dependent largely on the unveiling of character, but this was to become effective only in later performances.

Then, toward the end of the act, and continuously in the second act, the tension grew. Total absorption could now be felt. Peter and Anne, their scenes modulating from childish exploration to awareness, to anger at all that was around them, to clinging support of each other, were shattering. Yet as the play lifted, the grotesque quality of the comic actress playing Petronella Van Daan began to break the spell, to interfere; each time she had a line to speak I was gripped with fear for the entire enterprise. When inappropriate laughter came, there would be a shushing throughout the hall, but I still might be accused of writing a burlesque of a tragedy.

In a scene toward the end, where the entire group sits with lights out, expecting at every instant to be arrested, and they whisper their final desperate thoughts to each other, in virtual summation of the Holocaust experience, Mrs. Van Daan, in her terrified, pathetic way, declares they all ought to commit suicide and put an end to their torment. That line, from the comic actress, brought a gale of laughter.

Like some living organism striving to survive, the drama wobbled, and then rose again, coming to the closing scene with Anne and Peter at his garret window watching a massive Allied bombardment of occupied Amsterdam, and a dogfight with German planes, with Peter savagely shouting "Kill! Kill!" and Anne uttering her last, eternal plaint, "Oh, why do they make more gigantic planes, still heavier bombs, and, at the same time, build houses to replace those they destroy? Oh, why do some people starve, while in other places food is rotting in the storehouses? . . ." And with the music of "God of Compassion" rising underneath the crashing of the bombs— the catharsis was achieved.

All defects were washed away. As Anne's continuing voice

became ethereal, and her figure faded into mist, into apotheosis, the audience sat silent, stunned. I was weeping. I had, thank God, for at least this evening's interval in all these long years, been released from my personal obsession. I had totally forgotten politics, producers, betrayals, vindication. I was returned to what had happened to humanity.

The silence broke into an ovation. I found Shoshanah in the wings, in uncontrollable sobbing. Hugging the girl, I felt her entire body quivering as though she could not cease uttering those last lines of Anne Frank, her immortal, shattering outcry against mankind's increasing destructiveness.

"Oh, why do they make more gigantic planes, still heavier bombs—"

Every night it was to be like that—Shoshanah could not overcome her sobbing, her shuddering.

The reviews in Israel don't appear at once. But unlike the traditional course of events in the theater, where the second night is likely to prove a letdown, it was the second performance that struck every chord perfectly. The rhythm was there from the start. Even the mistaken laughter for Mrs. Van Daan failed to arise.

As the re-echoed "God of Compassion" began to be heard under the crashing of bombs, as the stage dimmed out, leaving only fire-flashes behind the window, and Anne's words of transfiguration came distantly while her form was barely glimpsed, ghostlike, at the window, in the profound after-silence, a rhythmic clapping began, the accolade of the European theater, but here like an assertion of survival. It went on and on, endless.

If only Otto Frank were there. If only I could have cried

out to him, You see, you see what I meant—your daughter's words—all these years—

It was still not too late to release the true Anne, the true Margot, the true people of the Diary to a kind of resurrection on the stage. All the bitterness, the hatred toward me, could at last be washed away, and with it, my obsession. If only a Judge Rifkind, a Myer Mermin, had been there. Even the Hacketts, it seemed to me in my euphoria, would have said, "Let this be seen."

A few days later we gathered the reviews. Some were almost blindly enthusiastic. Some mentioned, with understanding, the shortcomings of a few actors. But as for my text, there could remain no question: ". . . the artistic and theatrical value of this drama exists even without the lesson of the Holocaust that it brings us . . . this combination of imagination and form, this display of mastery" . . . "populated with living human beings instead of facsimiles" . . . "closer to the original . . . more honest" . . . "almost an exact transmission of the Diary."

Since these reviews bring into focus the entire issue of this narrative, of my obsession, of the degrading experiences of all these years, and even of the continued suppression of *Anne Frank,* they should perhaps be more fully presented, in what they had to say about the play itself.

AL HAMISHMAR (On Guard):

Last night nine hundred soldiers thirstily drank in the play at the Soldiers House in Tel Aviv. Were I only to stress the value of the idea and the "message" of the play, I would demean it and do it an injustice, for the artistic and theatrical value of this drama exists without the lesson of the Holocaust that it brings us. It is precisely this combination of imagination and form, this display of mastery, that adds substance and value to the entire play . . . There is no

270

moralizing in it, there are no terrors, persecutions, tortures, trials; here everything is restrained in the ordinary flow of life . . . Here hover the dreams of a young girl who couldn't resign herself to her prison and the wickedness of man and society . . . frail and solid, childish and grownup, dreamy and realistic, humble and rebellious, *Shoshanah Rozen* (Anne Frank) did not perform, she lived her role . . . Any effort at analysis in the face of this experience seems tasteless. In those two hours at the Soldiers Theater we live the short life of Anne Frank, moving, exciting, authentic.

MAARIV (Evening):

In contrast with the much less dramatic version which was approved by Mr. Frank . . . Mr. Levin's version of the Diary is populated with living human beings instead of facsimiles . . . Levin's characters achieve their full expression. The audience sat tensely through the performance . . . A profound experience.

JERUSALEM POST:

Meyer Levin's play differs considerably from the Goodrich-Hackett play which was presented on Broadway and later the world over (including Israel). It hews closer to the original; it stresses more the psychological element . . . It is on the whole a more honest dramatization than the slickly professional one we have seen before.

HAYOM (The Day):

The play as written by Meyer Levin is an almost exact transmission of the Diary. For two hours I identified myself with the theme, with the characters, with the story and the physical and spiritual hardships of the two locked-in families. The identification of the actors with the characters they embodied was unquestionable. Perhaps that is why they managed to make so powerful an impression, rising out of the concise text, every sentence rich in meaning, every word appealing to the mind and to the heart.

271

. . . Infinitely superior to the Hackett version, which put aiming for a hit above faithfulness to the sources.

The Tel Aviv correspondent of *The New York Times* cabled the story, including the "infinitely superior" quotation, to New York.

So there it was, proven, finished! I was released! It had all been a mistake in judgment from the start. No need for another version to have been written, for the suppression, for the hysteria that had come howling out of my throat, for the torments that had driven Tereska to the edge of the river.

I had fought it through. After a prolonged one-man fight, the world cries, Behold! The press tells once again the story of the man who would not give up! There would be a complete report in the theater section of the Sunday *Times,* serious discussions in the literary journals. Lillian Hellman would hasten to explain that she had made an honest mistake in evaluation. The New York Civic Theater would stage Levin's version of the Diary. The Pulitzer Prize Committee would discreetly square matters by giving my play, too, an award. All my left-wing friends who had dropped me would call me up with congratulations.

From Paul, Weiss, Rifkind, Wharton, and Garrison, there came a lengthy cease-and-desist cable to the Soldiers Theater: Meyer Levin had no rights to the Diary. They must at once close down the play.

Major B. confronted me. Didn't I have rights in Israel? In answer, I said, Did the Haganah have the right to bring surviving Jews into Palestine when the British forbade their entry?

"We cabled the lawyers that we're perfectly willing to pay royalties," the Major told me. "They insist on a closedown."

272

I explained about "proper use." I was ready, indeed eager, to have the principle tested once and for all in court.

Personally, the Major declared, he fully agreed with my attitude. He would cable apologies for the army's unwitting transgression and, pointing out the enormous educational value of the work, ask permission to continue. Again offering royalties.

Meanwhile the educational aspect was in use. Afternoons, the theater was filled with high school students brought in busloads. The performance over, question-periods ensued, sometimes with the players on the stage, sometimes with history teachers, sometimes with survivors of the Holocaust.

If these youngsters of Israel had so much to learn about the psychology of Jews in the Holocaust, how great then was the need for this experience among young American Jews, already half-alienated? And among non-Jews? In the scenes that portrayed what we now call the generation gap, the scenes between Anne and her mother, between Peter and his father, even in the final strained dialogue of the scene between Anne and her father, the empathy of the Israeli audience was total. It brought them to realize aspects that were glossed over in common discussions of the Diary—largely these aspects had to do with the effect of the experience on Peter Van Daan. Thus, in the last part, Peter reaches the rejection of all values and even of his identity, bursting out, as Anne recorded in her Diary, that after the war he would change his name so as not to be known as a Jew. "But Peter! That's not honest!" Anne cries out. And in counterpoint I had had her respond to Peter with her own remarkable avowal of faith, "It is God who has made us as we are, we are Jews, and we want to be . . ."

Wasn't this the crux of the entire Holocaust experience? The human being's right to his own identity? Against multiplied degradations that led to the final effect of his rejecting it? This the young audiences in Israel saw, and discussed as an illumination. And it was for this, more than for any other scene, I was sure, that my work had been suppressed by the politicals.

More threatening cables arrived. And now a noted law firm in Israel had been hired from New York to press for the closing.

I, too, was receiving cables but of another sort. Could the Israeli Soldiers Theater come to America to tour in the play?

An Israeli publisher wanted to bring out my text. I had to explain that Otto Frank owned it. He wrote to the owner. The reply was no.

Davar, the paper of the dominant Socialist Labor Party, wrote, *"The Diary of Anne Frank* is not the private property of her heirs, and there is a lack of taste in the legal actions against Levin over this play." Only, in Hebrew, "lack of taste" is closer to "shamefulness."

Major B. came for a talk with me. There was high-level pressure from friends of Otto Frank in America. Big donors, he hinted, were involved. I had to understand his position. In a sense the entire project of the army educational theater was now at stake. He was still with me, and he would drag things out and keep the play running while carrying on the intercontinental exchange of communications, but as to taking the issue to court, he had to inform me that the army would not do it; I had put them in an awkward position by neglecting to inform them that I did not have a clear legal right.

But what if I myself went to court? Even *Davar* said—

No, no. The idea had been mooted. No. It would not be seemly to engage in legal action involving Otto Frank. Through the army I had at last had my hearing. Now they most seriously asked me to refrain from any court action.

There were bookings as far as three months ahead in various towns, schools, camps, kibbutzim. He doubted that the run of the play could be drawn out that long. Perhaps a month. He wanted my assurance that when the pressure was

274

so strong that they absolutely had to close down, I would "make no trouble."

And why didn't I howl, fight, fight even the Israeli brass, picket, or go on a hunger strike? Here was suppression worse than before. Suppression of a proven work. The tormented nights were on me once again. Perhaps Major B. and all the others were right: I had been vindicated—now I could drop the damned affair! What more could I want?

All these years I had been haunted by the lawyer's remark, "You'll never know." Now I knew. What further need would I invent to cling to my obsession?

Why, that irreducible need, freedom of expression.

Ach, a slogan.

Pathologically obsessed or truly burdened, I could not drop the pack. You climb a peak and at the top you see a higher peak that you must climb before you can get to the other side.

During rehearsal weeks I had virtually abandoned my writing schedule, but now I went back to Beit Yanai, doing my three days a week on *Gore and Igor*, trying to work out my venom in the parable of a suppressed writer from Russia and a suppressed writer from America, both in wild flight, meeting as truck drivers at the Dead Sea fertilizer works.

Again, protest letters and letters of explanation to Otto Frank and press releases swarmed through my head. Every Friday as soon as I got back to Herzlia I started typing stencils. One of the clerks in my bank in the Old Herzlia, I had discovered, did mimeographing on the side, with a Gestetner in the front room of his little house at the edge of an orange grove. Each Friday, as soon as I appeared, he'd ask me, "Any results?" and shake his head over the silence that greeted my news releases, petitions, open letters. He had become thoroughly involved in my cause and would charge me only for paper and ink. What a scandal! to have the Israeli Army theater suppressed—and for performing *Anne Frank*! I must write to Ben-Gurion, I must appeal to the Minister of Culture! Once, he suggested that I get petitions signed by children of the age Anne had been, as they saw her in the play, and that I send these petitions to Otto Frank. Forthwith, we wrote the petition. Hundreds signed, and I sent them off. Nothing.

The world press was well represented in Israel, with special envoys and local correspondents, some of whom I knew. Perhaps long ago they had written me off as a nut on this Anne Frank thing. I wouldn't nag them, but almost every weekend as the last month went by, I left releases in their boxes at the P.I.O. Only one correspondent, a reporter from a Danish paper, called for an interview.

Had my obsession even warped my news judgment? Or had they checked with the army and been requested to let the issue drop? At last I asked a few old friends in the craft. Well, if the matter came to court, doubtless it would have to be covered. Petitions from children weren't enough.

Each time I came to the theater the actors surrounded me, begging for news. They simply could not believe the play would close down. Day after day they anxiously asked: How much longer?

I had promised Major B. I would not go to court. But this time I must at least consult a lawyer.

Now that timorousness, that fright and cowardice that is reached if one goes far enough into my nature, came into play. Something in me well knew that the kind of advice I would get—to fight, or to give in—would depend on the lawyer I approached. On the surface I had got myself the reputation of a tough fighter, and, given the timorousness I have struggled against since childhood, I suppose I have put up a respectable fight. But I am still the little Jewboy, terrified of the neighborhood wallios, who only after long torment nerved himself to rush with flailing arms at an enemy, and

276

then, astonished at knocking him down, ran away before the wallio could rise and murderize the Yid.

Here, I had landed one telling blow. I had presented the play before critics. I should flail on. Picket. Call out the cast to picket. But they were soldiers, subject to military discipline. They'd be sent back to their units. The fact that this was an army production, at first an advantage, was now a handicap.

As for Peter Frye—he was abroad.

I knew several Israeli lawyers; I could have gone to an aggressive young attorney who had, a few years before, fought and won before the Israel Supreme Court the right for our Reform congregation to be accorded a public place of worship in equality with the Orthodox in our town. But instead I went for advice to a highly cultivated, successful neighbor in Cfar Shmaryahu, a man of German origin like Otto Frank. Applebaum settled me in a deep leather chair in his booklined study, facing his peaceful tree-shaded garden, so characteristic of this tree-immersed village that had been settled by the early wave of German refugees in the thirties. "I must tell you from the outset," he warned me, "I don't believe in going to court. I agree you are right, and will use every possible means, but I don't want to go to court."

Neither did I, I said. I only wanted freedom for my work.

"Let me try." He would accept no fee.

After a few weeks Applebaum said he had encountered nothing but blind refusal. He would quite understand if after all I did take the issue to law.

Good God, was it I who was obsessed, or they?

The pressure to close down was now unanswerable. A date would have to be named, Major B. said. Would I come to a meeting at the Advocate General's office?

There was one other lawyer I knew, a man of solid temperament with a strong sense of justice. From South Africa, unwilling to live in the land of apartheid, Brody had come to Israel to settle. So we all sat in the Advocate General's office.

277

A closing date had been fixed on. A dozen performances beyond it had to be canceled. Everyone was indignant. The Advocate General even gave me the names of civilian cultural leaders to whom I should appeal for protests after the army was out of it. My lawyer knew several of them; I knew one myself, the wife of the Mayor of Tel Aviv. All were part of the Israeli establishment, not unrelated to the American Jewish establishment. Doubtless they, too, would be privately indignant.

As though in some fated ritual marking the close of a time-circle, the final performance, I learned, would be at my old kibbutz, Meshek Yagur, where I had first stayed in 1927.

I was greeted by a number of old-timers, the *vatikim,* my comrades of those days: Bialystoker, who a few years ago had remembered to invite me to the Passover seder; Weisman, the short husky chief of the threshing crew; Dvora, the little woman who had virtually spent her life with the poultry. Yehuda was no longer there. Some I did not remember.

We recalled the despairing day in 1946 when the British had descended on the meshek, ripped the grounds apart, and torn the tiles from the floor of the baby-house, uncovering the Haganah's arms caches, and I had arrived in my war correspondent's uniform to watch it all, to watch the men being clubbed and flung half-conscious into the British vans, to watch the women being torn aside as they clawed the invaders, to watch it all so as to report it to the outside world.

Yes, they knew something of my literary battle, but now, apparently, it had to be their turn to stand and watch, in sympathy. What more could they do? Pass a resolution?

The performance was in the enormous auditorium where I had been for the seder. It was packed not only with the chaverim of Yagur, but with visitors from surrounding kibbutzim and villages.

278

There came to my mind the tradition of last-night performances in professional theaters, when the actors play all sorts
of private jokes onstage, in an effort to "break each other
up." Here, the converse took place. A rite was performed. It
was as though a touch of the sense of doom that pervaded the
Diary had come to each of the actors in the face of this closing
night. There were a few soldiers in minor roles who had been
unable to rise above stiff recitation; this night even they
assumed character. Mrs. Van Daan had never before achieved
the depth of feeling that she had this night; there could be no
fear of a laugh in the wrong place. And Margot—there came
into her being a warmth, a sisterliness toward Anne, as though
in presage of their last days in Bergen-Belsen together.

At the end, after the long rhythmic acclaim, a member of
the cast stepped forward simply to say that this was the closing, and to thank the audience.

It was over. The entire project of a Soldiers Theater was
being abolished. A few of the cast were being kept in the
army's pool of entertainers to do skits in the camps. When the
"bad experience" had been somewhat forgotten, Major B.
said, he hoped to form another group—perhaps in a year's
time. They would perform only the classics.

The director of the New York City Center Theater, Jean
Dalrymple, to whom I had sent a copy of the text, said they
could be interested in staging the play, but only if there were
no legal difficulties.

I'd hunger strike in Amsterdam, at the Anne Frank House
itself!

And then what? They'd be delighted. In the end I'd have to
give up.

My sickness again. Survivors' guilt. To bring their hunger
on myself.

Every night, plans, statements, recapitulations. All night.

A trio of radio commentators who conducted a "controversy" program scheduled an interview. I could not control the shrillness in my voice.

One of them suggested I take the issue to the Ministry of Education and Culture. Why did I have to pursue every suggestion? But I had to.

A subminister replied with personal greeting; he was Anne Frank's own teacher, whom I had met a few years before when I visited Amsterdam. It was his department, he wrote me, that had advanced funds to the army for the production. But he didn't see what could be done now. Except—did I know that several of Anne's schoolmates were in Israel? Perhaps if one of her own friends appealed to Otto Frank?

He gave me the address of Anne's closest, dearest confidante, Lies, the very girl she had seen in her nightmare and about whom she had written, "Why should I be chosen to live and she probably to die?"

In response to my note I received a call from Lies's husband. In these last weeks Lies had had a recurrence of hysteria, and she was again in treatment. Then there was no question of bringing up the whole subject, I said. But he was interested in my text; they had seen and been shocked at the other play. Would I send him a copy? I sent it.

He called again. Yes, he saw the difference. He wished he were free to help. I could only extend wishes that his wife would soon recover.

I had even, at the suggestion of my mimeographer, written to President Shazar. Himself a man of letters, he had asked the Israeli Ambassador in the Netherlands to see what might be done. When such measures failed, couldn't I finally dismiss the whole matter from my mind?

An offer came from Behrman House in New York to publish my text. Again, the "owner" refused permission. It occurred to me that in the Soviet Union, writers defied such acts of suppression, at risk of decades of imprisonment, and had copies of their works circulated through the underground.

280

I would have the work printed, in Hebrew and in English. I would write a cool and factual preface. No shrillness must intrude. I'd send the books out "for literary discussion." Indeed, both dramatic versions should be printed side by side. But when it came to printing their version, I did not, of course, have the same moral right. Mine, I would give away. Anyone interested in comparison could easily procure the other, and I would suggest this.

My bank-clerk adherent sent me to a friend named Dan, a printer in Tel Aviv, for the Hebrew. At the basement shop I was startled to see Dan take my bundle of papers between two handless stumps, and begin expertly to leaf through the job. The following week the booklets were ready. We talked a bit. Would there be war? As I made out the check, I said I was probably being foolish, spending money in a personal fight when big trouble loomed. With his stump-device, Dan struck a match, lit a cigarette. He eyed me. Then he held aloft his handless forearms. From the War of Independence. "This gave me a good excuse; I could have given in," he said. Then added, "I'm married, I have two children, I built up this shop. Mr. Levin, everyone has his personal fight, no?"

Dan insisted on carrying half the bundles to the car.

The Egyptian troops stood massed in Sinai; the U.N. truce force had vanished at Nasser's demand; the Straits of Tiran were closed. Each day a man went off from among our neighbors. The electrician was gone. The bakery's delivery service ceased. In the local cinema, the film would be interrupted while code words were heard from the radio; then in the dark one could make out the forms of young men, and older ones too, squeezing their way to the aisle and going out.

I received accreditation to cover the "situation" for NANA. As Abba Eban returned from his last futile trip to Washington to stave off the war, I drove the roads that were becoming emptier each day of civilian traffic. I drove north to the kibbutz of the Fighters of the Warsaw Ghetto and sat with Antek, their leader, as he gave directions for the emplacement of sandbags, while the radio repeated Arab promises of a war of total annihilation, another holocaust.

And even in all this I could not let go! Dan was unequipped to do my English text, so I had taken it to another printer; now his typesetter was gone, but his daughter was trying to carry on.

One night our doorbell rang; in first surprise we did not even recognize our daughter Dominique, arrived on the last plane from Paris. "I have come to die with you," she announced.

The next morning the war had begun; I dropped Tereska at the Tel Ha-Shomer hospital where Ruth Dayan had arranged for her to drive an ambulance, and I took Dominique along to Tel Aviv for press accreditation, as *L'Express* had asked her to send material. She was standing for her tintype photo on Rothschild Boulevard when the air alarm sounded; there was a shelter a step away, but the photographer preferred to finish the photo. At the P.I.O. entrance I introduced her to Paul Shutzer of *Life,* whose eyes gladdened as always at the sight of a pretty girl. He was rushing off to fix up with Moshe Dayan about going forward in a halftrack. A quick boy from Brooklyn, he'd reached the peak in photojournalism, but his work was more than that—his camera seemed to pick up what was inside of people. A few years before, Paul had done a story in Israel, and stayed on for some months, "for himself," and now he had rushed back without waiting for an assignment.

Another friend darted up in the corridor, hustling as usual —Ben Oyserman, once a Londoner, long an Israeli. He had been our assistant cameraman on *My Father's House.* Just now he was covering the war for Canadian television. "Meyer, I want to talk to you, soon as we get a chance. I've got a project—" Ben always had a project, a television series, a

282

film— He was off in a little car with a few other correspondents—no room for us; Dominique and I climbed into the tourist bus now marked *Press,* and headed for the Gaza area.

In Nahal Oz we counted the dead cattle after the dawn shelling from Gaza and stood with the kibbutznicks in their bunkers watching the puffs from the Israeli tanks attacking Napoleon's Hill.

Back at the P.I.O. we learned that Paul Shutzer had been killed there, riding in a forward halftrack. Ben Oyserman's little car, attempting to reach Gaza across an open field, had come up against a rock. Ben, as was his way, jumped out to help a soldier clear it; the rock was booby-trapped. Both died.

Yet I went to my printer—I'd been to the front? What had I seen? We were winning, yes?

Despite all, he was running off my job.

We hurried to Jerusalem; sitting on a tank before Damascus Gate, Dominique saw a boy from her schooldays in Kfar Schmaryahu. "We did it!" Eli cried. "We! Can you imagine? We!"

The Press bus took us to the northern front, across the Bridge of the Daughters of Jacob onto the edge of the Golan Heights, the newly smashed bunkers before our eyes. But the story of the Six-Day War has been told, and told best of all by those who fought it. The same Eli of Dominique's schooldays wrote out for me his step-by-step experiences in the battle of Jerusalem, and I incorporated his story into *Gore and Igor.* Another soldier, Ronnie, the next-door neighbor who had once been in love with Dominique, came back from Sinai to days of depressed silence. Then at last, to Dominique alone, he told what had happened. A few days after the battle, he and some comrades had halted at an Arab roadside place and been warmly welcomed by the aged proprietor, who served them their shashlik and then pulled out a pistol and shot dead Ronnie's comrade sitting there beside him, and still another, before he could be brought down. "And then in our rage we couldn't stop, we killed every Arab in the whole place."

6

WE RETURNED for our year in America, in the half-and-half pattern that seemed to fit the role in which I rather portentously saw myself: as a writer-link between the two large Jewish communities.

In Israel I had built my long dreamed-of seashore house, and now we started to remodel a West Side brownstone, in a redevelopment area that was to have both racial and economic integration. With the building being stripped to the bare walls all around me, I held back a corner of one floor where I set up a few crates and made myself a little office. Here, so it would not trouble Tereska, I deposited the bundles of the printed play, and carried on my obsessive campaign. Very well, let it be a *meshugas*. This much I had found out—that as long as I was doing something on the issue, I felt relief. Otherwise it festered.

From the brownstone I mailed off copies of the play to colleges and libraries, and to a haphazard list of authors, including with each my petition for freedom of production, and noting that it had already been signed by Albert Camus, Norman Mailer, and a dozen other "big names." Not to forget the earlier endorsement by hundreds of rabbis!

An odd assortment of signatures began to come back. Some were from writers who were personal friends and who might simply be humoring me. Others were from professors of drama—among these was a sheet signed by a score of students at a Southern Methodist college.

What was I going to do with all this? There had never been any results from such petitions—did I expect things to change now? What I really was asking for, I knew, was confirmation that I wasn't mad. If a professor at some remote college was moved to sign the statement, I must be rational.

At home I could not even speak of what I was doing. To carry on a campaign in this half-secrecy, in this half-demolished corner, my graying hair white with the dust of crumbling plaster, made me feel really cuckoo. Yet I was doing my work; with *Gore and Igor* on the way to publication, I had meanwhile taken the lecture route again. Only, once or twice the head of the bureau, Sam Freeman, said he had had some complaints because I kept bringing up the Anne Frank case—all people wanted to hear about was the Six-Day War, so would I shut up about the Anne Frank case? All right, I said, I wouldn't speak about it unless, in the question period, someone asked. Almost always, someone did. When I got to the political side, there would usually be at least one disgusted-looking listener, youthful to be sure, who ostentatiously got up and walked out. Meyer Levin the red-baiter.

I had proved myself in court, my work had proved itself on the stage, nothing more could be done—they were too big, too rich, too powerful, for me. I knew perfectly well these petitions and appeals were futile—why couldn't I let go?

Back to analysis. Back to Dr. A.

I was trying finally to get into solid work on the big pioneer novel. For this I needed my habitual half-week workplace away from home, and as Dr. A was now living in Princeton, I found a place there, a room in a fixed-up barn. In that isolated room I went through the most unproductive and depressing of winters. Within a few weeks I had run into a total block on the novel. Nothing helped. I would struggle through the morning, shuttling between desk, armchair, and cot; sometimes I would try to get a running start by revising passages that had accumulated over several years. Or else I would jump ahead to a scene that would fit into the latter part of the work. No use. After a few paragraphs, a page, I'd be struggling to write half-sentences, mere notes, and at last would sit staring out at the desolate little yard where a few graduate students who lived in the main house parked their cars.

Then, the same struggle in the afternoon. At last I'd release myself to walk over to a diner, where I ate at the counter in silence.

The therapy hour came on the second evening of my stay, and presently I found myself all that day each week distracted by the anticipation of the breakaway from the solitary workroom. The day after, I told myself, I'd be able to work, but next day I was already anticipating going home.

As to the analysis, it also seemed blocked. Again and again we shredded apart the Anne Frank obsession and Tereska's fears that I had a persecution mania, and all the rest. Yet weren't facts facts? Wasn't it the proven truth that the trouble had been started politically? Didn't their text itself provide the proof? Hadn't that literary agent told me I was already being worked on with *My Father's House*? How could all this be paranoia if it was true?

Again the personal tack: what did Otto Frank represent for me, a bad father? Dr. A was herself German-Jewish; what about my transference, was I perhaps hostile to her?

No, I had always deeply felt that she wanted to help me. Yet surely I resented her for her failure with Mabel. Everyone had failed with Mabel. And was it still my guilt about Mabel

287

for which I punished myself at every turn? With the Anne Frank affair coming right after Mabel's death? Hadn't we long ago found that I was masochistically self-destructive?

What is really known of the mysterious process of analysis? Some detective–story-like cases we know, cases in which the clue came in a word, a dream, an incident recovered from prememory, and a trauma was dissolved away. And yes, I did know a few persons who had been helped by analysis. I had in the past in some way myself been helped by Dr. A, mostly in our early sessions in Jerusalem. Now I was stuck, as surely as I was stuck in the novel.

This was the time when Dr. A, with a way she had occasionally of springing a shock on you, toward the end of an hour declared to me severely, directly, that I was suffering from a paranoia that would become progressively worse. Unless? There seemed to be no unless.

Perhaps I do her injustice. Perhaps I purposefully, masochistically, misunderstood. But not long afterward Tereska went to see her in her New York office and was given the same dark prognosis. To Tereska it seemed that there was one faint "unless"—I must overcome my obsession by totally and at once dropping and forgetting the Anne Fank case. All the evil was there. I was somehow in love with Anne Frank. My wife even cried out bitterly, "Anne Frank, or me!"

No use for the thousandth time to explain "But Anne Frank as herself has nothing to do with it! I have no more personal feeling for her than for any other victim. And even Otto Frank has nothing to do with it! I am simply a writer fighting a case of suppression, as every writer must do!"

Maybe I was still fighting the Catholic Church for the suppression of *Model Tenement* in Chicago. Maybe I was so persistent this time because I felt I hadn't fought hard enough that time. And anyway, I wasn't even sending out petitions anymore. But when requests came for the play, could I do less than respond?

288

It was a deadly lost winter. In spring, *Gore and Igor* appeared, and for a while looked like it was becoming a success. A different Meyer Levin began to be written about, avant garde, hip. Then suddenly all went dead. As though choked off, it seemed to me. Return of paranoia?

* * *

Once again in Israel, I drove off, one Friday afternoon, on my mission. Southward from Tel Aviv the highway already had a pre-Sabbath emptiness. A last bus, racing to reach Ashkalon before the Sabbath eve sundown. A thinning out of trucks and cars.

This pre-Sabbath dying down of traffic was in itself an oddity, I told myself for distraction from nervous tension, since tomorrow, on the actual day of Sabbath, the highway would be busy with excursionists, private cars, motorcycles, and truckloads of kibbutzniks ignoring the rabbinical regulations. Yet now, just before the Sabbath fell, everything came to a halt. Even the irreligious seemed to seek a Sabbath eve quietude.

In this way, with these speculations, I tried to stave off the uneasiness that grew in me as the road grew emptier.

The kibbutz for which I was headed, alone in the little car, lay along the border of the Gaza Strip, second or third in the chain extending southward. I had not been in the area since the Six-Day War, but scarcely a week passed without mention in the news of a tractor, or an army patrol vehicle, or a passing car, striking a terrorist-planted mine in the Gaza region. Or for variation there would be items about grenades tossed at passing vehicles.

But not mines on the main road, I kept telling myself, and I was driving on the main coastal road. There had nevertheless been a few instances of tossed grenades, just where this road swept past Gaza itself; an isolated car could be a target. But my turnoff was well before Gaza.

289

I missed the turnoff. ("Self-destructive?" ask all my analysts. And I?)—Author Killed on Way to Performance of Suppressed Play. At last the hush-up would be broken. Headlines! MEYER LEVIN HIT BY TERRORIST GRENADE . . . Levin was alone in his car on the way to a performance at Kibbutz Kisufim of his dramatization of *The Diary of a Young Girl,* a version that has been forbidden production by the owner of the Diary, and over which the author has carried on a fifteen-year battle . . .

Then cunningly I began to invent plans that would break out the story and yet permit me to live and relish the effect. I could disappear. Suppose I simply pulled aside into an orange grove and waited out the Sabbath? I could even drive back a distance, to Ashkalon, and spend a few anonymous days at the beach. The kibbutz, after I failed to appear on time for the performance, would call my home. An alarm would be sent out—Author Vanishes, Attack Feared—

Suddenly I noticed that I was passing the pottery stands just before Gaza. Young Arabs along the road glanced with hard eyes at the car. But the plates were not Israeli; the car was on a French TT license, and they would not be likely to throw grenades at a French car, I told myself. Provided they knew it was French. I pulled into a gas station—the lone vehicle there—and asked my way, feeling additionally terrified as I said, "Kibbutz Kisufim." His face and voice expressionless, the attendant gave me directions. No need to go back all the way to the missed turn, there was a connecting crossroad.

Time was getting short. I decided to take the side road across the Strip. After all, since it was mostly traveled by Arab vehicles, it would surely not be mined. And why be cowardly? The seductive nether impulse was still awake in me—now the risk would be for real. Perhaps all this was "meant," fated, *beshert.* Don't avoid what is meant to be.

The distance to the linkup with the road on the Israeli side was only a few miles, but I drove it in heightening panic. I was

290

between densely lined orange trees—Arab groves. Not a road sign to be seen. Had I blundered again? Had the gas-station Arab purposely misdirected me?

At a dirt-road intersection, a few Arabs loitered. I stopped to ask directions, and one of the lads said he was going my way. (You're really over the border—intensity provokes puns —insane for sure! What's to prevent the fellow from cutting your throat? Then your cock whacked off and stuck in your mouth, tradition fulfilled, that's how you'll be when found!)

A few miles onward, the Arab hopped out, pointing straight ahead for me; we exchanged a half-wary "maas-salaam" and "shalom," and presently I reached the highway.

The road was entirely empty. My publicity schemes had vanished from my head, and I was in plain fright, trying to keep a close watch on the cement road for any spot that might in the last hour or so have been broken open for the placement of a mine. Kisufim was much further south than it appeared on the map; I accelerated, really, now, like some pious Jew racing the Sabbath sundown. And almost exactly as the sun came to rest on the horizon, silhouetting the outer guard-tower, I turned into the kibbutz lane.

Swinging the gate open for me, with a quick wave of relief, was a frail-looking chaver with the thin-lipped sensitive face of the culture-lover; just so I recalled the secretary of a Jewish community center in—Syracuse, was it?—anxiously waiting on the doorstep as I arrived tardily for a lecture. "Moshe?" I asked. It was he, the director of the play. "Were you getting worried? I should have started earlier."

It wasn't for my safety that he had been worried, he said, for there had been no incidents on the main road. (I suppressed any mention of my detour.) No. The trouble was a cable from New York. A cable on two pages, forbidding any performance. A long legal pronouncement signed by a whole list of names.

"Paul, Weiss, Rifkind, Wharton, and Garrison," I said.

There had been a meeting of the central committee. It was decided to go ahead anyway with the performance—

I breathed. How could I even for a moment have doubted them? But Moshe was still worried. He felt responsible. Could the lawyers really cause the kibbutz any trouble? Or expense?

Na! I said, and if there was legal expense, I'd pay for it. Yes, the enemy was behaving true to form. A small, isolated kibbutz in the most dangerous spot in Israel, all its length against the border of the Gaza Strip, continuously exposed to infiltrators, and to this remote place the mighty American law firm dispatches a terrifying cable forbidding the kibbutz to perform *The Diary of Anne Frank*!

"To tell you the truth I was waiting at the gate not only for you, but in case they might even have sent somebody to stop us. A court order or something." It struck me that chaver Moshe felt less able to deal with the threat of Paul, Weiss, Rifkind and company than with the constant threat of the fedayeen. However, Moshe rattled on, as I parked and we crossed the yard to his dwelling, however, the central committee had decided on a line of defense, if trouble came. "It's like we were only using the play in our own home. A kibbutz is like a family, this is our home and they can't stop us from doing what we want in our home. This is not a public performance."

All right, I said, though I was a touch taken aback by the casuistry. If trouble came, why not raise the real issue, the public right to make use of the Diary? Meanwhile, Moshe asked in wonder, how could those people in New York have known about this performance?

I confessed. "I myself sent them the notice." And they had reacted just as I had expected.

"You could have got us stopped!"

"No. I sent it only a few days ago, so there wouldn't be any time for them to get any kind of stop order." Moshe seemed somewhat put out, but I had two reasons, I explained. First, I

292

did not want them to be able to accuse me of doing anything underhanded, as with the army theater performances. Secondly, I believed that somewhere, sometime, a legal test had to be made. The army had been pressured out of doing it, but perhaps a kibbutz would feel differently. "If they make any move against you for doing this play, I'll be responsible; if there are any expenses, I'll pay them," I repeated.

The worst that could happen, I felt sure, would be that on a legalistic basis the kibbutz might have to pay perhaps twenty-five dollars in royalties to the owners of the dramatic rights to the Diary.

The fact that the play was forbidden had at least been no secret to Moshe. As librarian of the kibbutz he had received one of the copies I had sent out when the army production was closed down; my preface contained the whole story. Moshe had decided to do the play anyway. His enthusiasm returned. "I think I've got really a good cast. Our Anne—wait till you hear her! We've rehearsed every night, even though we're in the picking season." He had put in his hours in the orchard, even today, in spite of the lengthy meeting over the cablegram, and I could see he was exhausted.

We had reached his dwelling, the room-and-a-half in a standard kibbutz structure; the living room with the couch-bed was crammed with books.

Moshe's wife was waiting, a golden-skinned girl, soft-eyed, from Morocco. He himself was American, as were most of the founding members of Kisufim. Raised in Philadelphia, Moshe had joined a Zionist youth group, but already at that time had been drawn to the theater and had even studied for one season in New York. "Your play is beautiful!" he suddenly exclaimed, with no accent of flattery. "I just had to do it, no matter what! You know, there is so little to be found that we can perform, in our Jewish dramatic literature."

All at once I was back in my own young days with an amateur dramatic group in a Jewish community center in

293

Chicago—and how I had searched for authentic material! For outside of *The Dybbuk* and *The Golem* and *Green Fields,* so little was available at the time. This prolonged and bitter struggle over the Diary, wasn't it, then, partly a continuation of that early community activity of mine? Only someone like Moshe here could fully understand this particular feeling: this material was ours, ours where we had so little—and now even this was being taken away from us.

We went to the *cheder ochel,* the dining hall, which would also serve as the theater. It was meanwhile set for the Sabbath meal, with white tablecloths. I met the kibbutz secretary and his wife, both also from America, founder-veterans who had come some years before Moshe. A lively, aware couple; the wife was to play Mrs. Frank.

Immediately after the meal, the tables were moved back, the benches and chairs rearranged to face a platform on which there was a row of seats. It was to be a recital performance, as the kibbutz had no staging facility.

The performers came on and took their places. Almost at once, I forgot all the strife, the intrigues, the personal involvements, that had brought me here. I was within the events of the Diary again, but afresh, as though for the first time. The girl reading Anne was Anne, with such a total interior identification that even the emotional identification of Shoshanah Rozen, the Persian girl in the army performance, was no longer present with me.

True, there were lapses by self-conscious readers who had been dragooned from the limited kibbutz membership to fill the minor parts. But in compensation there was the performance of the mother, far more touching even than in the army's production. At last Mrs. Frank's personality emerged, her tense bewilderment before her younger daughter, her desperate clutching at religious faith, her occasional release in superiority remarks against Mrs. Van Daan. And here in this simple kibbutz dining hall alongside the Gaza Strip I felt healed of a particular bitterness that had nested within the whole Anne Frank affair, a bitterness connected with the Broadway portrayal of Anne Frank's mother. As I listened to this American-Israeli woman in the reading, there came a release from a side-aspect of the story that I have until now repressed in this account, for to have told it in its chronological place would have seemed a piling on of ugliness.

What had happened was this: shortly after the Broadway production opened, I received a clipping from a Los Angeles English-Jewish weekly in which a survivor from Germany exposed the past of the actress who was appearing as Mrs. Frank. He remembered her from before the war, and he had looked up her record and found that she had performed all through the Nazi régime, in plays and in films, and had been a member of the party-controlled actors' guild. At the end of the war she had married a captain in the American army— a Jew. True, I felt, her membership in the Nazi actors' guild might only have been perfunctory, a necessity if she was to work in her profession. But of all the actresses available in New York for this role, wasn't it an affront to have chosen this one to play the mother of Anne Frank! In addition, she was not a particularly good actress and was stiff and cold in the role. Yet the producers had insisted on putting her into the film of the Diary as well. In the theater program, in the film publicity, there was no hint of her wartime career, and this was to me perhaps the most infuriating aspect of the entire incident. For had the producers, obviously with the consent of Otto Frank, meant to make a "universalist" point by placing a German actress in this role, then all should have been done openly. As it was, the theater program declared that her career had abruptly ended when the Nazis entered Austria.

There were Jews who, having seen her in the play, later learned of the actress's background and felt the way an observant Jew feels when he has been tricked into eating *trayf*.

Indignant, I had written of the situation in my newspaper column at the time, and this had not gone unnoticed. Once, called to speak at Temple Emanuel, the Fifth Avenue synagogue with the highest-status membership, I was requested not to mention the Anne Frank case, and so refrained. But among the people coming up to the platform after the talk to greet me, there was a burly man who growled, as he held back his hand, that he was the husband of the actress in question. That was all he said. I did not reply.

At times, I had wondered whether I would have reacted in such outrage over the casting of the mother, had it not been for my whole involvement. Here, in Kisufim at last, as Mrs. Frank was given her full self by a woman of the kibbutz, I felt released from that part of the question.

When the performance was ended, the girl who had played Anne broke away from her congratulators. Like Shoshanah Rozen, she was atremble, sobbing.

Late in the morning, after he had attended a committee meeting, Moshe took me for a walk over the kibbutz fields. Despite the forbidding legal cable, the committee had decided to put on the play once more, he said; two weeks from now, at the furthest kibbutz along the Strip, there was to be a commemoration for two chaverim who had died a year before in border incidents. Each kibbutz in the area would have a share in the program. "For our part, we will do *Anne Frank.*"

I strolled with Moshe along a dirt road that marked the border. Every dawn, he told me, two minesweeping tractors checked this road, as well as all the paths in the fields. "So far we have been lucky, no casualties"—though a couple of tractors had been damaged.

We came to the perimeter road of the kibbutz, which had a new tar surface, soon to be extended along the border stretch where we had walked. This was being done for all the local kibbutzim, he said, as a protection against mines. "Of course it it a big expense, but later on, the roads will remain useful."

We passed a schoolhouse, and Moshe indicated a repaired section in the wall. "A bazooka hit one night. Luckily, there wasn't a meeting going on."

At the noon meal I sat with the secretary and his wife; we had a long talk. They had read several of my novels. Why did I keep up my back-and-forth life, half in America, half in Israel? the secretary asked. Why didn't I finally become an Israeli?

I repeated what I had written in *In Search*—that I felt my particular task as a writer—though I hadn't fulfilled it very well—was to be a link between the Israeli and American communities, since these were now the principal reservoirs for Jewish continuation. His wife nodded. True, she agreed, that was the proper task for me.

The memorial performance at the neighboring kibbutz had a deep effect, I later heard from Moshe. No, there had not been another cable. Probably—as I had not alerted them—the firm of Paul, Weiss, Rifkind, Wharton and Garrison had not been aware of Kibbutz Kisufim's brazen repetition of their crime.

* * *

This is the part most difficult to keep from leaving out, for it touches the borderline. I must now deal with the no-answers. I can tell it best through my own behavior toward another person, gripped in an obsession so close to mine that it seems either a parody or an object lesson, or both.

A few years ago in Israel I received a letter from a Mrs. G. in Haifa, who asked to see me; it was a reasonably written letter saying that from what she had heard of me, she felt I might be willing to help her in a problem of public interest.

Mrs. G. arrived, a compact, middle-aged woman with a bounce to her step and, from close up, a certain softness in her cheeks, as one saw in people who had taken the world's beating. What she set forth was a story at times in the same words as my own.

A woman active in Jewish affairs, in California, she had conceived the idea of a lofty Peace beacon on the Israeli shore, a "Statue Shalom" which would not only shine as a world symbol, but would in itself become a bringer of Peace. Energetically, she had enlisted the support of "big names," senators, governors, do-gooders of every kind. She had raised some money, she had secured a design for her wondrous symbolic beacon, she had come to Israel and obtained the blessing of the Haifa authorities, and even an offer of a site near the Druse village along the ridge of Mount Carmel—a magnificent height. Her beacon would be visible from far out at sea: the first glimpse of Israel would be Statue Shalom. At its base would be meeting halls for peace organizations. This would become a pilgrimage place drawing tourists from all over the world; great good would come from her dream project.

And then the site had been withdrawn. Support had begun to seep away. Gradually she had become convinced that word was being passed, that backers were being discouraged, that unseen powers in the establishment were against her. Why? What possible harm could there be in her vision? And didn't the public have the right to bring into being so beautiful an emblem, a beacon for Peace, in the one land, the Holy Land, whose great prophet had cried out: Hammer your swords into plowshares?

I heard her out, though my brain had begun to throb. I took each document from her hand, and agreed it was valid; I looked again at the impressive list of sponsor-names.

No, no, it's not the same as with me! I denied to myself.

And what she wanted to ask of me, Mrs. G. pleaded, was whether she should go to court? She knew about my case. She knew, she had been warned, and she dreaded court action. She

298

had used up all of her money, she had separated herself from her family and was staying on here alone to fight this thing. Many times, she confided to me she had been on the verge of suicide, but there was a principle here, the right of the public—

No, no, not the same! I shouted in myself. And pointed out to myself that although there were superficial similarities, the crux of her case was entirely different. There was the simple matter of inappropriateness at this time. Israel would be open to ridicule for spending millions on a peace monument, just now in the unresolved tension of the Six-Day War, while Arab refugees still crowded the camps. The beacon would seem not a light of peace but of triumph. Obviously this was why her project had been discouraged, and there was no similarity here to the political act of repression at the root of my own obsession. And yet—? And her persistence—?

Hadn't I already dealt in *The Fanatic* with this undermining fear of self-recognition in other victims of obsession? Hadn't I described Maury Finklestein's self-doubts when, on the way to the printer to pick up his own protest material, he passed, at the subway entrance, some sign-carrying nut parading a grievance against the gas company?

As gently as I could, I advised Mrs. G. to go easy, to avoid the courts. I tried to show her that there was no point in her subjecting herself to personal suffering, in breaking up her family—but she kept gazing at the sketch of her Statue Shalom. It would be so meaningful, so beautiful!

From time to time I received letters from Mrs. G. She was going to court after all, as it was her last resort. She would sue the mayor of Haifa for interference, for causing the site to be withdrawn. Could I send her a few words of support?

The trial had come. She wrote again, in the midst of it. She was in an ordeal such as only persons like myself, who had been through it, could understand. Dark impulses had come to her, but for the sake of the public's right, she was determined—Would I send her a word of encouragement?

I kept her letters for weeks, half-hidden under other papers on my desk. I didn't, I couldn't answer.

—And was it for the same reason that people didn't answer me? "Don't feed Meyer's obsession."

—Then how was it that many did answer? A citation from Josef Rosensaft, leader of the survivors of Bergen Belsen, where Anne died. And the kibbutzniks who performed the play? And Rabbi Judea Miller, from the Boston area, who presented *Anne Frank* in his temple? No, no, Mrs. G's case and mine were not the same! One had to fight this kind of negative seduction, too.

—Still, what about the no-answers? The many no-answers?

—Oh hell, people just followed the great motto of our time: don't get involved.

—But there are people who start to get involved and then fall silent. Like you with Mrs. G.

—Exactly which people?

—All right, we'll skip all the drama critics who on principle ought to be interested, but take people like Brustein at Yale and Arthur Miller, and that Brechtian expert, Eric Bentley . . . All these people are constantly coming out against repression. They never answered.

—Sure, but they have personal friends on the other side.

—Take Edmund Wilson. He answered, and said you certainly should have the right to have your work performed. You asked him to sign your petition, and there it stopped. No answer.

—Sure, the same week a columnist mentioned him at some literary party with Lillian Hellman.

—All right, your personal devil appears. Everyone knows everyone, and the highest minds put personal connection above principle.

300

—No, not necessarily above principle. But I still have this odd feeling that something is being said about me, something I still don't know, but so rotten that it puts everyone off.

—Wow! Paranoia!

—Then what stops them?

—What? You've just put your finger on it. The Mrs. G. syndrome. A tone in your own letters, your own appeals. At some point it stops them.

—I admit it, I know such insistence creeps in. Like that time on the Israeli radio program when I heard my own voice going shrill. And on the phone once with a news-paperman I could hear it. But what has that to do with the issue itself? It simply means that I can't help getting tense and at times overreact.

—What's so different about you and Mrs. G.?

—Good God. I keep going to analysts. I keep checking myself out. I grant you that one of them had a pessimistic evaluation, but the others all said it was real, real, a reality problem. Maybe it's simpler in the Soviet Union, where if you fight repression they just send you to an asylum.

Perhaps it would be well to try a male analyst, Dr. A agreed.

Walking with a writer-friend, I asked out of the blue, "Who's your shrink?"—every writer had to have one—and he gave me the name. Though he wasn't going any more, and wasn't sure he had been helped.

Dr. A said the choice was excellent.

So, with Dr. Bychovsky, once more the rehearsal of early years, marriage and divorce, the suicide. The absorption in things Jewish, perhaps overcompensation for that first marriage to a gentile? And the second marriage to the daughter of a con-verted Jew, herself baptized at birth. Rebellion, guilt, and hence my obstinacy over the Jewish content of the Diary?

And so the whole Anne Frank story all over again in all its wanderings.

301

—No, maestro, not a paranoia; paranoid tendencies as in all artists, he tells me benignly. (Mere reassurance?) But the affair itself, he says, is reality.

As for my work problem, Dr. Bychovsky prescribes a pill.

I am working this time in an idyllic setting, a cottage on a wooded height overlooking the Hudson, half an hour from New York. Found through an ad. There I shut myself in for my workdays; a few times I have even been snowed in.

The first morning I take the pill, I feel slightly as though I'll fly apart; energy sizzles in me, but doesn't channelize, and the morning passes before I can steady down. His pill seems to be a mistake.

The next day I try only a nibble. I work fine all day. Clear-minded, energized. At the end of the afternoon I am drained; it is as though the pill had concentrated my total energy-store into the working hours.

It goes well. I settle into this routine. For my work it works.

Could the entire difficulty have been simply organic? Solved by a pill?

After a few months Dr. Bychovsky dismisses me with his last "maestro." He is sorry, in his friendly way, that certain things in my life are the way they are. But, as we agree, the main thing is to get my work done. Book One is ready and I seem, from the reaction of my editor, indeed to have succeeded in reaching the epic tone. I must continue on through Book Two, so that we'll have something really big, overwhelming, to present. I tend to agree, and provide myself with a sufficient supply of pills, as it is time again for our year in Israel.

Not until *The Settlers* was finished did a young doctor, in a chance conversation on a beach, hearing me mention my Ritalin pill, tell me, "Man, you've been on speed!"

It was done. It had come off, completely.

All during the writing I had held down the obsession by

making myself a kind of promise. Only let me finish this. I'll take up the fight again.

A student named Harvey Cushing who had heard me speak the year before at Boston University meanwhile had asked me for my play. Without applying for permission to the Diary owners, he had produced it at a summer camp. The performance had been the most impressive event in the thirty-year history of the camp, Cushing wrote. The owner of the place had embraced him, ecstatic, in tears. But it was the effect on the audience that he wanted to tell about. "Catharsis was complete and unequivocal. Small children, adults, even the hardened 'sophisticates,' openly wept. After seeing this, it is difficult, if not impossible, to convince myself that *Anne* is only a play." Touchingly he told me that his own father had recently died, and that their last conversation had been about how good it was that he had done this play.

How could I give up?

Another student, who wanted to present *Anne Frank* at a Midwest college, applied to the owners for permission and sent me the form letter of refusal that he received from the lawyers. My work, the letter said, had been rejected by four-teen Broadway producers, I had dragged Otto Frank into the courts, and the judge had ruled that I had produced no evidence whatever, and basically upheld Mr. Frank; in view of this, it could be understood that permission to perform my play could not be granted.

But I would not be interrupted; I would finish my work.

In the *Jerusalem Post* there appeared a question about the Anne Frank house in Amsterdam being used by an international youth group for discussions that were largely pro-Arab.

It was at this time, as I have already mentioned, that a letter came from an American young woman saying she had been told I would be able to explain to her what had happened with the Diary. It was on reading the Diary at the age of fourteen

303

that she had first become really aware of herself as a Jew. This had brought her to Israel. Recently, on a trip, she had visited the Anne Frank house in Amsterdam and received a shock. In the way things were presented there, the Jewish element seemed to be of no particular significance.

No, I must not get into all that again. Not until *The Settlers* was safe.

I had done the writer's part. Now came the publication part.

There were a few early signs that caused me misgivings. First came the *Kirkus* review, three months before publication. Sneering.

The *Kirkus* is a trade journal, presumably without bias; its purpose is to alert bookdealers to what will sell in the coming season. When a book gets a "good Kirkus" the publishers tell the author that the journal has enormous influence. When a book gets a bad Kirkus, they tell him it is unimportant, that it has lost its authoritative voice since the founder, Virginia Kirkus, sold it. But that first word can still start the word going, good or bad, on a book. Worried, I went early to New York.

Signs were excellent, my editors said. The Kirkus meant nothing. No, I wasn't set on any big talk shows as yet. No, we didn't get on the *Today* show, but they rarely took novels. In any case, I must promise not to talk about my troubles.

Very well, even though the play was just then being produced at Brandeis University, I would keep silent. The issue had gone on for twenty years, it could wait another few months. Only, if the whole affair was a fantasy, an illusion of persecution on my part, how was my book going to be hurt if I talked? By whom?

And so back to therapy.

I didn't go back to Dr. Bychovsky; I respected him, he had helped me, probably without his pill I couldn't have got

304

through the long, heavy task, but I felt I had said all I could to him—we would go around in circles; he had in fact dismissed me.

My former landlord, Dr. Reuben Fine, had asked me to speak at a psychiatric symposium on the creative process; another of the speakers at this symposium was Dr. Erika. I had already met her in writers' circles; this encounter seemed an omen.

At our very first session, as I began to go into the political background of my troubles, she waved me down. "I know exactly. You are absolutely correct about what happened. Of course people don't believe you. That's something else."

I must use tactics. Strategy. My editor was right, I must stop all mention of the Anne Frank thing until months after the book was out. "Pile up your ammunition! When you no longer risk their taking revenge on your book, let fly!"

Was she humoring my obsession?

In a letter Tereska wrote, "At least you now admit it is an obsession."

I never denied it was an obsession. From the first I recognized and fought as best I could the obsessive nature of the trouble within myself, while also trying to fight the cause of it outside myself.

Even my wife saw me only in the image of the obsessed. "Unfortunately Levin has developed an obsession over the matter," Otto Frank had told a friendly American rabbi, as though this erased all that had been done on their side. And the image of the obsessed then engendered a succession of images. Meyer Levin was a disgruntled, incompetent dramatist. Even after the drama had proved itself, that image lingered. A second image set afloat was that Meyer Levin was "always in the courts," "litigious." Ephraim London's "seven years of legal abstention," no matter what the injustice, had long ago passed, but at a stop in England an agent had said, "I was told you sue everybody." So he had asked, Who? "They couldn't answer except to say that you sue everybody!" In Paris, our own daughter jestingly greeted me with "Who are you suing now?"

Then there was the image of Meyer Levin so completely in the clutches of his obsession that he couldn't write. No amount of published work had any effect on this image. Until I gave up my obsession, I obviously wouldn't be able to write.

A new, sinister note had appeared during the last election campaign. One day, when I got back from a lecture trip, Tereska mentioned that Fred Morton had been around collecting names to put in an ad of Jewish writers supporting Paul O'Dwyer for Senator. As our son Mikael was working in O'Dwyer's campaign, she had assumed I'd add my name. I didn't especially like the idea of listing Jewish writers against Senator Javits, whom I in any case thought a good man, so I asked Fred if he could take me off the list. "Don't worry, you're off," he said, adding that a peculiar thing had happened. When he had gone to campaign headquarters to have a look at the final list, he had noticed my name was missing.

"But I brought you Meyer Levin," he told the woman in charge.

"Oh," she said, "I checked the list upstairs and they took him off. They said he was dangerous."

In literary circles it was now widely decreed that Meyer Levin had been a talented social novelist in the thirties when he wrote *The Old Bunch* and *Citizens,* but unfortunately when he got involved with his Jewish themes, his writing utterly deteriorated.

In one magazine after another, just then, appeared substantial articles about the new literary élite clustered around *The*

New York Review of Books. This was now the center of the intellectual establishment. That fascinating young couple, Jason and Barbara Epstein were described in *Esquire,* their magazine was analyzed in *Commentary,* their life-style was described in the *Sunday New York Times Magazine.* They even appeared in a book, *The Jewish Mystique,* by psychiatrist Ernest Van Der Haag (not one of mine!) who found that their literary power had become frightening. The frequently first-rate articles in their *Review of Books* had come, he said, to serve "as a figleaf for New Left politics." And in the Sunday *Times* article the influence of their dinner parties was noted. Among their illustrious guests one was always sure to find Lillian Hellman.

Jason and Barbara Epstein had, not long before, extended their domain by becoming partners in the ownership of the influential *Kirkus Reviews,* guide to the book trade. They had announced that the *Kirkus* would remain editorially independent.

> *The Kirkus!* cried the Obsession. That was where the sneering preview of *The Settlers* had appeared, to set the tone.

Barbara Epstein, the article continued, had, as Barbara Zimmerman, begun her career at Doubleday, where, with virtually all of the top executives opposed, she had insisted on the publication of *The Diary of a Young Girl* by Anne Frank. It was she who had got the brilliant idea of having Eleanor Roosevelt sign the introduction.

But it was that quiet little Barbara Zimmerman, now the so-dear friend of Lillian Hellman, to whom I had openly unburdened myself about my worries over the treatment of the Jewish material in the Diary if the Broadway politicals got hold of it.

307

"Yes, you picked a good little mousie," says Dr. Erika. "A quiet little mousie to sing to!"

Did I think Barbara Zimmerman was political-minded? Even way back there at the start of my trouble?

"Look, I don't know what she was. I never gave it a thought. Since I read this article, I've asked around a bit. I hadn't even known that Jason Epstein had also worked at Doubleday back at that time—it seems that's where their romance took place. Maybe over the campaign on Levin."

Could it somehow have been through them that Lillian Hellman had been brought in to convince Otto Frank to ban my work? What difference did it make, exactly how the affair started? I had been open enough in my views so that the trouble would have come from one political or another. Certainly Barbara had come to be very close to Otto Frank. I would probably never know exactly how the manipulation was carried out.

Then, the following Sunday, a tart letter appeared in the *Times Magazine*. Though Barbara Epstein claimed credit for putting through the Diary against executive opinion, the writer said, he himself as the Doubleday representative in Paris had bought the American rights for the Diary from Otto Frank before Barbara ever heard of the book, and not only he but a number of executives had been most keen on it. Besides, he pointed out, it was a review by Meyer Levin that had made the Diary an overnight success.

Something in the tone of the letter made me feel the writer had more to tell. The address was Quogue, on Long Island. I called up Mr. Price.

A man alone in a car, driving on a Sunday morning past hotdog stands on the Montauk road, where it changes from its suburban highway character, and truckfarms begin, with boxes of fresh tomatoes along the roadside, and where the towns retain a touch of early America. I was like some character in a Hitchcock thriller, the lone persistent non-detective don, following out an after-clue, the hanging thread that remained when all seemed cleared up. It always led to an obscure cottage off a dirt road in the woods, and there an eccentric elderly scholar with clumps of wiry hair on both sides of his domed head would come politely forward saying, "I've been expecting you."

Mine was, instead, a tall, still youngish man, who was indeed expecting me, since we had an appointment. The paved road had brought me to a circle of neat homes within strolling distance of the sea.

We had met before, Francis Price remarked—I'd forgotten it—on that day in Paris over twenty years ago when I left Otto Frank with him to sign the Doubleday contract.

Yes, he still worked in publishing, though just now he was writing a book. At one point he remarked, "I hope you don't mind a non-Jew saying this, but there are some Jews who are the worst anti-Semites."

"We've noticed it ourselves," I said.

A whole page of his letter to the *Times* had been omitted because of space limitations; he showed it to me. Mostly, it was about Eleanor Roosevelt. Through a happy accident, Mr. Price had met Mrs. Roosevelt in Paris and given her a copy of the Diary in English. Intensely moved by the book, she had agreed to help. And about Mrs. Roosevelt—did I know she had written to Mr. Frank after I had seen her, asking him if he couldn't somehow straighten matters out with me?

"She did?"

"He showed me her letter, in Paris."

I was glad to hear it. She had after all made a last effort to help.

Mr. Price had something more to tell me. "When Otto

Frank came back from New York, you know, just after the book was published, I asked him what had happened to Meyer Levin's play—why wasn't it being done?"

"Hellman and Bloomgarden persuaded him that it was unactable," I reminded him.

"That's not the reason Otto gave me. He said they told him your play couldn't be done because it was too Jewish."

"He gave no other reason?"

"None."

7

THERE HAD COME the time with Dr. Erika, too, for me to go back into my personal life, and there came the day of the weeping. Over what, in those words of my sister's, had I wept?

In my mind there rose up a story—Franz Werfel's, wasn't it?—of a ship's doctor, musing alone one night by the rail, recalling the love of his childhood nursemaid, recalling how she had always kept track of him all through his medical-school days, and on into his manhood, though in a world so far removed from her own. And then when she had died, her little hoard had been found, her life savings, all in pure gold coins, gathered and left for him. And so, remembering her, he poured the gold into the sea. *The Pure in Heart* the book was called.

It was for the pure in heart that I had wept. For those like my brother-in-law Meyer Steinberg, the good little doctor, for their departure, for the horror of their absence in our world. I had wept because of Bess's belief, and her Meyer's belief in me, and in justice from God, in that world where one encounters only betrayals and hostility from so many, even from those who should be most understanding. And so I was choked with my grief for such love, the rare love of the pure in heart

311

that still manifests itself at times in our besmirched and murderous world of man.

Was it because Anne Frank, too, had symbolized for me the pure in heart?

On the way back to Israel there was an overnight stop in Amsterdam; in the morning I found the Prinsengracht a few steps from my hotel, and walked toward the Anne Frank Memorial House. In a shop along the way I stopped and bought something for my son Gabriel in Boston, a bit of coiled glass with a colored fluid rising in the warmth of your hand. What in the world did I have to be angry at? My big work was done; it was being widely read. I was alive and walking around. I had three sons and a daughter, all good people.

Here was the church, the Westertor whose tolling bells had pleased Anne.

On this canalside she had watched the ragged wartime urchins.

This ordinary door was where the burglars had broken in, and up this narrow hallway they must have come, almost to the secret bookcase door.

And at this point the place became a depersonalized museum. At the entrance hung an admission box. I put in my fee.

What had they done with the millions from the Diary? Stop! Don't bring that in!

Arrows guide the visitor through the front building, which had once housed the business establishment; the walls are arranged with commentated photographs showing the background and progress of the Second World War. The pictures are arresting, many of them familiar, and the comments are almost archeological in their stiffness. I would have imagined that fragments from the Diary might have better served.

312

I try not to be biased, yet I am struck by a considerable section given over to the heroism of the anti-Nazi underground in Germany. True, true, but it seems almost as much emphasized as the material about the Jews. As one moves along the walls, the pattern becomes clear: it is the device of showing the Jewish story "in its proper proportion." There are the early phases of degradation: dignified Jews forced to scrub the streets, Jewish shops with anti-Semitic daubs on the windows, burned synagogues. And finally the death camps. But all this is worked in amongst so many other horrors, so many political explanations, that the sheer fact of the Holocaust as a further meaning in the human capacity for evil—this uttermost and essential fact and experience belonging to this very place—is submerged.

This, then, was what so shocked the young American girl who wrote to me, the girl whose life had been altered by reading the Diary at fourteen.

Let us de-emphasize, reduce, all this Jewishness.

In the end you are not even memorialized for yourself, for your clinging to yourself, for being killed as yourself, but must be dissolved into ideological purposes.

Yes, yes, I know. Universality, universality. The German people suffered too, and among the Germans there were heroic anti-Nazis; let us not forget them, here in Anne Frank's house. She stands for universal love. "Perhaps it is through our Jewish suffering that the world will learn—" Omit it. Chauvinism.

Yes, but in this particular house the Jews—

Jews, Jews, why always with your Jews! What about the homeless Arab refugees?

I passed through the short second-floor corridor that led into the rear hiding house. Here too the furnishings had been removed, but still on the walls of Anne's room her pinned-up film stars remained. Clipped from magazines, some with faded print. Dick Powell was here, and Greta Garbo twice.

I copied names from the wall.

Then up the pitched steps to Peter's attic, and the window from which they watched the Allied air raids, when Peter cried out "Kill! Kill!" and said that if he lived, he didn't want to be a Jew, didn't want to be anything!

So with enough punishment we shall purge ourselves of identity, all.

On the way out of the attic, to one side like an afterthought, there was a small panel of photographs depicting phases of the Zionist movement and settlement in Palestine—Satisfied?

At the exit, downstairs, was a counter with literature. An elaborate history of the Diary was there, and in it I came upon a curious bit of information. The one time the Diary had been acted in the Soviet Union had been by students at the Moscow University. The director, however, had turned from the Broadway play to the Diary itself for the dialogue.

I had to smile. For in Israel one of the newly arrived Russian Jews had asked me for a copy of the suppressed version to send back through the underground to the Soviet Union, where it would be translated and passed along as *samizdat* literature.

In America too the play had become an underground item, and thus perhaps the only example of *samizdat* used in both lands.

After it had been illegally presented at Brandeis University, a reviewer, Shoshana Pakciarz, had written in a publication called *Genesis:*

. . . what makes this version so different and in a sense faithful to the original diary is the presentation of Anne's search for herself as the search of an adolescent Jewess, and the struggle of the people living in the attic as a . . . struggle for Jewish identity, in

314

addition to their struggle for elementary survival. Their scream for justice and peace is in a sense the uttering of the sacred words of the *Shemah*.

And in regard to the Broadway version:

I don't like the schmaltzy sale of universal messages through identity genocide. Universal messages are all right with me, insofar as they are concerned with a humanism in Judaism or in blackness . . .

But not, she pointed out, as a way to smother identity from behind.

In the new generation there were those who clearly understood.

Once after a lecture, at which I had told something of this long experience, I had gone with the chairman and his wife to their house for coffee; there came a moment after we were settled when the wife suddenly remarked, "I know what you are! You're The Jew."

* * *

Raised in an American and Jewish culture that stresses ethical values, open relationships, frankness (even though today it widely practices the reverse), the use of conspiratorial elements of deception, connivance, of sneaky, twisty ways is for me an ultimate abhorrence. That is why I fought so obsessively.

The real conspiracy of our times is mind manipulation. As a psychologist put it to me, we are all being lobotomized. The feeling of being increasingly in the grip of gigantic power structures from the right and from the left, in our society and in rival societies, generates the *schrecklichkeit,* the terror, of contemporary life.

315

Thus there developed my justice obsession. The obsessive aspect is perhaps now more manageable, but I would not want to lose its concomitant, the search for justice. Yes, I cling to it. For in its broad aspect the justice obsession represents an essential resistance to those who are the most cruel and the most arrogant of all, those who permit themselves every use of deceit, and the infliction of every torment, under the excuse of idealism. They will bring us Messianic times, they imagine, through total control. All this cant had to be applied, fanatically, even to the point of censoring the inmost beliefs of a young girl who died in the Holocaust.

"We are Jews." God, whatever his form or formlessness, whatever His impulsion or design, has made us Jews, "and we want to be." My effort has been not only to encompass an obsession, but to resist suppression. Overt, or hidden. In my case, or everywhere. Anne Frank's affirmation, stifled in the throat of her every resurrection, is the key to a universal human sense of continuation. My experience is an example, a presage, a warning. Our sense of self can be slowly expunged if the opponents have their way. In the Jewish case, gradual but overwhelming assimilation can be the end. In the coldest calculation, considering all that the Jewish spirit has given and continues to give to the world, is such extinction for the good of the international world of man?

And so when I walked out of that museum house, again along the canals of Amsterdam, I realized why, through all those years of horror, I had striven to make heard the Jewish cry of affirmation.

In the Jewish conception the era of justice and peace is not to be brought about by lies, suppression, or even power. Our Jewish Messianic belief is a belief in universal illumination.

316